To Prison
with
Love

The True Story
of an Indecent
Indictment and
America's
Adoption Travesty

By
Sandy Musser

TAP

This is a true story covering specific events surrounding the indictment of The Musser Foundation. There were eye-witnesses to every event that occurred. Names, however, have been changed, in most cases, or not used in order to protect individuals from becoming targets of governmental investigations.

9 8 7 6 5 4 3 2 1

Printed in the United States of America

Library of Congress CIP 94-79336
ISBN 0-934896-37-2

The Awareness Press
PO Box 41
Cape Coral, FL 33910

Dedicated to:

My Entire Family
who walked with me
each step of the way

• • • • •

My Supportive Friends
who reached out
and touched me

• • • • •

My Husband
without whom
I could not have
pursued my dreams

"In all reform movements, there

comes a time when individuals are

called upon to stand strong in their beliefs.

. . . Musser demonstrates clearly the

depth of her moral fiber in this book

which is written from the heart."

Annette Baran, M.S.W.
Co-Author of *The Adoption Triangle*
and *Lethal Secrets*

ACKNOWLEDGEMENTS

"PEOPLE WHO NEED PEOPLE
ARE THE LUCKIEST PEOPLE IN THE WORLD"

A GREAT BIG HUGE WARM THANK YOU TO THESE
WONDERFUL PEOPLE WHO CAME THROUGH WITH LOVE
AND SUPPORT DURING MY DARK HOURS!

TOGETHER THEY PROVIDED THE
'ONE SET OF FOOTPRINTS'!

Abby – Adam – Al – Alan – Albert – Alberta – Alicia – Alvie – Alison – Alix
Amy – Andrea – Andrew – Angel – Angela – Anita – Ann – Anna – Anne
Annie – Annette – Anthony – Arlene – Arthur – Ashley – Avril – Barb – Barbara
Becky – Bert – Beth – Betsy Betty – Betty Ann – Bettye – Bev – Beverly – Bill
B.J. – Barbara Jean – Bobbie – Bob – Bobby – Bonnie – Brandon – Brenda
Candy – Carl – Carla – Carol – Carole – Caroline – Carolyn – Carrie – Carroll
Carson – Cassandra – Cathy – Char – Charlene – Charleen – Charlie – Charles
Charlotte – Cheron – Cheryl – Chiquita – Christine – Christopher – Cindy
Claire – Clare – Colleen – Connie – Crystal – Curry – Cyndi – Cynthia – Dan
Dana – Daniel – Danny – Darlene – Darrin – Daryl – Dave – David – Dawn
Deanna – Deb – Debbie – Deborah – Debra – Dee – DeeAnn – Denise – Dennis
Devin – Diane – Dixie – Dodie – Dolores – Dominick Don – Donna – Doreen
Doris – Dorothy – Dot – Dottie – Doug – Edie – Edith – Ed – Edna – Eileen
Elaine – Eleanor – Elinore – Elizabeth – Ellen – Ellie – Emily – Eugene – Faith
Felicia – Frances – Francis – Fred – Fredda – Gail – Gale – Gary – Gene – Genie
George – Georgia – Germaine – Ginger – Ginny – Gladys – Glenda – Glenn
Goddess – Gordon – Grace – Greg – Gretchen – Gwen – Hal – Harold – Harriet
Hazel – Heidi – Helen – Henrietta – Higher Power – Hila – Holly – Iris – Jackie
James – Jamie – Jan – Janay – Jane – Janeal – Janet – Janice – Janine – Janis – Jared
Jason – Jay Jayne – Jean – Jeanice – Jeanne – Jeannie – Jeff – Jeffrey – Jeannette
Jennie Jenny – Jerry – Jesus – Jill – Jim – Jimmy – Joan – Joann – JoAnne – Jody
Joe – Jon – John – Josie – Joy – Joyce – Judith – Judy – Julia – Julie – June – Kandy
Karen – Karyn – Katherine – Kathleen – Katie – Kathy – Katrina – Kay – Keith
Kelli – Kelly – Ken – Kim – Kimlee – Kristi – Kristin – Kristine – Larry – Laura
Laurie – LaVonne – Lawrence – Leah – Lee – Leanne Leeann – Leigh – Lesley
Leslie – Lin – Linda – Lisa – Liz – Lori – Lorraine – Lou – Louann – Lucy – Lynn
Lynne – Madeline – Madelyn – Maggie – Marcia – Marcie – Marcy – Margaret
Marge – Margie – Maria Marian – Marianne – Marie – Marilyn – Marjorie
Mark – Marla – Marlene – Marsha – Martha – Mary – Mary Ann – Mary Jo – Mary
Lou – Mary Sue – Matt – May – May Nell – Megan – Melanie – Melinda – Melissa
Michael – Michelle – Mickey – Mike – Mildred – Millie – Mindy – Mimi
Mom – Morgan – Nancy – Nickie – Nikki – Noreen – Norm – Norma – Oleen
Pam – Pamela – Papa Joe – Pat – Patricia – Patti – Patty Paul – Paula – Peggy
Penny – Phil – Phyllis – Pollie – Rachel – Randy – Ray – Raymond – Rene
Rebecca – Reuben – Rhonda – Rich – Risa – Rita – Robert – Roberta – Robin
Ron – Ronald – Rosalie – Rose – Rosemary – Rosemarie – Rusty – Ruth – Ruth
Ann – Sally – Sandi – Sandra – Sandy – Sara – Sarah – Scott – Shannon – Shanti
Shari – Sharon – Sharyn – Sheila – Sherri – Sherrie – Sherry – Sherwin – Sheryl
Sondra – Sophie – Spirit – Stan – Stanley – Stephanie – Shirl – Stephen – Steve
Steven – Sue – Susan – Susie – Suzy – Sylvia – Teresa – Teri – Terry – Theresa
Tim – Tina – Todd – Tom – Tony – Trish – Val – Valerie – Vera – Veronica – Vicki
Virginia – Wanda – Warren – Wendy – GOD!

Note: If you slipped through the cracks, forgive my humanness, but please
let me know so I can include you in the next printing.

TABLE OF CONTENTS

Preface
Forward by Reuben Pannor
Introduction by Elaine Noll
My Turn

Chapter 1
    Indecent Indictment — 3
Chapter 2
    The Awakening & Finale — 17
        The Background — 17
        Moving South and Starting Over — 19
        The Founding of ALARM — 20
        Expanding to a 'Real' Office — 23
        Getting Baptized Into Search Work — 23
        The Development Stage — 26
        A New Search Connection — 27
        Fateful Phone Calls — 28
        The Musser Foundation is Born — 30
        The Talk Show Circuit — 33
        The Infamous Set-Up — 34
        A Shocking Discovery of Deceit — 36
        New Office to Expand and Grow — 37
        Reunions Worth Going to Prison For — 40

Chapter 3
    The '93 Conference — 47
        The Real Story — 51
Chapter 4
    Akron Bound — 57
        Pre-Trial Jitters and a Revelation — 65
        An Interview at the Border — 71
        '93 March on Washington — 71
        Gearing Up For Trial — 72
Chapter 5
    Standing Trial — 77
        Trial Begins — 79
        The Fictitious Scenario — 87
        High Hopes, But Another Set-Up — 107
        Last Day of Testimony — 110

Chapter 6

Over The Edge — 119

The Final Travesty of Justice — 121
A Genetic Disease Rears Its Head — 123
Crumbling Marriage & Spiritual Beginnings — 124
A New Roller Coaster Ride — 125
Face to Face with Insanity — 127
Personal Experience Leads to Understanding — 136
Seeing the World Through Rose Colored Glasses — 137

Chapter 7

Trial Aftermath — 143

60 Minutes Pays a Visit — 145
Sentencing & CERA Conference Coincide — 145
"You Are Sentenced To..." — 147
No Stay — 153

Chapter 8

The Prison Experience —- 155

To Hell and Back in 3 Days — 156
They Took You (and me) Away — 158
Mini Experience of Prison Life — 164
60 Minutes Film Crew Visits Prison — 170
A Typical Day in Camp — 178
UNICOR - The Federal Prison Industry — 179
The Latest American Phenomenon — 185

Chapter 9

Mini-Visits and Reform Voices — 189

Chapter 10

The Leadership Speaks Out — 209

Jim Gritter — 210
Annette Baran — 211
Reuben Pannor — 215
Penny Partridge — 217
Jon Ryan — 225
Nancy Verrier — 229
Lynn Giddens — 238

Chapter 11

What Now? — 241

A Reform Platform — 241
Making A Beginning — 243
The 14th Amendment — 244
A Policy Statement for Consideration — 245

Chapter 12

The Homecoming —- 247

Party Time — 248
House Arrest & Renting Shackles — 249
Hope Springs Eternal — 250

Educate for Awareness — 252

PREFACE

Many people reading this book may not be familiar with the adoption reform movement, the sealed records controversy, or the fact that there are now hundreds of search and support organizations throughout the country. The following will provide a capsulized overview.

Adoption records (also affecting step-parent adoptions) have been sealed in 48 of the 50 states since the early 40's. What exactly does that mean and how does it affect us?

1) It means that when an adoption takes place, the adoptee's records are sealed "forever," causing, some believe, a form of genocide or ancestricide. Entire family genealogical histories are wiped out by virtue of an archaic adoption law.

2) It means that an entire segment of our population, known as "the adopted," are unable to have access to copies of their original birth certificates or other legal documents concerning their own lives. Accordingly, the 14th Amendment does not apply to them.

3) It means that adoptees are being denied basic God-given rights that the rest of us enjoy - our heritage, our medical history, our genealogy, and the ability to find the answer to the age-old question - "Who Am I."

4) It means birthparents who surrendered their children in good faith have had to suffer years of anguish wondering what ever happened to the child of their womb.

5) It means that adoptive parents are also being denied pertinent medical, psychological, genetic information necessary to the parenting of an adopted child.

6) It means that those who "facilitate" adoptions have been free to do unscrupulous deeds and then hide behind the confidentiality law; i.e. tell birthparents their child died, tell adoptive parents the child was "abandoned and unwanted," alter and falsify adoption documents, sell babies to the highest bidder; the list goes on and on.

7) It means that individuals all over the country who want to assist in family reunions are putting themselves at risk because of the "sealed record."

Jean Paton, an adoptee, now in her mid- 80's, first "broke the silence" during the early 1950's; but it's only been since the early 70's that a growing movement, dedicated to the unsealing of these records, has emerged. As a result, adoption search and support organizations have sprung up all over the nation.

This story has to do with a particular organization known as "The Musser Foundation" and the Indictment of 1993. The following excerpt from the *American Journal of Adoption Reform* provides a backdrop to this story. The complete text is found in the chapter entitled *The Leadership Speaks*.

"The Federal government has officially begun to suppress the search efforts for family members who have been separated by adoption. In a case filed in March 1993 in the United States District Court for the Northern District of Ohio Eastern Division, Sandy Musser of FL and Barbara Moskowitz of OH were each charged with a 39-count indictment for violating sections of the United States Code.

The indictment culminated an investigation that began in August 1989 and continued through January 1992. An investigator with the New York State Department of Health, Thomas J. Flavin, posed as a birthfather trying to obtain information about his child who was placed for adoption years earlier by a girlfriend. Based on telephone calls that Mr. Flavin taped and promotional materials from The Musser Foundation that went through the U.S. Postal Service, the government sought to indict Barbara and Sandy on conspiracy, wire fraud, mail fraud, and theft, retention, and sale of government property.

In June, Barbara pled guilty and agreed to testify against Sandy when she went on trial. For her cooperative efforts on behalf of the government, Barbara received a sentence of two months in a halfway house, two years probation, and a fine of $1600.

Sandy pled not guilty to the charges and had a trial in July. A jury of eight men and four women found Sandy guilty on 35 of the 39 charges. She was found not guilty of mail fraud.

On October 1st Sandy was sentenced to four months in federal prison, two months house arrest by electronic surveillance, three years probation, and ordered to do no more adoption searches."

During four years of operation, The Musser Foundation was responsible for over 500 families being reunited. This is the story about the indictment, the subsequent trial, the intricate relationships, and the imprisonment of the Founder, Sandy Musser.

Except for the names mentioned in the transcripts, which are already a matter of public record, most of the names have been changed. The only purpose for changing them is to protect those who might otherwise become targeted by agents of the Federal Government if their names were to be revealed.

Note: Throughout the book, when the term 'government' is used, it refers to the investigative branches of the justice system; i.e. agents and/or informants of the state and federal government.

FORWARD

Sandy and I first met at an Open Adoption conference in Traverse City, MI in the early 1980's. In talking with her, I came to understand that she believed strongly, not only in the need to humanize adoption practices, but passionately about the need to help those who have suffered from the effects of sealed records.

She identifies with adoptees who have been deprived of civil liberties and told that they have no rights to identifying information about their birth parents - rights that those who are not adopted take for granted. She identifies with birthmothers who have been deprived of the right to know what happened to the child that had been relinquished for adoption, or even to know if that child is dead or alive. She identifies with the adoptive parents as they, too, struggle with a system that even deprives them of information affecting the children they adopted.

The people who came to Sandy for assistance had been turned away from social agencies when they sought help. The legal system would not listen to their pleas. Out of frustration and desperation they turned to search groups made up of people who had been victimized by the same system. Together, they gave people hope that they could stand up to this dehumanizing system and could find ways to ease the pain and suffering.

For this, Sandy Musser was indicted and went to jail. The system that created these problems should be indicted. Sandy's actions were those of a brave and courageous woman. They were in the best tradition of the civil disobedience movement. As such, she is in good company.

Henry Thoreau, for example, in *Civil Disobedience* (1849) said that individuals should refuse to obey any government rule they believed unjust. In 1845 he refused to pay poll taxes and went to jail. Mahatma Ghandi, who was influenced by Thoreau's teachings, said that non-violent resistance was justified to bring about social change. Ghandi believed it was honorable to go to jail for a good cause and those of us who know history, know that Ghandi spent many years of his life in jail.

The Nuremberg Trials that followed World War II (1945-1949), held that a person did not have to blindly obey laws that were unjust, but had a responsibility to follow his own conscience. If these examples were not convincing, one need only to look at the leaders of our own civil rights movement led by people like Martin Luther King, who believed that unjust laws should be challenged. In following her conscience in challenging sealed records in adoption, Sandy was acting for all of us whose lives are in any way touched by adoption. She has my unqualified support as she goes about her work of reform.

This is not only Sandy Musser's story, told as only Sandy can tell it, but it is part of a historical record of the adoption reform movement. Most importantly, it represents a turning point in the struggle to open adoption records.

Reuben Pannor, M.S.W.
Co-Author of *The Adoption Triangle*
and *Lethal Secrets*

INTRODUCTION

When Sandy first asked me to write a prelude to her story, I felt honored. Though we now live 1200 miles apart, we have maintained our bond of friendship which began 23 years ago at a local church where we both taught Sunday School. I recall when she first told me she wanted to go to Bible School; her desire was to learn as much as she could, so she registered for classes at Philadelphia College of Bible (PCB). She hoped to become a 'missionary' someday. Though she had not even thought about opening the adoption closet door, God was already preparing her for missionary work in the adoption reform arena. She completed her courses at PCB just prior to being invited to her first Adoption Forum meeting.

I suffered with her through many ups and downs; the mountain-top experiences and the valleys. I was her sounding board as she decided to "go public" with her birthmother experience and as she embarked upon an emotional search for the daughter she surrendered in 1954. I was there when she found Wendy in 1977; and in 1978, I offered encouragement as she struggled to put her story into words. The final product became *I Would Have Searched Forever* which was published the following year.

Her traumatic divorce in 1979, after 20 years of marriage, was an extremely painful experience. She jumped that hurdle and managed to raise four teenagers on a meager secretarial salary.

In 1980, we sat together and shared ideas as she began to formulate her first organization known as Adoption Triangle Ministries. In the summer of 1982, she published her second book entitled *What Kind Of Love Is This*. Our lives parted that year when she moved to Florida in the late fall.

Her life has had more than its share of heartache, pain, and sorrow, but she has always kept her positive spirit; and within that spirit, I sensed a fierce drive and determination - not only to survive, but to also succeed in the work she set out to accomplish. I've always been amazed at the amount of energy, dedication, and genuine commitment she has displayed in her efforts to help bring about adoption reform.

This book capsulizes 18 years of her life. She told me recently that the years between 1988 to 1993 were some of her most enjoyable as she became a catalyst and a willing vessel for the reunification of so many families. A scripture verse on The Musser Foundation brochure says it all - "...He has given us the ministry of reconciliation." (II Corinthians 5:18)

When you finish reading this book, it is my hope that you will know her as I have known her - as a sincere, honest, caring person who "went to the wall" for the cause she believed in.

Elaine Noll
August 1994

MY TURN

The title, *To Prison With Love*, probably sounds enigmatic. It rings of conflict, of opposites. Choosing a title is never an easy task. To an author, it's as important, and as difficult, as naming a child. I chose the title *To Prison With Love* because it felt right. Its meaning is simple and two-fold.

From the time I became enmeshed in adoption reform work, I always knew deep within my soul that I would be willing to go to jail for the cause of adoption reform. I believed so strongly in the work because I came to understand that the adoption laws in our country are so unjust and so wrong. I loved the work enough to be willing to pay whatever the required price was. For me, there was no cost too high. There's a current country song that says "When it comes to love, you don't count the cost." Ultimately the cost for me was prison and so I went to prison - and I went with love.

While I was in prison, my family, my friends and hundreds of people I'd never met wrote to support me. They were writing to me in prison and they were writing with love.

This is MY story about MY experience. I do not purport it to be anyone else's story but my own. As I began to write, I questioned myself as to what I wanted to accomplish through this book. In searching my heart and soul as introspectively as possible, this is my conclusion.

The primary purpose is to take "my turn" to explain the events surrounding The Indecent Indictment of 1993 (a phrase we coined in our office soon after the indictment). My intent is to lay out the events as I recall them occurring; to present my reactions to those events, as well as my perception as to how others reacted; and to share some poignant thoughts of a few leaders who march in the forefront of the adoption reform parade holding high their batons.

There are three major goals. The first is to provide a history and background concerning the founding of The Musser Foundation; the second is to explain the events which led up to my arrest and subsequent imprisonment; and third, to provide documentation in the context of the political ramifications - never before had anyone in the reunification movement been sentenced to prison for their reformation work.

To Prison With Love will also provide you insight with which to draw your own conclusions concerning my guilt or innocence, should you feel so inclined to do so. Though I was "on trial," I was, nevertheless, incapable of testifying on my own behalf for several reasons which are explained within the context of the book.

The purpose of this book, however, is not an attempt to prove my innocence. That will always remain subjective. The law is primarily about assigning blame and pointing a finger at a responsible party. In this particular scenario, the responsible party was neither my codefendant nor myself. The responsible party was (and is) the illegal, immoral, unconstitutional, and corrupt system of sealed adoption records.

I was found guilty and sentenced to four months in federal prison, two months house arrest and three years probation. In addition, I would not be permitted to be involved in adoption search work nor allowed to associate with The Musser Foundation during the term of my probation.

I want to stress one point very strongly; I do not blame nor judge my codefendant for what happened to me. In spite of the fact that she testified against me, I realize that she had to do what she felt was "in her best interest," just as I had to do what I had to do. i.e. It would have been impossible for me to plead guilty to an offense for which I believe I was not guilty. It seems dishonorable to have to admit to wrong doing if you truly believe in what you do, no matter what the cost. I believed in what we were doing. I believe that the end justifies the means. I believe that immoral laws **cannot** be broken by virtue of the fact that they **are** immoral or, to flip the coin over, they **must** be broken because they **are** immoral.

To "cooperate" with the government by giving them the guilty plea they wanted would have gone against my very nature and the ideals I believe in. I have always tried to practice the "higher law" concept, and follow my heart's command in making the hard decisions in my life. I never had, nor do I now have, any grandiose ideas of myself as a "martyr," as some have charged. There is no question in my mind, however, that I was a scapegoat. I was setup by a NY State investigator and then targeted by the federal government to be an example, as clearly stated by U.S. Attorney Thomas Getz when he told a reporter - "We hope that this will send a chilling effect to people who do these kinds of things."

Many have questioned why I was singled out when it was a known fact, both before and after trial, that many, many others were (and are) doing the same type of work with the same investigator. It has been mentioned by some of the leadership that it was primarily because I had become too "visible" and often spoke out openly and harshly against our government practice of sealed records; thereby, setting myself up as "an easy target." Our 'freedom of speech' in America is shot down when we become too vocal.

Whatever the case may be, the federal government accomplished what they set out to do - they brought a screeching halt to adoption reunions and split the movement (provided it was ever intact). Had it been united and strong, it could have fought the battle - and possibly won the war. As it turned out, it was unable to even endure the skirmish. Maybe this will provide an opportunity for the movement to regroup and plan some new strategy tactics.

In the past two decades, I have been committed to three primary goals:

1) **Open Records**
   I am no longer idealistic enough to believe that open records will occur within my lifetime - in fact, I'm sure they probably will not, unless a miracle occurs.

2) **Reuniting Families**
   The government has forbidden me to have any part in reuniting families and forced me to disassociate myself from my own organization during the time of my "supervised release."

3) **Family Preservation**
   Family Preservation is a goal we must continually work towards. Current adoption and its unhealthy practices should be abolished. Closed, sealed, secret adoption should be outlawed since it has no place in a free society. The practice of separating a child from its mother of origin "forever" is unnatural, immoral, and holds irreversible consequences for both parties.

Going to prison was a heavy price to pay - but prison is prison. Locking up my body was certainly no more traumatic than the 23 years I had already served - mentally imprisoned by an archaic adoption system. It was the price I was forced to pay when I surrendered my child in 1954. Only after I completed my search and found my daughter was I finally set free. I have paid my dues many times over for the "crime" of being an unwed mother. No one should be subjected to such a cruel and unjust punishment for giving the gift of life. But millions of our foremothers have suffered for unjust **'man-made'** laws.

Susan B. Anthony was sentenced to prison on November 5, 1872 for attempting to cast a vote, and it took nearly 50 years until the 19th amendment was ratified, finally giving women the right to vote (1920). It was 90 years from the time the Civil Rights Act of 1866 was passed (which placed the federal government squarely behind the enforcement of equal rights), until 1955 when Rosa Parks sat in the front of the bus which began the crusade against the Jim Crow laws.

In the final analysis, the creation of this book will provide a historical record and documentation of an important point in time - an era when birthparents lost their children to an unjust, immoral institution called adoption, performed under the guise of "child welfare"; and a time when one lone birthmother was sent to prison for daring to reunite loved ones who had suffered the same kind of injustices. I realize that I may, once again, be putting myself at risk simply by speaking the truth in writing this book. Though we presume to live in a free country, those who speak out eventually suffer the consequences.

Nevertheless, history will show that, on the time line of life, a mark will have been etched forever. It will prove that this event and outcome was a turning point in what we now call "adoption reform." The only question is - how much longer? How much longer will the chains of adoption continue to bind us?

A CUB friend sent me the following little story just before I went to trial. It's called The Goose Story and carries an important message for all of us - no matter what the 'cause' may be.

> "In the fall when you see geese heading south for the winter flying along in a "V" formation, you might be interested in knowing what science has discovered about why they fly that way.
>
> It has been learned that as each bird flaps its wings, it creates an uplift for the bird immediately following. By flying in a "V" formation, the whole flock adds at least 71% greater flying range than if each bird flew on its own.
>
> Whenever a goose falls out of formation, it suddenly feels the drag and resistance of trying to go it alone, and quickly gets into formation to take advantage of the lifting power of the bird immediately in front.
>
> When the lead goose gets tired, he rotates back in the wing and another goose flies point. The geese honk from behind to encourage those up front to keep up their speed.
>
> Finally, when a goose gets sick or is wounded by a gun shot and falls out, two geese fall out of formation and follow him down to help and protect him. They stay with him until he is either able to fly or until he is dead; they launch out on their own or with another formation to catch up with the group. If we have the sense of a goose, we will stand by each other like that."

There is no doubt that I have been "shot down" and have been deeply wounded by this difficult experience, causing me to fall out of formation. There are many close friends who dropped out of formation so they could stay by my side and help care for me. I will be forever indebted to them for being constant and steadfast. They know who they are and they have my deepest gratitude. At this writing, I have no idea what my future holds, but possibly the day may come when I can return to formation.

Sandy Musser
June 1994

P.S. Coincidences have always fascinated me. As mentioned above, Susan B. Anthony and sixteen of her friends were arrested for attempting to vote on November 5, 1872. 121 years later, to the day, November 5, 1993, I was sent to prison for the 'crime' of conspiracy in my work of reuniting families.

LAWS VIOLATING

MORALITY

ARE NOT BINDING!

Pope John XXIII

"By whatever name you prefer, the birth family, the biological family, the genetic family, this gathering of souls is inherently important. That's part of why we have search and reunification - because the individuals involved need to reconnect with what has been lost. We need to be looking to programs that prevent the loss to begin with. **Healing is wonderful, but the better path is not to contract the disease.**

Traditional American adoption practices constitute a diseased system. It is sick behavior to participate in the unwarranted separation of parents and their offspring, and over the decades, that has happened endlessly. Among its many aspects, the search and reunification movement has been cast into the role of the physician. As a result, we have the responsibility to educate ourselves as to the nature of the diseased system, how it came to prominence, and the available populist, legal and professional means that can be used to put it into remission."

Hal Aigner, Author

● ● ● ● ● ● ● ● ● ●

"My biggest disappointment and most scathing criticism regarding adoption reform is reserved for professionals because they must bear significant responsibility for the ongoing unsound adoption practices. The evidence is in - closed records and closed adoption hurt people."

Ray Ensminger, MSW

THE INDECENT INDICTMENT OF 1993

It was Saturday morning, March 27, 1993. I heard the phone ringing, but thought I was dreaming. My husband and I had been out late the night before so I was exhausted and had planned on "sleeping-in." It was still dark outside and as I glanced at the clock, I noticed it was only 5:30 a.m.! Who would be calling at 5:30 a.m.? Worried that something might be wrong with one of my children or grandchildren, I quickly fumbled for the phone by the bed. The first words I heard were "Sandy, the story is in our paper this morning - the Cleveland Plain Dealer - the headline says 'Foundation Head Indicted for Fraud'." It was Bobbie, one of The Musser Foundation's best investigators.

"Yeah?" I responded, still unable to fathom what I thought I just heard!

"Cary's on the line too," she replied. "I don't know if you remember him, but he's a good friend of mine."

"I don't understand why you're calling me at this time of the morning?"

"Because we've got to decide what we're going to do."

Suddenly, Cary spoke up and said "Bobbie, this is going to get national media attention. Sandy's had a lot of experience with the media, but you haven't, so you need to start thinking about it." (How did he know it was going to get national attention or why did he think so? He had been involved in a state case several years before - did he have 'special' insight?)

"Listen guys, I'm going back to sleep. I'll talk to you later." My mind was having difficulty absorbing what I had just heard! I wasn't even sure I'd be able to go back to sleep, but I needed time to think and wanted to do it alone.

3

"But we've got to talk about what we're going to do. Aren't you worried or upset?"

"Bobbie, it's 5:30 in the morning. I can't even think at this hour. I'll give you a call later." That was the beginning of the end - or was it the end of the beginning?? Only time would tell. One thing I knew for sure - I had a strong inclination that it was going to be a long year!

As I lay in bed, now wide awake, my mind began to drift back, recalling the first time Bobbie and I had ever spoken. It was the summer of 1980 and I was living in New Jersey; and she in Maryland. In addition to raising four teen-agers and working full-time as a school secretary, I was still reeling from the effects of a marriage that had collapsed after 20 years. My activities as a CUB leader (Concerned United Birthparents) helped to keep my mind occupied and my hands busy. My commitment and work with CUB was a direct result of my "birthparent experience."

In 1976, I made a conscious decision to search for the daughter I had surrendered in 1954. My search was completed in 1977 - the same year I became involved with CUB. The personal story of my search and reunion is told in my book entitled *I Would Have Searched Forever*, first published in 1979.

I had been an active CUB leader for three years when I first received a call from Bobbie. Someone had suggested she get in touch with me for peer counseling. The content of our conversation concerned a son she surrendered for adoption who had recently contacted her. Though she was thrilled about being found, she had never told her husband of her son's existence and wasn't sure how to break the news. Now it was time to face the music. I offered a few ideas, shared some thoughts, and encouraged her to 'go for it'. That was the last I heard from her until eight years later when our paths crossed again. Ginger, my Golden Retriever, plopped on my stomach and brought me back to the reality of the present moment.

The phone rang again. By this time, it was 8:30 a.m. and Mother was calling to let me know where we were meeting for breakfast. It was a ritual for my mother, sister, myself and a few friends to meet on Saturday morning for breakfast and conversation. Then we would go our separate ways - food shopping, craft shows, errands. The story had apparently hit our local newspaper, so on this particular morning, our employees joined us as well. Pat, my dear friend and right-hand assistant brought extra copies of the paper.

We began to try to unravel the bits and pieces of the story as written by the "*News-Press Staff.*" The story was about me. My name was interwoven throughout the context of it. Nevertheless, none of us recognized this person who was being accused of these horrible charges?

4

The headline on the front page read "Adoption/Reunion Specialist Indicted."

I recall two feelings emerging simultaneously - numbness and outrage! Why hadn't I been notified?? The article said "Ms. Musser could not be reached for comment." What a joke! I had an answering machine at my office and at home. No one had tried to contact me or if they had, they hadn't bothered to leave a message. It was my suspicion that no one had even tried. To say that I "could not be reached for comment" was one of those coined phrases the media likes to use for "effect" or when they can't be bothered due to the time element. Once they decided to print the story, they didn't really care about my input.

Why did it take an inaccurate story about myself to realize that newspapers often print false and/or misleading information? I had been as naive as many others who believed most of what I read. What I know now is that a reporter is seldom able to get all the facts straight. He or she can only report what they perceive to be "the truth." As Cary predicted, the media hype had just begun.

With shocking disbelief, bewilderment, and utter amazement, we read a story of "criminal conspiracy, wire fraud, mail fraud, and theft of government property." This was absolutely crazy!! In actuality, The Musser Foundation had reunited hundreds of families, and distributed thousands of pieces of literature in an effort to reform the system. That had always been the primary purpose and the goal of the organization - it was as **pure and simple** as that!

The National AAC (American Adoption Congress) conference was being held the following week in Cleveland - how ironic (or was it?) that this Grand Jury indictment came out of Cleveland also! I was going to be a presenting a few workshops. Had they planned to serve me "the summons" while I was attending the conference?

Pat and I had already made our travel arrangements to leave the following Wednesday, March 31st, which was only four days away. Though our conference fees were paid, the hotel room reserved, and the plane tickets purchased, we now wondered whether or not I should even go. Would it be "in the best interest" of The Musser Foundation or myself? After an agonizing discussion, the general feeling and consensus of the group was that, in light of the 'current events', it might be better if I didn't attend, but who could go in my place?

Neither Rosie or Terry could take time off from their other jobs on such short notice; Andrea was still in her senior year of high school; Diane had obligations at home that would not allow her time away. All of a sudden, Mother piped up and said "Why can't I go?" We all looked at each other with shocked expressions and then burst out laughing. We were startled that she would even offer. "Do you want to go?" I asked, still surprised by her outburst and the generosity of her offer. "Yes, I'd like to go." "Well great!" We all laughed and said "Mom, you're elected!" And so it was that my 80 year old Mother would attend her first adoption conference, even though she still had not met her granddaughter, surrendered in 1954.

Upon leaving the restaurant, I immediately went to my office which was just down the block and across the street. The answering machine light was blinking; there was a message from Mark Rollenhagen, a reporter from the Cleveland Plain Dealer. He wanted to know if I wanted to comment on the indictment charges and asked if I would return his call. Again, I felt confounded and confused. I had not received a warning notice or a summons of any kind - only an early morning phone call, an article in my local paper, and now a call from a reporter in Cleveland.

Within a short span of time, I returned his call. He wanted to know if I was aware of the indictment and I explained that I had just learned of it a few hours earlier by reading it in my local paper. I expressed my dismay and humiliation at seeing the story on the front page of the Ft. Myers News-Press without any prior forewarning or notice. We discussed the fact that I had not even received a summons. He then informed me that the court has the right to "notify the parties involved" by publishing the story - especially when the indictment is from another state, as in this case. It's called "Notification by Publication." I called it "guilty until proven innocent."

As a result of our brief conversation, Mr. Rollenhagen wrote another story the following day. He asked specifically if I had knowledge of what Bobbie was doing. I remarked that I did not know nor did I care. I then said something like "the end justifies the means." When he asked what I meant by that, I said that I didn't believe I had done anything wrong. What was important to me was the fact that people were being reunited and those results were what mattered.

Since he was going to be writing about our organization, I asked if he would like to receive some literature and he said he would. Did he know about the national conference being held the following week in Cleveland? I told him I had been planning to attend, but in light of circumstances, I would be contacting an attorney for advice as to whether or not I should. "But if I do attend, I'll be holding a press conference and you're invited!" He claimed to have no knowledge of the conference but, in an off-the-cuff manner, he said "maybe they're planning to give you the summons while you're here in Ohio." I have a strong feeling he may have been right and suspect he may have even known it - since he was not only the one to "break" the story, but he also became a witness for the prosecution.

Mr. Rollenhagen then offered to fax a copy of the indictment. Since I had never seen an indictment before, I wasn't sure what to expect. The 20 page document was in my hands within a few minutes and, like the newspaper article, I still didn't comprehend these blatant, ridiculous charges. The primary goal of The Musser Foundation was simply to reunite families; apparently the government didn't choose to see it that way. The most glaring and outrageous part of the indictment was the heading which said -

The United States of America
vs.
Sandy Musser
d/b/a The Musser Foundation

I vividly remember thinking to myself "Did everyone in America agree to this absurd indictment?" I was now experiencing the same heartsick feeling Bobbie must have felt just a few days before when the FBI made a personal visit to her home.

She had called me earlier in the week. Her voice was much softer than usual and cracking. It was Tuesday, March 23rd between 5:30 and 6:00 in the afternoon and I had just come home from my office. I'll never forget her first fateful words - she said, "it's all over." "What's all over?" I asked. Then she told me the news - the FBI had just left her home! She said they handed her a summons, walked through her entire house confiscating files, and asked many pertinent questions concerning other people in the movement.

She said it was apparent they had several leads to other individuals and groups and wanted to know what her connection was to them. The Musser Foundation, she said, was included in that scenario and obviously at the top of their list (or did she put it there?) Needless to say, she was quite shaken over the matter, as anyone would have been. They inquired as to whether or not she was the person known, in the movement, as "The Searcher" and she replied emphatically "NO!" The government was about to make its first deal and it was cut and dry.

They told her they were looking for the person known as "The Searcher" and all she had to do was "cooperate" and things would go a lot easier for her! They wanted information and believed she was the person who could provide it. When they inquired about her relationship to The Musser Foundation, she told them she worked for us. The statement was somewhat misleading since she was not an employee of The Musser Foundation but, in fact, had worked on a contract basis case by case. She worked for many other groups and individuals and

7

had been doing so since the early '80's. Likewise, we had other investigators we contracted with and did some 'in-house' cases as well. But we didn't begin to do searches until late in 1988.

Before ending the conversation, she asked if I would be willing to testify on her behalf and I told her, with no uncertainty, that I would. The next day I wrote a letter on her behalf, as she had requested, and sent it to her for her perusal. I have always felt a strong sense of loyalty to those I considered family in the adoption reform movement. Deep within my spirit, I knew I would go to bat for any one who might find themselves in 'hot water'. I had, of course, always hoped they would do the same for me.

I remember my sick feeling as we spoke, and how terrible I felt that this was happening to her. She was known in the movement as the "searcher's searcher" - and considered to be one of the best in the field. I tried to find words that would somehow alleviate her tremendous anxiety - unaware that in three short days, I would be drowning in the same anxiety-filled boat. As our conversation came to a close, I assured her once again that I would do anything within my power to help her in any way I could.

The days immediately following the article about the indictment were a blur, but the first Monday (March 29th) was memorable. The Maury Povich Show reran the twins' reunion show which had originally aired November 6, 1992. The first show displaying our 800# brought 11,500 calls (and a huge phone bill) and now the phones were ringing off the hook again. But it felt like soothing salve to a deep wound. There was little time to feel sorry for ourselves - we were too busy answering to the needs of people who wanted nothing more than to be reunited with their loved ones. Another 6,500 calls resulted from the second show. Our phone bill, of course, was in the thousands. The phones continued to ring for the next several months. While all that was going on, the office had a circus-like atmosphere with various things happening at the same time.

On Tuesday, we received a beautiful bouquet of flowers from a sister organization in a New England state. We were touched by the thought, but especially the message - **"You'll never walk alone - we are with you."** Other groups and individuals were calling with their own caring comments and thoughts.

Within a few days we were contacted by 60 Minutes. When Pat told me 60 Minutes was on the line and wanted to talk to me, I thought she was joking. 60 Minutes!! I knew this was a big story, but I didn't realize that 60 Minutes knew it was! Needless to say, we were all very excited about it. We considered it a golden opportunity, believing that we would finally have a podium for getting our issues before the public.

Over the next several weeks, we received calls from several other investigative-type shows including 20/20, Eye to Eye, Inside Edition, and Dateline. Though 60 Minutes could not guarantee that they were going to run the story, they nevertheless asked us not to talk with the other investigative shows. They wanted an exclusive and believing it was our "best shot," we complied. In retrospect, we're not so sure. But at the time, we felt that we'd get the best coverage from 60 Minutes so we agreed to the "exclusive" story they had requested. I had been in prison for two months when the show finally aired on January 2, 1994.

Dateline had been particularly persistent and though we refused an interview with them, we did provide them with several reunion stories. When the show aired on September 15, 1993, we were pleasantly surprised with the results. As it turned out, their story was a more honest portrayal of the truth than the 60 Minutes story. At the same time, we were shocked to see that they had included an interview which I had given to Broadcast News Network three months before, while in Ohio.

Later in the week, I spoke with Tom Murphy of Video Technologies Network who had been working on a video project for us. We had decided to put together a 30 minute video to be used as an educational piece by support groups, shown at seminars and workshops, or distributed to the media, etc. It was going to be called **THE REUNION STORY / Breaking the Adoption Seal.** The 'actors' were already lined up - they were all individuals who had been reunited through The Musser Foundation work. Though it was going to be a costly project, we believed it would be a worthwhile one. The indictment came just as we were beginning the project. It didn't take long for us to realize that we were no longer in a financial position to complete it.

Tom had seen the story in his Naples newspaper, contacted me, and referred me to a local attorney who might be able to give me some direction. He also suggested that I come down to his 'studio' and do a taped interview since we had already given him a considerable deposit for the project.

I contacted the attorney Tom had suggested and explained that I needed a consultation as soon as possible. An afternoon appointment was arranged. She, too, had seen the article, so it wasn't necessary to go into a lot of detail. It still bothered me that the story hit the paper without my knowledge, so that was one of my first questions. Why hadn't I received a summons? Can an article just be published about you without your consent? She reiterated what the Cleveland reporter had said about 'notification by publication'. In a few words, she summed up my two choices succinctly:

9

1) I could turn myself in; or
2) I could wait to be arrested.

She suggested it would be better ("in my best interest") if I turned myself in, rather than wait to be arrested. "And how do I do that?," I asked. She said she'd call the Northeastern District of Ohio to let them know I was willing to "surrender" (sound familiar, birthmoms?), which she did. The primary intentions of the government were also spelled out in that conversation. As the U.S. Attorney in Akron, OH, spoke, the local attorney scribbled the following notes on a yellow legal pad:

- •levy a fine to discourage her
- •no restitution/no victim
- • use financial guide to determine fine based upon # of searches, records, activities. No amount that will shut her down; (which they ultimately did)

She informed me it would be less expensive if I obtained an Ohio attorney since a Florida attorney would need to be reimbursed for travel fees, etc. A possible change of venue was never mentioned and in my dazed state, I hadn't thought to inquire. I had little or no experience in dealing with the legal system and didn't even know what kind of questions to ask. She wished me well and provided me with a substantial bill for the one hour consultation.

I spent the rest of that day as well as the next several weeks trying to decide whether or not I wanted an attorney - or whether I wanted to try to defend my own case. When I discussed the idea of defending myself with my two sons, they let me know loud and clear what a stupid idea it was! My oldest one suggested I use a public defender; his theory being that they try harder to make a name for themselves. I still wasn't sure I wanted to go that route, but I was also concerned about the exorbitant costs. I knew I would have to make several trips to Ohio. Contrary to popular belief, I was not well-to-do, nor was the organization; most adoption reform leaders can bear testimony to the financial strain of operating costs.

The employees suggested we raise the funds by establishing a Legal Defense Fund. We had only a few days to get the envelopes printed in order to have them ready for the Cleveland conference. I had also written a statement called "The Real Story" to be read at the conference on my behalf.

Since I had never needed an attorney before, I had no idea how to begin to locate one - particularly one who could handle a federal case.

Naturally I began to have lots of regrets over the fact that, in all my years of reform work, I had never bothered to develop some good attorney contacts. Nor, did I ever think it would be necessary.

Within a few weeks, three referrals came my way. The first one was from a local talk show host whose father had once practiced law in Ohio. The second one was from a friend in Ohio who had been through a state case of a similar nature; and the third was from a well-known adoption reform author and friend.

I began the process of calling each lawyer and getting a "feel" for them on the phone. One of the key questions, of course, was the cost factor. It was extremely important for me to have a "bottom-line." It turned out that Mr. Keith, the first lawyer I spoke with, was the only one willing (or able) to give me a firm quote. Price became the deciding factor. If I had been true to my first inclination, I would have chosen the second and probably could have worked out the finances with her. If I had big bucks to spend, I might have chosen the third. As it turned out, I felt comfortable knowing exactly what it was going to cost and how much I would have to raise. I'm a "bottom-line" type person. Some believe it cost me the case.

During the following week, news reached us that two more indictments had been handed down. They occurred in New York State and affected two more birthmothers. It seemed as though the New York investigation team was on a roll and were working exceeding hard to stop adoption reunions from taking place and/or to 'hang' birthmothers.

Bobbie was calling the office three to four times a day. Every call was a major crisis and she was always in a panic-stricken state. I'd be right in the middle of a project and feeling fairly "up" - then she'd call and drag me down to the pits. By the time the conversation had ended, her continual bullying and intimidating manner would leave me completely drained. I was angry at myself for allowing her to 'get to me'. Still, I felt sorry for her. I even wrote her a short note telling her that "this too shall pass" and that she should be proud of the fact that she had been responsible for so many reunions. In the meantime, our office continued to carry on its work of reuniting families and adoption reform, even during this difficult period.

After awhile, Bobbie began playing emotional games. She would call to tell me who said what to whom, when, where, and why, but the straw that knocked me over the edge, and made me decide not to accept anymore of her calls, was her insinuation that this whole dehumanizing matter was my fault! My attorney had given me a copy of the Discovery Papers from the government, so I knew that she was being investigated long before I ever walked into the 'search' arena. The fact that she was

11

now laying all the blame at my feet made me see red.

Anger welled up within me (which seldom happens) and, in a loud, curt tone, I advised her to take a look in her own back yard. I had become convinced, for various reasons, that it was an "inside" job. At that point, the **person with whom I had originally contracted to do searches** spoke up and said "what do you mean by that?" Till then, I had no idea anyone else was on the line, but was not surprised since that had been Bobbie's style. She enjoyed making third party calls with one party unaware that anyone else was on the line. I was chagrined that this 'third party' on the line was my **original search contact**, whom Bobbie had eventually 'cut out' of the middle.

Following that episode, I began to refuse her calls. I had an office to run and an indictment to deal with - I didn't need her playing head games with me. Pat took her calls for awhile until she could no longer deal with her either. When she couldn't reach either of us at the office, she began calling us at home. Because we were both under stress and unable to deal with her, our husbands took over, but nevertheless, she continued to call. Finally they told her we had gone away for a rest, but didn't know where. They had hoped it would solve the problem, but it didn't. Pat's husband, Jerry, finally told her straight out to stop calling and said "Bobbie, this is not open for debate - you will not call here anymore!"

My husband even told her he was considering a divorce because of everything that was happening - that rumor took off with the speed of light through the 'movement' grapevine. He felt it was the only way he could get her to stop calling. The calls finally stopped and the silence was golden.

A very dear and close friend helped carry me through those first few crazy weeks. Our friendship dates back to the mid '70's. We "grew up" together in the movement and have developed a strong bond. In the early days, she was my mentor and I still gain insights from her quite often. Though we are 3000 miles apart, we are always close in spirit and during those dark hours, she became my lifeline. We had many late night conversations hashing and rehashing the series of events and how the negative could be turned to a positive. We have both always clung to "the bigger picture," and talking with her helped me keep the picture in focus - difficult as it was, it was becoming more vivid than ever.

Since Bobbie could no longer reach me, it was only a matter of time before she began to contact my friends. Mary Jo was one of them. Mary Jo attempted, quite vigorously, to be a mediator, but it was pointless. Though I was too blind to realize it at the time, the handwriting was already on the wall. Bobbie had entered a guilty plea and, in order to save her own skin, agreed to provide the government with whatever information they wanted, needed, or requested. Ultimately, what they demanded was her full cooperation in order for them to land me. Though it should been obvious to me that I was being setup as the "fall guy," it wasn't. It was not until much later that I understood that they needed her testimony for two primary reasons:

1) Without it, there could be no conspiracy charge since it takes two to form a conspiracy; if she had refused to testify, they would have had to drop their case against me;
2) Other than her testimony, there was no concrete evidence for them to convict me.

It was my original hope that we could both get through this crisis unscathed, but that was not going to happen. One of us had to be the **sacrificial lamb**. The government wanted and needed a scapegoat. Mr. Getz, the U.S. Attorney, made that clear when he stated in a newspaper article during the trial, "I hope this (example) has a chilling effect on anyone who does these kinds of things." But would it or could it stop people from wanting and needing to find their roots. Of course not. You cannot turn back the hands of time. The momentum may be slowed down, but the avalanche is so great that nothing can stop it from picking up speed.

I was saddened that we were being pitted against one another. Though she had a controlling and intimidating personality, I learned to accept it as part of her makeup and we managed to have a fairly decent working relationship. She performed the job we asked her to do. She was not an employee, but an 'independent contractor' whom we hired to do individual searches on a case by case basis. There were a dozen others we worked with on the same basis.

By contracting most of the search work out, The Musser Foundation was able to carry the torch of adoption reform. We accomplished this mission via many avenues: the printing and distribution of educational material - books, speeches, tapes, advertising, talk shows, selling t-shirts, cards, bumper stickers, pins - anything that would send the message that adoption was desperately in need of change. We even established an 800 # to make it easier for people to reach us to request our free information packet. In the meantime, hundreds of families were being reunited. We often received letters from college students working on their thesis; because of the amount of educational material we had printed, or acquired, we were able to provide them with a wealth of information.

There is no debate or question that the organization was sustained by search fees. They provided us with a solid base enabling us to carry out our primary goal of adoption reform, which was to change and improve an archaic system. It was through The Adoption & Family Reunion Division of The Musser Foundation that we accomplished those goals which had been spelled out in our Articles of Incorporation - to reunite families and reform the child welfare system!

From the time the indictment was made public until this present day, there have been several close friends who have gone the extra mile. One of them contacted me as soon as she heard the news and offered to do whatever she could do to assist. She sent out letters to all the support groups in an attempt to raise funds for my defense; she contacted several high-profile attorneys on my behalf; when I've been weak, she's offered her strength and encouragement. Her efforts are ongoing.

Lynn and I met several years ago when she invited me to speak at a conference for the Adoption Information Exchange, an organization she founded in 1980. Because of some internal problems in the mid-'80's, she took a sabbatical for about five years and only recently reentered the reform arena. This circumstance gave her a strong opportunity to become reinvolved. She has been and remains one of my closest and most trustworthy friends.

Another friend who contacted me early on was Hal Aigner, an adoptee activist and author. Hal is in his second year of law school and offered to do research work for my attorney. He was also willing to come and give expert testimony since he's quite familiar with search techniques and the legalities. Hal and I had many long conversations. Sometimes he would just call and say "How are you doing - I'm thinking about you." Those kind of calls were important and I was fortunate to have so many friends who, by reaching out, gave me strength.

Then there were wonderful supportive groups from around the country who wrote to me while I was in prison. Many of them sent cards and had all their members sign it - those were especially meaningful. Though I wish I were able to mention them all by name, my major concern is that it might put them in a precarious position. Deep bonds and friendships with adoptees, adoptive parents and other birthmothers had been forged over the past 18 years. The last thing I would want to do would be to put anyone in jeopardy of going through what I had to go through.

One evening, soon after the indictment, I wandered into the room in our office that we called "the lounge." It was the room where we took our coffee breaks and 'rested our minds'. A soft comfortable sofa allowed us to sit and chat with those who occasionally stopped by, or provided a place for a quick catnap.

On this particular day, after everyone had left the office, I went in and laid down. My mind began to wander and wonder. How did I get to this place in my life? At what point could I have changed the course of events? How conscious was I about my actions or reactions and the decisions I chose to make? My awakening had occurred in 1976 after years of suppression; that year was the turning point, as well as the point of no return. As my mind drifted, it became clear to me that I was living out my destiny. Come along as I share with you how I got from there to here.

they said

they said i had to go to a home for unwed
mothers - they never asked me what i wanted
to do; they said my baby should have a mother
and a father - they never gave me a choice to
help me see it through

they said the line on my belly would disappear -
they never mentioned the wound in my
heart; they said go on with your life and
pretend it didn't happen - they never told me
i would grieve all the years we're apart

they said i should be happy now that i'm free
they never admit my flesh and blood has
been amputated from me; they said i could get
married and other children would call me
mother - they never said one person does not
replace another

they said why worry she has a good life -they
never listen to how the pain of not knowing
cuts like a knife; they said it's against the
law to search and find her -
they never knew this was my heart's desire

they said she's still young and has other
things on her mind - they never say you're
getting older you've been waiting a long
time; they said when she has children she'll
want to know me - they never concede i missed
sharing her life, she never sat on my knee

they said if i loved my baby i'd sign the
paper and leave that day - she said
"don't tell me you love me, you gave me away!"

sheila ganz

16

THE AWAKENING AND THE FINALE

It's difficult to have a clear picture unless you know something about the background of an organization - how it came into being, events leading to its existence, its primary purposes and goals, and the person at the helm. Knowing background helps to fit pieces together; and, in this case, helps to make sense out of the chaos which was presented by the prosecution.

This chapter capsulates, in just a few pages, the past 18 years of my life within the arena of adoption reform. It explains the progression of the organizations I spawned in chronological order. By following the chronology, you may find several clues that suggest that the downfall of The Musser Foundation could have been prompted from 'inside' the movement.

The Background

In April of 1976, I attended a support group meeting of The Adoption Forum of Philadelphia. It was to be my first such experience, but many more would follow. I had been invited to the meeting by Penny Partridge, Founder of the Forum, who had met her birthmother just a few months before. An article about her reunion story prompted a call from me and she extended an invitation to attend the meeting. I'm certain I must have been "ripe" for 'coming out' because, although I was nervous at first, it was a fairly easy thing for me to do.

In a very short period of time, I became an active Board member of the Forum. I also wasted no time in making a decision to search for the daughter I had surrendered 22 years before. She had always remained within my heart, and very often on my mind. I located Wendy in April of 1977, almost a year to the day that I had joined the Forum.

At the first Forum conference that same month, my path crossed with Lee Campbell, Founder of Concerned United Birthparents. She had formed CUB about six months prior in her home state of Massachusetts. During the conference, we spent a lot of time together and had a good rapport.

Soon after she returned home, she contacted me and asked if I would be interested in representing CUB as Branch Coordinator, establishing CUB branches around the country. At first I was hesitant because I wasn't sure of my own capabilities or what would be involved. She suggested that I take a little time to think about it.

One of the major factors which helped me decide was the opportunity and challenge it presented, so I called Lee and told her I'd accept. I began by starting my own CUB branch in South Jersey in the summer of 1977 and by the time I left CUB in 1981-82, 25 branches were actively functioning.

In 1979, the first American Adoption Congress conference was held in Washington, D.C. The AAC had been formed as a umbrella organization for the 300+ grassroot search and support groups around the country. It's primary purpose was to promote Openness & Honesty in Adoption. Since I had a grandchild due the same weekend as the conference, I only attended one day. But it was there that I had the opportunity to meet a few people who became lifelong friends - Mary Jo Rillera, Founder of Triadoption Library, and Emma May Vilardi, Founder of ISRR, who has since passed away. Penny Partridge was voted as the first President of AAC and, since we lived fairly close, I offered to do whatever I could do assist her.

During the spring of 1980, I attended a CUB Board meeting in MA and came away feeling disappointed and discouraged. Some of the new CUB leadership seemed to be very angry and "radical" (for lack of a better word) and I was still in my nicey, nice niche. Obviously they saw the bigger picture long before I did.

Throughout the summer of 1980, I mulled over ideas in my mind for an organization that could somehow reach out to the religious community. It was an area that was "fertile ground" and an area I knew well. For several years, I had been an active member, Sunday School teacher, and eventually Superintendent, of a Baptist Church. I had also attended Philadelphia College of Bible School in the evenings and received an Evangelical Teacher Training Certificate. Everything seemed to be going along fine until I made a conscious decision to open the closet door, step into the light, and speak out publicly.

I was quickly taken back to 1954 for an immediate recall of the chastisement from the community. A special meeting of the school board was held to determine my 'fate' as to whether or not I should remain in

18

school? I was sent away - out of town, hidden from my family and friends. My pastor decided I was in need of "counseling" for the "sin" I had committed, while the birthfather, a member of the same church, walked off into the sunset needing no counseling at all! Interesting! Especially since our intimacy had occurred on a youth church retreat!

Yes, just as the church preached its message to all who would listen, I now felt that they were the ones who needed to hear a message - a message that adoption needed to be reformed and the church should have an active role in its reform.

In the late summer of 1980, I began to formulate ideas for an organization called Adoption Triangle Ministries (ATM). The primary purpose of ATM, as stated, was an attempt to educate the church community with educational material about adoption issues. A wonderful school teacher friend donated $35 as 'seed' money; she felt confident it would grow to accomplish great things. She was right. It did.

By way of beginning to educate the church community, we developed 30-35 tracts written by various triad members. They were printed and distributed by people around the country who became ATM representatives. We hoped these little tracts (which we called leaflets) would give the reader a new perspective within the short span of time (about 5 minutes) it took to read one. They seemed to fit the bill. We received glowing comments about particular favorites like "The Grave at the End of the Search", "Your Birthday" and "Dear Daughter". Triad members ordered extras to send their family and friends; some even mailed them out with their bills. About a dozen of the popular ones were kept in print and mailed with each information packet we sent out.

Moving South and Starting Over

In November of 1982, I made a permanent move to Florida. My Mother had moved to Cape Coral in 1962 and I had made several visits over the years. Leaving the cold north and moving south was something I always knew I would do - now the time had arrived. My youngest son had just turned 20 and was sharing an apartment with his older brother. My two daughters were also on their own. It was time for me to "move on". The home where we had lived for 17 years held too many sad memories and the cost of the upkeep alone was more than I could afford. I left everything behind except the things I could fit in my '69 Toyota.

The trip was great. Many of my friends in the reform movement had invited me to stop and visit along the way, which made for a pleasant and enjoyable trip. I had already planned to stay with Mother until I could get on my feet. My younger sister, Terry, was still living at home

19

so we shared a room for about a month and then moved into a duplex.

By the spring of 1983, I had settled in and decided to set up a support group. I made contact with the Ft. Myers News-Press and they came out and interviewed me. The result was a full-page story which received a tremendous response. Within a few weeks, the first meeting of the Adoption Triangle was held in my apartment.

I had been attending a Baptist singles group and late in November of the same year, I met the man who would become my second husband. Since I had stars in my eyes and been bitten by the lovebug, I had precious little time for anything else but my new love. For the first time in seven years, adoption reform took a back seat. Norm and I were married four months later in April of '84 and recently celebrated our 10th anniversary. Except for running the support group and speaking at a few conferences, I took about a year and a half sabbatical from my volunteer work of adoption reform. I worked part-time as a secretary in a family owned electrical business, and my husband and I bought a small two-bedroom ranch-style home, where we still reside.

Toward the end of '85, I began to reconnect with many of my adoption friends. I had brought my donated Apple Computer from NJ, set it up in the living room and began to create various data bases, wrote letters to legislators, and corresponded readily with the 250+ (at that time) support groups in the country.

The Founding of ALARM

In 1986, I was invited to speak at a conference in Louisville, KY. It was one of the most moving and well-planned conferences I had ever attended. A group of us were sitting around on Saturday evening having a brainstorming session and wondering - wondering why things weren't happening more quickly - why had nothing changed - what were we missing? Someone brought up the fact that there was no lobbying effort going on. That was it! Everyone in the little group agreed that lobbying definitely should be the next order of business and, undoubtedly, should have been all along. Most of us had been too absorbed in our own pain to "see the forest for the trees". We were having great conferences; we got together and had lots of fun; laughed and cried and helped each other through the pain, but we had dropped the ball when it came to developing any kind of lobbying effort.

Some individual members had been doing it in small ways, but there was no single organization to carry the national thrust. Most of us had the mistaken belief that lobbying was one of the primary functions of the AAC but, at that time, it definitely was not. There was seldom any mention of legislation or lobbying at any of the AAC conferences. There was no national push at all, except by Bill Pierce, Chairman of the National Committee for Adoption. He was right there in Washington lobbying to make sure the records remained sealed. He also had the big bucks from the private agencies behind him - something our movement greatly lacked and have never had - the funds with which to do a concerted national effort.

On the airplane back to FL from KY, my mind began to formulate an organization that could become a grassroot lobbying group. I toyed with a name which was originally Adopting Legislation for Adoption Reform Movement. But later it was changed to Advocating Legislation for Adoption Reform. It was quite a mouthful, but the acronym ALARM seemed to work well. In fact, we were able to use it to our advantage in our advertising pieces.

Over the next several weeks, letters were sent out to all the groups announcing the formation of the organization. The response was not great, but enough to warrant a decision to move forward with the idea. However, I wasn't sure I was the one to be leading such an effort or that I wanted to take on the task. Nevertheless, the organization was established in May of 1987. While in the process of laying the groundwork, I decided to put together a proposal to the AAC that they "adopt" ALARM as their lobbying arm. That proposal was presented to the AAC Board at the national conference in Calgary. Aside from the fact that they turned down the offer, it was the first time that I could recall being "snubbed" by the AAC Board, but never knew why. They declined the offer by saying that they wanted their legislative effort to be done "internally".

In the meantime, several triad members from different parts of the country had expressed an interest in ALARM by volunteering to represent their state as a coordinator. A logo (a tree with question marks on the branches) was designed and a 'motto' - "FREE BY '93"! Setting a date seemed to help spark motivation and gave us a goal to work toward. A newsletter called the *FREEDOM RIDER* was sent quarterly for a $35 membership fee.

The State Coordinators were responsible for developing their own chair people and committees for a state lobbying effort. The national office provided the technical help and direction; letters with supporting documents and material were sent to any state legislators and committee chairs who were sponsoring bills or had bills pending.

The bill we proposed was an "Access to Records Bill for Adult Adoptees" or an "Open Records" bill as it is more commonly called. It would make it possible for an adopted adult to obtain a copy of his/her original birth certificate, upon request, once majority age had been reached. Kansas is one of the two states where this has worked for years,

21

being the only state in the country which has always allowed adoptees to receive a copy of their original birth certificate. They were never sealed. Alaska, the other state, initiated the same option in their state law in 1980.

The flyer we distributed carried a strong, "to the point" message:

The ALARM Is Sounding!

We are **ALARMED** that ADOPTED ADULTS do not have access to their own original birth certificate, or court and agency records concerning themselves!

We are **ALARMED** that ADOPTED ADULTS birth and adoption information has been altered and falsified, then protected (hidden) by the confidentiality law!

We are **ALARMED** that ADOPTED ADULTS are unable to obtain a current medical history - especially in light of 3000 known genetic diseases!

We are **ALARMED** that ADOPTED ADULTS are often given false and misleading information about their background by social workers, attorneys, and other "helping professionals" in the field of adoption!

We are **ALARMED** that ADOPTED ADULTS must pay agency fees to receive NON-identifying information; state fees to be placed on a state registry; and attorney fees to petition the court system in an effort to receive what is rightfully theirs - their IDENTIFYING information!

We are **ALARMED** that confidentiality laws have stripped ADOPTED ADULTS of their own, their childrens' and their grandchildrens' entire genealogical history and genetic heritage causing a malady known as ancestricide!

We are **ALARMED** that in a free and democratic society, these basic, human, God-given, constitutional rights, promised to all Americans, are denied to all ADOPTED ADULTS!

We invited anyone interested to join ALARM'S campaign to free the adoption community from the bondage of our repressive adoption laws. The ALARM Network was originally responsible for generating

22

legislative activity in several states, particularly in FL, MI, NJ, OH, IN, and OR. In the fall of '87, we sparked the interest of a Democratic Senator in FL who was ready to sponsor an open records bill. Since Florida is only in session for 60 days, we had to find a sponsor from the House so the bill could run concurrently. We never succeeded.

Expanding to a "Real Office"

During this time period, my husband suggested I look for office space since our small two-bedroom house was being overrun with adoption material. At the same time, my parents had retired and closed their small business, so I needed to find another job or create one. Having my own office would provide me with the opportunity to devote more time to my 'love' of adoption reform work, but how was I going to support it? Obviously I would have to setup a "profit-making" company in order to support my volunteer work.

Since my profession was secretarial work, it made sense to establish a small typing business. So November 1, 1987, I nervously took the plunge and hung a shingle called S.O.S. which stood for Secretarial Office Services. S.O.S. provided typing and computer services i.e. resumes, term papers, leases, legal documents, etc. Since business was slow, I had lots of extra time on my hands. It afforded me the opportunity to communicate with the ALARM coordinators, legislators and the media about our proposal for open record bills.

Because of my personal involvement in the reform work since 1976 and the publications of my books in '79 and '82, I've always received a large volume of mail. Most of the letters were from individuals who were "in search" and needed help. Since I had only been involved in the educational aspect, but never in the 'search-end', I felt inadequate to assist - though I had great empathy.

Getting Baptized Into Search Work

During the early part of '88, a gentlemen came into my office for some typing work. He was employed part-time for a large genealogical tracing service so I mentioned my work with adoption reform. I explained that many people wrote asking for search assistance, but I had been unable to help them. He suggested I call their Home Office to see if they might be able to assist. He gave me the name and address of the person to contact.

The president of the company returned my call and asked me to send him the particulars on a few cases. He would look them over and then forward me quotes. He said I should add a referral fee since I would be responsible for handling the funds. The company worked on a "no trace/no fee" basis, but the money had to be placed in an escrow account before the search could begin. This was my **baptism** into "search work". I was excited about this new venture because S.O.S. was not bringing in enough income to substantiate the office. I knew I wouldn't be able to remain open much longer.

I was surprised when I received the first few quotes because they averaged between $3,000 and $5,000. As it turned out, we did not do business with them because they were unable to do a "straight adoption case" - or, as we came to call it, "a no name search." Most adoptees who contacted us for search help did not know the name of their birthmother, or the person they were seeking, since that information was in the "sealed record."

It had been rumored for several years that there was a person who could get "sealed" information. He was known as "the searcher" or "the underground" and called by various names. However, it was necessary to have a "contact" or a connection to get to him. The flat fee was $2500 cash and I was told that, in the early years, the money was placed in a shoe box and mailed to a P.O. Box. Now it is Fed-exed to one of five or six contacts in the country.

Since the genealogical service charged over $3000 to complete a search, I reasoned that it would still be less expensive for an individual to go the "underground" route if I had a "contact" - which at the time I did not.

There was also a group of individuals in the movement known as Independent Search Consultants. ISC's specialized in adoption searches so I decided to send a letter and questionnaire to each of them. I inquired about their particular areas of expertise and fees, as well as their willingness to receive cases from me. (In essence, my organization would be their client). I was informed that the Founder of ISC was upset over it and sent out a special newsletter discouraging her members from responding. About 20 consultants sent back the form and I began to work with those individuals.

One of the best contacts to respond to the ISC mailing turned out to be a woman from OH who we'll call Jeannette - the name the court clerk chose for her during the trial. I had met Jeannette at a few conferences, didn't know her real well, but found her to be friendly and anxious to help with cases. So it was that late in 1988, I began to work with Jeannette and others to help reunite individuals with their families.

My daughter, Sherri, started coming into the office a few days a week. She was a tremendous help and I depended on her more and more as the work load increased. We were also having regular support group meetings each month. One young girl in our group had given up her baby only a year before and was having a lot of difficulty dealing with the experience; particularly with angry feelings toward her mother.

A few weeks later her mother came in to talk with me. She hoped to gain a better understanding of what her daughter was experiencing as a new birthmother, and her own guilt feelings as a birthgrandmother. We became friends and she began to drop by often. Before long, Doris was helping out on a regular basis, putting data onto the computer. She also had a great personality on the phone; she related well to each person she spoke to. But her best skill was organization - something I've often prayed for, but have always lacked.

The three of us began to formulate the program. The first thing we did was to draw up our Philosophy Statement which follows. It was sent out as part of our information packet to each person requesting material.

THE MUSSER FOUNDATION PHILOSOPHY STATEMENT

The Adoption & Family Center serves all individuals who have been touched in some way by the "adoption experience" as well as individuals who are separated from family members due to divorce, foster care, family illness, mental breakdowns, wartime depression years, or family disruption of any kind.

Our Center believes that at the core of every human being is a God-given, innate desire to "connect" with birth family from whom we've become separated. We are not concerned about the reasons for the separation, but only to begin the healing which we believe comes about through the process of reconciliation.

1) We believe that loss and separation from family members caused by divorce, foster care, or adoption has created severe psychological problems and weakened our family structures.

2) We believe that the severing of genetic roots is not healthy and that all individuals have a right to know their siblings, the "missing" parent(s), birth grandparents, and all other genetic relatives. We also believe that parents who have "lost" their children (for any reason) have a need and right to know of the welfare of their children.

3) We believe that all family relationships should be inclusive and not exclusive. Therefore we believe in the concept of extending and expanding the family circle; and believe

that blending our families will strengthen them and our world as well!

Our Purpose and Goal

To provide emotional support for families in crisis through private consultations; to offer search assistance and direction for individuals seeking missing relatives; to provide a network referral service; to promote open adoption as a viable alternative to the present closed system which severs roots; to provide new ideas and thoughts for those desiring personal growth.

The Development Stage

While we were in this formulative stage, we found that the most difficult part was setting the fees. We had all agreed that the cost should be a fixed cost; that it should remain firm so the client would know right from the beginning what the "bottom line" was going to be. We first had to consider how much the individual investigators were going to charge; then we had to figure in enough to cover our fixed operating expenses such as rent, printing, phone bills (our 800#), equipment, supplies, i.e. letterhead, envelopes, computer disks, anything necessary to operate an efficient office.

We decided that the person searching should sign an agreement form which would provide them with an exact quote. Aside from a small deposit (half of which was refundable if we didn't find within six months), the balance would be paid only when and if the search was completed. **ALL CASES WERE DONE ON A "NO FIND, NO FEE" BASIS**. The investigators and consultants, with whom we contracted to do searches, had all agreed to work with us on the condition that they got paid when we got paid - when the search was complete.

We were especially sensitive to the fact that many people 'in search' are often vulnerable. There is a strong desire to reconnect, and sometimes desperate need, to meet their missing loved one. Since we were all part of the adoption triad family ourselves, we did not want anyone to feel they were getting "ripped off". While we realized it was not possible to give an ironclad guarantee that the person being sought would be located - we, nevertheless, were able to guarantee that if we did not complete the search, the person searching would not have to pay! It was the best 'deal' around!

The fees for services were worked out with each individual investigator. They would tell us how much it was going to cost and we would decide if we could handle it. Very early on, it became obvious that Jeannette was producing the best results in the shortest amount of time. She said that the cost would be $675 for adoptees searching - a $75 deposit and $600 due at the time the search was complete. We initially set a "flat fee" across the board of $975.

At that time, she was not able to do "birthparents" seeking the child they surrendered, unless they had relinquished in the state of Ohio. As time went by, we offered various fees based on the information the adoptee had. The more information, the less the price. A "no name" search for adoptees at the time we were indicted was a flat "no find - no fee" of $1800, except for a half dozen states.

Occasionally when I'd be talking to Jeannette on the phone, she'd mention the name "Bobbie". I didn't inquire because it didn't matter. I didn't feel it was my business to know who she was talking about since it was her contact. But I did wonder - could this be the same Bobbie who had called me back in 1980? Other than the original phone call, there was a brief encounter in the fall of 1988 when I was invited to speak at a regional conference in Cleveland. My husband had attended the conference with me, and since the bookroom always became busy with 'inquiring minds', it was great to have him along to help out.

Bobbie came to our book table, purchased a book, and introduced herself. Since we had never before met face to face and had only spoken on the phone briefly, I had no way of knowing who she was. The principle reason I recall the incident so well is because her $15 check for the book she purchased was returned. The only other time our paths crossed was early in 1989 when I was invited to do an AM talk show in Cleveland. She came to my hotel room where others were already visiting. We had not had any conversations about search work on either occasion.

After several months, it became clear that Jeannette was working with the same Bobbie, but I still didn't know who was doing what - nor did I care - nor did I ask! Why would I have needed to? Jeannette was handling the cases and the work was satisfactory. I realize in retrospect that, because of the many years I had spent working for reform, some people thought I knew who the various liaisons were in the "search" arena. The fact is - I did not.

A New Search Connection

It was about this same time that someone put me in touch with a woman in NC by the name of Charlotte who was a contact for "The Searcher". The searcher had a reputation in the movement for working miracles, especially when there was very little information to go on and particularly for birthparents searching for their offspring. Charlotte said the cost was $2500 cash, but agreed to give us a 10% referral fee because of the number of cases we would most likely be sending her. She said that the searcher was the only person in the entire country who could do a "no name" search in any state. As time went by, we found a few other investigators who could do "no names" in specific states, but for the most part, it appears she was correct in her statement.

Within the first six months of 1989, we had reunited several families. Though we were using other investigators during the same period, Jeannette was the one who was turning the cases around in the shortest amount of time. Sherri, Doris and I all communicated with her and found her to be a pleasure to work with. As she completed each case, we'd send her a company check. The search consultants and investigators were responsible for their own taxes since the work was subcontracted to them, and unless they had a company name, we were responsible for sending them a 1099 at the end of the year.

The first weekend in August, I attended the first March on Washington called H.E.A.L., which stood for Honesty and Equality in Adoption Laws, sponsored by the AAC. The public "speak out" was held on Saturday, August 5th, and I gave a brief speech entitled "This Time Must Come", (reprinted in The Leadership Speaks chapter). The title was taken from a wonderful poem written by Mary Anne Cohen, a birthmother with much foresight and insight.

In that speech, I spoke of Susan B. Anthony and told how she and 16 other women marched to the voting booth in 1872 and exercised their God-given right to vote. She was prosecuted and fined- a fine she refused to pay. I then posed a fateful question - **"How many of us are going to have to stand trial, pay fines, and be prosecuted for exercising our God-given right to our original birth certificate or other records concerning our own lives?"**

Never in my wildest nightmares did I realize that in only four short years, I would be sitting in a federal prison! The discovery papers said that the investigation began in August of 1989 - is it just another strange coincidence that my speech in Washington coincided with the beginning of the investigation? Big Brother was undoubtedly present!

Fateful Phone Calls

While I was in Washington, Sherri received a phone call from Bobbie. Bobbie told Sherri that she was aware we had been referring cases to Jeannette, but since Jeannette's husband was very sick, it would be better if cases were sent directly to her (Bobbie). Sherri also received a call from a young man in Indiana by the name of Jim. Jim informed her that he was a good investigator and would like to try a few of our cases.

When I returned from Washington, Sherri told me about the phone calls. Jeannette had previously mentioned that her husband was quite sick, so I knew that was true. Though Bobbie's call came as a surprise, it did clarify the fact that Jeannette and Bobbie worked closely together. I still didn't know who was doing what - and again - I didn't care. Reuniting families was our primary goal and it didn't make any difference as long as families were being reunited. Sherri then mentioned Jim's call and said she had given him a few cases. Since I trusted her judgement, I thought no more about it - until later.

Sherri gave me Bobbie's phone number and I called her. She reiterated exactly what she had told Sherri about Jeannette's husband, and I said I understood. I sent Jeannette a "thinking of you" card, but didn't mention the phone call from Bobbie. It hadn't even occurred to me to do so - since I presumed they had probably discussed the matter beforehand.

In this original conversation, Bobbie asked a lot of questions about our agreement forms, etc. I explained that we always gave a flat fee quote so the person knew 'up-front' what the cost of the search would be. She then asked, "Who do you give your birthparent cases to?" "Usually we give them to the Searcher", I said. "And what do you charge for them", she asked. "Well, we charge "$2500, but we send $2250 to our contact and keep $250 for our expenses and overhead." She then made a suggestion that we run them by her first and if she could do them, her charge would only be $1000. "If I can't do it, you can still turn it over to 'the searcher' since your client is already committed to $2500."

Undoubtedly, this was a generous offer and I thanked her. Since we had recently installed an 800#, we were receiving a lot more requests for searches. This would not only help us cover our tremendous overhead, but it would also assist us in expanding our reform activities. i.e. putting together a video, printing educational material, and possibly reach some of our long-range dreams - a home where young mothers could keep their babies with them for at least a year until they could get on their feet. As it turned out, there were many she could not do so we had to forward them on to Charlotte.

She then informed me that she could get social security numbers, but that it was necessary to have the complete maiden name, date of birth, place of birth and parents' names. She never said where she was getting them, nor did I bother to ask. Seldom did anyone come to us with that much information so the fact that she said she could get social security numbers didn't mean a whole lot to me. What would I do with the number once I had it? At that early stage, I had no idea that the SS# could be run through a credit company and bingo! - up pops an address, provided the individual has established credit. I explained that I had no resource, at that time, to obtain the current information to complete the case. She said her cost to provide a social # was generally $50, but if I wanted her to go ahead and complete it, she'd charge me $150. As time went by, the price was lowered to $100. For that type of a search, we charged $350.

The young man named Jim from Indiana called about the same time. He had worked on a few of our cases successfully, but now he was calling to say he was in trouble. He had been indicted for impersonating a judge and was seeking support. I didn't know Jim at all, but said I'd do what I could to help. (Did that mean I was guilty of conspiracy?) I wasn't sure what I could do other than offer emotional and possibly some financial support. In a subsequent call from Bobbie, Jim's name came up and she said she did some cases for him, but he owed her quite a bit of money so she was very angry with him. Apparently they had a big blowup and Jim said something about "getting her". Jim's legal problems began in the fall of '89 and, I was told, gave testimony in January of '92 - the exact dates we were being investigated. Another coincidence?

The Musser Foundation Is Born

In October 1989, a new birthmother attended our support group meeting on an evening when a birthparent couple were sharing their experience. The DiSarro's had married after relinquishing their firstborn son, and came to share their experience of meeting him after 19 years. Pat was so touched by their story, and the peace they had found, that she made a decision that evening to search for her daughter. She went back north for the holidays and we didn't see her again for a few months. When she returned, she came to stay and work.

We were getting so busy with cases, we decided we should develop a new brochure. So in November of '89, I took the ATM brochure and ALARM flyer to Cal, a local graphic artist. I explained to Cal that I had opened a small typing service the previous year, but most of my time was spent working on adoption reform and family reunions. We had originally had our phone listed in the name of Adoption & Family Awareness Center, but because most of the calls we were receiving were from prospective adoptive parents, we changed the name to Adoption & Family Reunion Center. Would he try to design a dynamic brochure that would tie ATM, ALARM, and the Reunion Center together?

About two weeks later, Cal called and said "Sandy, I think you ought to consider incorporating under the name of The Musser Foundation or The Musser Institute, and maintain the other names as divisions". Using my name was something I had never considered and, in fact, felt uncomfortable with **even** the suggestion of it. When I began to examine my fears closely, I realized that my main concern was that my friends in the movement would think it was presumptuous and pretentious. But Cal said "You've already established the name through the work you've accomplished". My next argument was "But it sounds so grandiose and doesn't really say anything - it doesn't say what we do - no one will know what it is!" He was becoming exasperated with me and he said "What does Coke say or do, or Sears? They've made a name for themselves and we all know who they are and what they do. You've made a name within your movement and you've done reform work for many years - soon others in the country will know what you do and what you stand for."

It took several weeks and many discussions with others before a decision was made. My dear and close friend, Mary Jo, was undoubtedly the catalyst in helping me to make the decision when she said, "People who use their name in business are putting their integrity on the line - if you're willing to do that, then go for it!" I was willing to put my integrity on the line and, in spite of what has happened, I've never regretted my decision. In fact, I am proud that The Musser Foundation, in a relatively short period of time, became synonymous with reuniting families.

Over the next few months, Cal and I discussed the content of the brochure. Naturally, we wanted it to be dynamic and classy; we also wanted to include our various services and be a self-mailer. We had decided that it would be 11 x 14 size folded in half, using card stock paper.

He began by developing an attractive logo which integrated a lighthouse with The Musser Foundation name and "Lighting the Way" became our byline. I suggested we use pictures of people who had been reunited through our service, with a small explanation beside each one - knowing so well that a picture is always worth a thousand words. My daughter's picture was placed in the first position inside the brochure and beside it was written "Finding my daughter, Wendy, healed my heart, changed my life and gave me renewed purpose and direction - and is the reason The Musser Foundation now exists".

Others included in the first brochure were a sibling who found a brother who had been given up for adoption; an adoptee and her birthmother; birthparents who had married each other and found their son; a young woman of divorced parents who found the father she had never known; and a picture of a family with an open adoption - included were both the birthmom and adoptive mom with their two year old twin boys.

Also on the inside cover across the top, in big bold letters, was written REUNITED... AND WHOLE AND LAST! Down the side of the brochure we listed our various services which included: Family Search Services,

Adoption Education, Support Groups and Private Counseling, Family Preservation, Literature and Tapes, and Public Speaking. Our Philosophy Statement was included with every packet we sent out.

People have often inquired as to how many Americans are affected by the adoption process. Several years ago when I was presenting a workshop in Tampa, that particular question arose. I knew that estimates of the number of adoptees in the country ranged from 5 million to 8 million. Writing on the blackboard and using the lower figure of 5 million, I began extending the figures by adding extended family members who are also affected by adoption. I was shocked when the estimated figure reached 135 million - over one-half of our entire population!

I mentioned these figures to Cal and showed him how they broke down. He, too, was amazed that so many people were affected by the institution of adoption. With tremendous ingenuity, he proceeded to create a tree which graphically demonstrated the 135 million. He placed the low estimate of 5 million adoptees in the center of the tree and branched out to include the 10 million birthparents and 10 million adoptive parents of the adoptee; the 10 million birth sibs and 10 million adoptive sibs (average of two each); he then added the 20 million maternal and paternal birth grandparents and the 20 million maternal and paternal adoptive grandparents, and finally branched out to include the 20 million birth aunts and uncles and 20 million adoptive aunts and uncles for a grand total of 135 million - one-half of our entire population!!

Our entire society is adversely affected by this process called adoption. An institution that continues to propagate itself by altering and/or falsifying birth records and vital certificates, then strips adoptees of their entire genetic and medical history by sealing records, thereby stealing their basic birthright, is a terrible shame and a sham in a country like America! Take note that the figure of 135 million DOES NOT include cousins, nieces, or nephews, nor does it take into account divorce and remarriage which would bring in a whole new set of family members. The reason these figures are so significant is because it is generally thought that adoption concerns very few people. In actuality, there are millions of people affected by family separation for many various reasons; for our government to put up the kind of roadblocks they do is asinine and continues to compound the problem.

When the brochures came off the press early in 1990, we were in awe at how impressive they looked. Yes, we were proud of them. We immediately mailed one to each of the 350+ support groups around the country. Several contacted us immediately to tell us how nice the brochure looked and how excited they were. As a result, many of them began to make referrals and we began fulfilling our purpose and goal of reuniting loved ones - the work we believed we were called to do.

We incorporated in the State of Florida as a non-for-profit organization on February 28, 1990. A few months later we applied for our tax-exempt status which was very costly and, took several months for the paperwork to be reviewed. We were eventually turned down because we "charged search fees". We were told we could reapply at a later date. We challenged this decision by questioning the fact that adoption agencies all over the country have nonprofit status; they charge fees to "place" babies for adoption and their fees are a lot higher than our search fees. We didn't understand why it was ok for agencies, but not ok for us - wasn't our work of reuniting families as worthy as placing a child with a new family?

Pat came to work with us early in the Spring. Up until then, Doris, Sherri and I had been carrying the ball. Since Doris had another job and Sherri had young children, they were both only working part-time. Therefore the majority of the work had fallen on my shoulders. The phone calls and letters were becoming more than I could handle. Because the workload had increased so much, I felt I needed someone on a full-time basis and since Pat was retired, I asked if she would be interested.

Keeping the books was the job I liked the least and that was the most trying for me. Accounting has never been my forte. I'm the type of person who rounds out the figures in my checkbook! I offered to pay her on a commission basis if she could work full-time as an Office Manager (eventually she became the Assistant Director). She agreed and it was a great feeling of relief to be able to share the workload. We had an excellent working relationship.

The Talk Show Circuit

In March, one of our local group members, for whom we had just completed a search, stopped in the office to share a letter she had received from her birthmother. She was very excited and "dying" to meet her, but her mother was in California and she was here in Florida. Neither of them had the funds to make a trip to meet. She wondered if we could contact one of the talk shows and initiate a TV reunion. We discussed whether they would both be comfortable doing a "public" reunion. She said that, from her vantage point, it would be easier to do in a fishbowl setting rather than privately. She checked with her birthmother who also agreed it was a great idea.

We decided to make a few calls and see what we could do. We had been talking to a producer of the Joan Rivers Show, and thought it was a go, but things fell apart. We learned very early on that TV talk shows are **always** tenuous. Caroline said she often watched a show called House Party, so we contacted them and arrangements were made for them to be reunited on the program. I, too, was invited to be a guest. The show was mentioned to Bobbie, and she said "Be sure to tell them that your best investigator from Cleveland broke the case". Her remark didn't surprise me since, in the past, she had said she sometimes resented not getting any credit. It seemed to be a valid point, even though she was being paid well.

The second week in April 1990, Caroline and I flew to New York for the show. It was exciting watching the producers frantically struggling to keep Caroline and her birthmother from running into one another. Finally it was showtime. Caroline and I were seated on the stage together. The host spoke to Caroline at length about her need to know her birthmother, her feelings about being adopted, and so on. He then spoke with me about our work of reuniting families. I mentioned the difficulty individuals have due to sealed records and the difficulty, in this particular case, was the fact that the date of birth had been changed by 10 days. Then offhandedly, I said something like "Our best investigator from Cleveland was able to break this case even though the date of birth had apparently been changed!" This seemingly innocent comment set the wheels in motion. Though I had not planned to make the remark, I knew Bobbie would appreciate this little bit of indirect recognition since she had specifically requested it.

The show brought hundreds of calls. For several weeks we were busy responding to adoptees and birthparents, siblings, grandparents, and a few adoptive parents. Each person who called received our brand new brochure along with a cover letter, an agreement form, a fee schedule, and miscellaneous leaflets from ATM.

The Infamous Set-Up

One of those calls was from a "birthfather" looking for a child given up for adoption when he and his girlfriend were in high school. He said the child was relinquished in NY so we considered it a NY search. Mr. Flavin (the alleged birthfather) was very friendly on the phone. As it turned out, Mr. Flavin was not a birthfather, but a NY State Dept. of Health Investigator. Doris had taken his original call and sent him the packet of information. She had even spoken to him from her home. He made several more calls to the office over the course of several weeks and spoke to each of us at one time or another. Unbeknown to any of us, he was taping the conversations; particularly the ones between him and I. Because I have a trusting nature and have always taken people at face value, I was totally unprepared for "the setup". By the same token, I made some adverse comments which were misconstrued and taken out of context, causing my innocence to appear questionable.

34

He also sent us the following letter:

> **Dear Ms. Musser:**
> While I was serving in Korea my girlfriend gave birth to a girl. She put the child up for adoption and has refused to give me any information about the birth or the adoption. I do know that she never had the child with her at her address in Rensselaer so she must have left the baby at the hospital. A member of my girlfriends family told me that my girlfriend went to Waverly, NY to have the child. This is the only information that I have. My wife and family is not aware of my desire to locate my daughter so it is important that if you wish to speak to me, please call me at home and speak only with me. I am normally home after 5 o'clock in the evening. Good Luck!
> **Tom Flavin**
> P.S. I have contacted the telephone company and they have only one hospital listed in Waverly, NY. Tioga General Hospital.

Within a short period of time, Bobbie realized she was not going to be able to complete Mr. Flavin's case. In the past, she had commented that she sometimes asked "The Searcher" for help when she got stuck on a case. This was one of those cases. I vividly remember the day she called to tell us that the "Big Guy" (the underground went by different names) told her to tell me to "get rid of the Flavin file - he works for the Department of Health"! Obviously he knew all the people who worked in the various departments, including the investigators. That advice came a bit too late since the damage had already been done and the rest is history. But I still have the file including the agreement he signed on May 18, 1990. At that time we were not taking deposits, so Mr. Flavin was able to pull off his bogus case without even spending a dime!

According to the discovery papers presented to my attorney, and subsequently given to me, as well as Mr. Flavin's statements at the trial, they had been tracking Bobbie for several years - at least since 1986/87. Mr. Flavin claimed that his wife told him about the show when he arrived home from work one day. He immediately called our 800# and requested our material. After receiving it, he proceeded to go to extensive lengths to set up a bogus case involving five other state and federal agencies. I imagine he wanted to stop our organization because we were "touting" our successes and speaking the truth - that adoption records should never be sealed. Since he was going to be retiring soon, maybe this would add a feather to his cap and he could wrap up his career with another notch on his belt. By going after both of us, he figured he could, not only "kill two birds with one stone," but probably bring down a whole flock.

He did well.

A Shocking Discovery of Deceit

The AAC National Conference that year was held in Chicago during the month of May. I was scheduled to give a few workshops and, of course, set up a table with our material. The evening before the conference begins is always a time for seeing old friends, and a hospitality room provides the opportunity.

I was not in the room very long when Jeannette approached me and asked if she could talk to me privately. Her husband had passed away a few months before and, though I had sent a sympathy card, I again offered my heartfelt condolences. The question she posed to me was shocking. "How come you guys aren't sending me any more cases?" I looked at her quizzically and said "What do you mean? We've sent many cases to Bobbie. She called the office while I was in Washington and told Sherri that, since your husband was sick, we should send all the cases directly to her! You mean she never discussed it with you? She never told you?"

I know I was as shocked as she was - mainly because Jeannette had been a much easier person to work with than Bobbie. The pained look on her face was unbelievable. It was a look of extreme hurt for being deceived, betrayed, and let down by someone she had considered a good friend. She wanted to know if we had proof that Bobbie had worked on cases without her knowledge. I said "Well, we've got the completed files and the cancelled checks we've paid her." My suggestion was that we confront Bobbie about it right then and there. My thought was that if we broached her about it together, she could not deny it, but Jeannette said "No, I'll take care of it in my own way."

When I returned home from the conference, I received a call from Bobbie with the suggestion that Jeannette come down and help us learn the ropes of the courthouses in FL. "You know she's really good at that and since FL has been such a tough state for me to break, maybe she could at least show you how to go in and pull the names." "Gee, that would be great," I responded. At the same time, I was thinking to myself, "What the heck is going on?" I was surprised that they were still speaking, considering how blown-away Jeannette was at the news she received at the conference.

A call from Jeannette followed shortly. She said she'd be glad to come down and show us the courthouse routine. We said "Great" and offered to pay her expenses, which we did. That summer, Jeannette came and spent two weeks - a week with Doris and a week with me. She took each of us separately "out on the road" hopping from courthouse to courthouse. I had been told that Florida adoption records were practically nil except for a few counties. After making the rounds of several counties, it was determined that FL records are generally held in much stricter abeyance than other states, with the exception of a few counties.

Aside from that, Jeannette's primary purpose for her visit, and rightly so, was to prove to herself that she had been betrayed by her best friend. Only when she saw the proof with her own eyes was she convinced. She asked us if she could make copies of the cancelled checks, which were paid to Bobbie, in order to have something to confront her with. Since we felt so bad that her "friend" had stabbed her in the back, we gave her the go ahead. (And maybe proof to show the government??) She sat in my living room in the summer of 1990, with my husband present, and said "I don't get mad, I get even and I'll get even with that bitch if it's the last thing I do." Before she left to go back, she called Bobbie on the phone and confronted her about it, but Bobbie tried smoothing it over by saying it was just a misunderstanding between them. She told Jeannette that she had only agreed to work on Ohio cases and split those with her - not the ones from out of state. But I had never/ ever talked with Bobbie about working on any cases until after she called Sherri and told her about Jeannette's husband being ill.

Obviously, Jeannette was going to take care of this matter in her own way, just as she had said at the conference when we first discussed it. I suspect she did.

New Office Space to Expand and Grow

In September of 1990, we began to look for new office space. Our lease was coming due and since we had some minor problems with the air conditioning and plumbing, we decided to try to find a larger office. We were growing rapidly and more room was what we needed desperately. We were fortunate to find space that was quite a bit larger than our old one for the same amount of rent. The only drawback was that it was on the second floor, but we all agreed it was nicer, brighter, and provided room for us to grow.

About this time, we invested in a fax machine, upgraded our copy machine, bought a few more desks, etc. Shows were beginning to contact us for reunion stories. As we began to complete searches, we asked if we could use their name and phone number as a referral. Within a short matter of time, we had compiled a list of referrals which we printed and distributed along with our initial packet. We told each person who had agreed to be a referral to let us know if they received any type of call that seemed harassing or out of the ordinary and, if so, we would remove their name immediately. No one ever asked to have their name removed.

The list had never been abused by anyone - EXCEPT the NY State Investigator!

By publishing our referral list, we had inadvertently provided him with the all the ammunition he needed to put the pieces together. Upon calling our clients and "impersonating" himself as an interested searcher, he was able to draw them out and provide him with the information he needed to cement his case. i.e. when he obtained the name of the person they had been searching for, he was able to match it up, in some instances, with Vital Records in NY and eventually the SS# dumps.

First, he deceived those he was speaking to (just as he had accused the investigator of doing) and then used the information to hang us. As an expression used in a speech by Annette Baran - we were hung by our own petard. Only the government is permitted to tape (and use in court) conversations without the knowledge of the other party; it is justified by citing "suspicious criminal activity"!

In May and June of 1991, there were two shows that increased our work load and brought about many reunions. The first was a Christian talk show I did in Fort Worth, TX called COPE. Since Doris had recently quit, my mother offered to come in and help answer the phones. Doris and Pat had been unable to develop a working relationship, but before she left, she was able to locate her birth granddaughter, thanks to Bobbie.

It soon became necessary for us to hire some part-time help to cover the phones. Rosie and Andrea were two of those special people who spent many hours on the phones answering hundreds of heart-rending calls for minimum wage pay. The other show that swamped us with calls was the Sally Jesse Raphael Show which aired June 27th. Though it portrayed one of our most negative reunion stories (only 2%), people were still excited over the possibility that we might be able to assist them in their own search. They didn't care that someone else's reunion had not worked out. We were amazed that such a negative show would bring such a positive response.

Reunions were abounding because of the terrific publicity. Families were being reunited, our organization was flourishing and we were beginning to help other organizations in our network; i.e. we donated a new fax machine to a sister group, we contributed funds for family preservation purposes to various groups; we maintained memberships in several organizations. We helped some local young mothers get on their feet; we bought airline tickets for two sisters who wanted to go visit their dying father. In other words, we were giving back.

More TV shows followed in 1992. The show that brought the largest response was the Maury Povich Show in November of 1992 when we reunited 3 sets of twins who had become separated. A few months earlier, we had received a letter from a 51 year old man who wrote:

"Fifty one years have passed for me and my twin sister; and we have never met. Christmas is coming and it is my heart's desire to be reunited with my twin if at all possible. Hence, I come to you in hopes that this goal may be obtained. Our mother was diagnosed with tuberculosis. Even though we had a father, the state, in it's lawful wisdom of that era, removed my twin sister and myself from the custody of our parents. Our father died in a fire in Cleveland, Ohio in 1959. Our mother died in Cleveland of tuberculosis in 1961. If you can be of any assistance in information concerning my long lost twin sister...then you will make an aching heart incredibly happy...whatever the outcome."

Because Gordon's mother was ill and his father a seaman, the twins were placed in an orphanage. His sister was placed for adoption and he went into a foster home. When he was 19 years old, he searched and found his mother. It was not until she asked about his sister that he realized he had a twin. His mother died a year later. Gordon's mother recalled the name of the adoptive parents and though he did not have the exact spelling, we did an in-house search and located his twin sister in a relatively short period of time - free of charge.

When we talked to the producer about the possibility of reuniting them on the show, she said she'd get back to me. When she called back, she said "If you can get me two more sets of twins, we'll do it!" She might as well have asked us for the moon! But all the planets must have been in conjunction that week because we did complete two more twin searches. One was an in-house search for twin sisters who had parted ways when they were 19; and were now 45. A kind, concerned sister-in-law had initiated the search and the cost was $75. The third set of twins we reunited were 28 year old male twins who had been separated at birth; the twin who initiated the search did not even know he had a twin until he received his non-identifying information from the agency and it said "multiple birth." It was a very moving show. Especially when the missing twin sister also got to meet the daughter she had to leave behind due to family circumstances. Her 25 year old daughter was there to make a plea for her mother, and was completely overtaken with emotion when her mother came walking out on the stage.

It's a well-known fact that the talk shows receive more calls after doing reunion stories than any other subject they do. I've known within my spirit that we will soon see a talk show completely dedicated to family reunions. Reunion stories are great for ratings. The Musser Foundation received more requests for reunion stories during sweeps week than any other time of the year. Maybe we are finally beginning to recognize how important our family ties and all our connections are to one another.

Reunions Worth Going To Prison For

The Dateline Show aired August 11, 1994 and one of the final questions posed to me was - "Was it worth going to prison for?" I responded that "Yes, it was ... and I hope some good will come out of it". As I thought more about that question, it dawned on me that what made it worth going to prison for were the wonderful reunions that were a direct result of our work.

What also came to mind was the irony of the fact that I went to prison for reuniting families and, in so doing, became separated from my own family. But I can honestly say that every reunion we ever completed was worth going to prison for. Even the 2% that didn't turn out well were still worth the price because the individuals involved now have peace of mind and are able to get on with their lives. Here are just a few that come to mind.

Paul was 27 years old when he contacted us for help. He was born in Miami, FL in 1964, but had very little information to go on. Besides the usual difficulty of sealed records, the southeastern part of Florida has always been well-known for black market adoptions. In those cases, of course, there is no record at all or a completely falsified record. FL was one of the six most difficult states in the country for doing a "straight no-name" adoption case. Since the underground was the only investigator who could do Florida cases, we explained to Paul that the flat fee would be $2500 if and when the search was completed. Paul had recently married, was planning a family and could not afford the fee. We told him to send us whatever information he had and we'd try to help him "in-house", but we held little hope. He sent a copy of his adoption decree which was from Mexico. We immediately became suspicious - why was he taken out of the country to be adopted? He had been born in Miami. But at least his birthmother's name was on it. Though very common, it was included in the body of the document. The name was Mary Jane Smith. Obviously with a name like Mary Jane Smith and an out-of-country adoption, this was not going to be an easy case!

Through some ingenuity, he received a copy of his mother's hospital record. There were 20 sheets of paper and 19 of them had Mary Jane Smith on them. Only one form, called a postnatal report, showed a different name which turned out to be her real name. We completed the case within a short period of time.

My question is this. How can attorneys, agencies and others in 'authority' falsify legal documents and get away with it, while those of us who are trying to set the record straight get indicted? I don't get it!

The apparent answer is that the laws are created by and for them, permitting them to alter and falsify legal documents, then hide behind the very confidentiality law they themselves created! Paul's mother was deceased, but he found five half-siblings.

A program called Homewood Bound sponsored by Homewood Suites Hotels brought the family together for a reunion on November 21, 1991 in Jacksonville, FL. Pat and I were invited, as well, and it was a wonderful experience. We were fortunate to have located Paul's family considering the fact that the attorney in this case had not only given his mother an alias name, but had also finalized the adoption in Mexico. The purpose of giving a birthmother an alias name is seldom ever the birthmother's idea. It is done by an unscrupulous attorney who can then sell the child to the highest bidder, guarantee the adoptive parents that the child will never be able to locate the birthparent, and do all this finagling under the protection of the confidentiality law. Adoption continues to flourish this way, even today, and is an absolute disgrace to our country. Sealed records and confidentiality are the culprits. Before Paul's birthmother died, she had told the other children about him and they were thrilled when they were contacted. Paul's story was told in the December, 1991 issue of the ALARM newsletter, The Freedom Rider. Another male child born in Miami in 1963, and also placed for adoption, is still being sought by Paul. This child would be Paul's full brother.

Another wonderful story that came as a result of one of the talk shows was a 52 year old adoptee by the name of Mary. Her birthmother was also found deceased, but she met two sisters who never knew of her existence. They welcomed her with open arms and wrote us a beautiful letter thanking us for helping Mary to locate them. They've developed a warm, fun-loving relationship. Since her adoptive parents have both passed away, these sisters are the only family Mary has. Her only regret is that she didn't start her search sooner, so she could have had the opportunity to look into the face of her mother. She waited for her adoptive parents to pass away. How sad.

We performed about 25 searches for adoptive parents who wanted us to help them find their adult childrens' birthparents. We always considered these adoptive parents very special as they sought to reach out to the birthmothers. Here are just a few: Fred was in his late 60's when he first came to our support group in 1983. He was the only male in our group at the time and had a wonderful sense of humor. But more than that, he had a special sensitivity to the needs of his grown son and wanted, more than anything else, to locate his son's birthmother before he passed away. Fred's son's birthmother was located in 1991. Fred passed away just a few months ago in a freak auto accident at the age of 78. As a tribute to Fred & Ann, and because it's such a beautiful piece, I am reprinting the flyer he wrote for ATM soon after he joined our group. It's called:

Thank You, Birthmother

Thank you, birthmother, for so enriching our lives these past 32 years through your supreme sacrifice, for whatever the reason. Words cannot express the feeling of joy, exhilaration and thankfulness to our Lord and to you, for making it possible for us to complete our family with a son. During our first 12 years of marriage and helpless attempts by all medical efforts to have a child of our own, we decided to adopt a child and share our love.

We experienced the normal flow of sadness and gladness, the tears and laughter, like natural parents -the baptism, the cub scouts, church confirmation, basketball games, parent-teacher meetings (of which there were many), and the hospital visits for broken bones and sprained ankles. We appraised him of the fact early in life that he was adopted, and that you loved him very dearly.

There were a few times during his teen years when he rebelled against our discipline by crying out in anger, "You're not my father and mother ... so there!" You can imagine our hurt to hear those sharp words because we loved him so much and wished only the best for him. But we realized that those words were said in anger, and that he did love us. Though apologizing did not come easily for him, he would pick all the flowers from our garden and say "Here Mom, I know you like flowers" or he'd come home with a bunch of french fries and say, "I know you love potatoes, Dad."

Each July, when we celebrated his birthday, we never ceased to forget that you were out there, somewhere, also remembering his birthday. Today he lives out west and we're retired in Florida. He now has his own 3 year old blue-eyed, blond daughter and we love her just as we know you would.

We are commencing on our own to search for you. We feel he has a right, as an adult, to all information concerning his background. Besides, we desire within our hearts to hug you, and kiss you, and thank you personally for the joy we've known because of you. Thank you, again, birthmother!

Fred & Ann

An adoptive mother from Tampa wrote to us and also wanted to help her grown child find her birthmother, especially for medical reasons. She had sent us the records from the hospital and wrote a note explaining that the name on her daughter's nursery records was the last name of the delivery doctor! She had been told, by the doctor, that this was the way they handled the records of babies being placed for adoption! "That's the way it's done!", he told her. Can you imagine? And right there on those papers was the doctor's name following Baby Girl! I guess that's what they mean when they say something has been "doctored"! Again, this adoptive mom wanted to obtain the information for her daughter before she passed on. Because of some wonderful clues, we were able to complete the case in-house.

As part of our desire to keep in touch and see how things were going after the post-reunion honeymoon, we sent out survey forms within three to six months following the reunion.

It had been six months since we completed a search for Linda, an adoptee, from Texas. We had found her mother deceased, but she had two sisters and two brothers. One brother lived only 10 minutes away, but she chose to make contact with an aunt, her mother's sister. The aunt warned her NOT to contact any of the children. She didn't. That was the current situation when I was doing follow-up and made contact with her.

When she explained what happened with the aunt, I asked her if she would like me to act as an intermediary and call her brother. She was thrilled. She had wanted to call him so badly, but was scared to death; especially since the aunt had told her not to. She also said she had not called us back because we had previously told her that we feel it's important for the adoptee to make the direct contact. But in a case like this when the person is so terribly frightened, we made exceptions.

It was surely fate. Her brother was dying of AIDS at that very moment and wanted to see her. She was at his home that same afternoon. Her brother died 10 days later. Linda's birthmother had told the children about Linda before she died. They had been looking for her! Linda met her two sisters on the Sally Show over the holidays, but had to sign an agreement that she would not mention our name!

Julia's story was told on Dateline. She lost her adoptive mother when she was 11 and yearned to know her birthmother. What she found was that her birthparents had married (though now divorced) and she had full brothers. But the point that Dateline failed to mention is that both Julia and her mother were in the New York State Registry for several years and a match was never made! The only registry that really works is the International Soundex Reunion Registry, PO Box 2312, Carson City, NV. Send a self-addressed stamped envelope and they will send you a form. There is no charge, but donations are welcome.

Usually it was a joy to call someone and tell them their search was complete. Even if a mother was deceased, we would put them in touch with another family member. There were only two times that we were completely stymied as to how to handle the situation.

The first was a birthmother whose daughter had committed suicide on her 23rd birthday. We received the news on what would have been

43

her daughter's 32nd birthday. It was the most difficult call I ever had to make. But somehow Mary knew. She, in fact, helped to make "the telling" easier because she knew how I was struggling for words. God had somehow prepared Mary for this outcome. She seemed to know ahead of time that her daughter was already gone.

The other difficult situation was the need for us to tell a birthmother that we had located her son in prison - and that he had been there for the past 20 years. He was only 17 when he went in. His uncle had custody of him when he was little, but the state stepped in and removed him when he was 3. He was placed in several foster homes and not adopted until he was 9 or 10. I had been in touch with the prison chaplain and, for a short time, it seemed as though the facility was going to release him to his family. I had talked with Shayne a few times on the phone and he was thrilled to know there was family that cared about him. The "feds" learned that his brother had gotten into some trouble, and decided it wouldn't be a good environment to send him home to. He is now 39 years old. These were the two most difficult cases for us to handle emotionally; especially as we put ourselves in the place of these two birthmothers.

We did a search for a 51 year old local man who had been searching since 1976 after both his adoptive parents died. He learned that his birthparents were still married when he was surrendered, but because of a pending divorce, the birthmother didn't feel she could raise him. Though we did locate her, she was not willing to have a relationship with Roger.

He then asked us to pursue a search for his father. This turned out to be one the most touching reunions we'd ever done. We located his 79 year old father in SC and in an article that ran in the Anderson newspaper on January 17, 1992, his father said *"I didn't know whether I'd ever hear from the boy or whatever happened to him or anything. Yet I had faith that I would and it came true. It changes your life. It really changes you."* Roger's father cried out of happiness for having the opportunity to meet his son before he passed away. He said he had only seen his baby one time, but he had a unique set of ears that he would recognize anywhere. He said he had thought about "the boy" for 50 years. What a joy to play a small part in such a great reunion!

Bonnie's birthmother was found just as Bonnie was turning 50. The likeness, talents, similarities and interests between Bonnie and her birthmother were uncanny.

Anna's mother was located in Puerto Rico. She had a friend call her birthmother and her birthmother said she had the wrong person and hung up! Anna called back the next day and her mother cried with happiness. She told Anna she was so glad she called back because she

44

hung up impulsively and, once she had, it was too late. She had been praying that Anna would call back. Anna met a huge extended family.

The moral of this story, of course, is not to give up. Birthmothers often have second thoughts and may impulsively say no. Give it another chance. Time and space is usually all that's needed.

Lisa is a young woman in her early 30's. She wanted nothing more than to meet her father, even though her entire family had tried to discourage her. Years ago, he had gotten into some trouble and spent time in prison so the family was, of course, concerned she would get hurt. We located Lisa's father and the first thing he said to her was "You know, I've been in prison, but I've been straight for 13 years." People deserve a second chance.

These have been just a **few examples** of the reunions worth going to prison for. The following poem is written by a friend who found "the grave at the end of the search."

MY LIFE WILL NEVER BE THE SAME

Today I turned 47 and remember clearly the
day I was pulled from you forever, and my
heart was broken in two.

Today I turned 47, which means 47 birthdays
without you!

Today I turned another year older and feel
I've aged a lifetime since we've been apart.

Today I am supposed to be happy but can only
mourn all the birthdays you and I were alone
and separated from each other.

Today I'm reflecting on the birthdays we
should have had together and could have had
if my records were not sealed!

Today as I read my cards from friends and
family, I pretend you're here sharing this
day with me as we did 47 years ago.

Today as I blow out my candles, my wish is
for you and I to be together once more, even
though I know that can never be.

You left this world before I found you, and
MY LIFE WILL NEVER BE THE SAME!

Sandi R. Grimmie
aka Rhoda Lee Conn

45

Following are the lyrics to a beautiful song written by Steve & Mary Jo Rillera. Mary Jo has been an active member of the reform movement for over 20 years. This song was played at adoption conferences around the country and triad members were always deeply moved. I can't begin to express how much this song means to me. It's entitled:

Come Together Now

She had a child, who's not a child anymore,
She said good-bye and tried closing that door;
But the past was every present, not forgotten with the years,
And still she sees each birthday through her tears.

They took a child into their hearts and their home,
And they became the only family she'd known.
But there were times & there were questions they could not
    answer if they tried,
But now they see there's nothing left to hide.

They're together now, all together now,
Just look around and see how much they've grown.
Come together now, join together now.
The time has come when no one is alone.

I was that child, I'm not a child anymore.
I need to know more than even before.
The time has come for confrontation,
My search is coming to its end -
And now I know there's no need to pretend.

© Steve & Mary Jo Rillera

THE 1993 NATIONAL CONFERENCE
NOT SOON TO BE FORGOTTEN

The American Adoption Conference held in Cleveland, OH in March of 1993, will probably be long remembered as the conference of confusion. Though I had been scheduled to do a few workshops, the series of events prevented and reversed my physical presence and participation. Word had filtered back via the network grapevine that the AAC President was concerned I would monopolize the time and it would become a media circus. I imagine she was quite relieved when she heard I would not be attending.

However, she was probably right. Had I attended the conference, I most certainly would have called a press conference. It seemed a shame that the national organization did not/would not choose to take advantage of this golden opportunity. We have always had difficulty getting the media to discuss our issues. This presented us with a fantastic podium for doing so! Instead, the AAC Board chose to stick their heads in the sand and, of this writing, that's where they've kept them ever since.

I had been advised, by the first attorney I consulted with, not to attend the conference. She explained "As long as you are present, someone can say they spoke with you and you said such and such. Even if you never spoke to that person, the fact that you were physically present will give the appearance that you may have spoken to them and said such and such. If you aren't there, obviously that can't happen." That made sense to me so I took it as good advice and did not attend the conference, though I wanted desperately to attend.

In lieu of going, I wrote a statement which was titled "The Real Story" and asked Lee Campbell if she would be willing to present it to one of the General Assembly meetings on my behalf. She readily agreed. "The Real Story" explained to my peers and attendees my perspective of what was actually happening and what it meant to us as a movement.

As it turned out, Lee was only able to present a few excerpts - fearful that the facilitator would cut her off in the middle of the presentation due to time restraints. Copies of the statement, however, were made available and widely distributed. Parts of it were carried in the newspapers and, eventually, reprinted in several adoption reform newsletters.

Since Pat was going to be attending the conference, she grew more nervous as the time approached. Because of the indictment, she had no idea what kind of reception she'd receive. She found out quickly. She said the very first feeling was that she had an active case of leprosy. The AAC leadership, who knew her well from past conferences, completely ignored her.

She and mother went about their business of setting up the book display and were warmly greeted by Judy Taylor and Joe Soll, Co-Founders of CERA (Council for Equal Rights in Adoption). Joanne Swanson, active birthmother and founder of Birco Publishing was also preparing her display and welcomed them with love and acceptance.

This was an entirely new experience for mother who had no idea what to do or what to expect. Pat had attended conferences with me in the past and setting up The Musser Foundation display/book table was always the first order of business; it needed to be done soon after arriving since attendees were always anxious to see what new books were available, as well as other fundraising items. The income generated from the sale of the 30 book titles and other merchandise we distributed, helped to offset the cost of travel, hotel and conference fees. We usually managed to break even.

CUB had called a special meeting due to a scathing article written by The New Yorker magazine about their organization. CUB President, Janet Fenton, asked Pat if she would like to take a few minutes at the meeting to say something about the problem The Musser Foundation was having. CUB printed flyers announcing the special meeting and had them placed on tables. At the bottom of the flyer, Pat wrote "Musser Foundation situation to be discussed". A Board Member of the AAC said it was not permissible for this meeting to be held and removed the flyers! The meeting went on as planned.

Mom decided not to attend because she was afraid she'd get too upset if anyone said anything 'negative' about me. There were about 100 people in attendance and, since the room was packed, many of the people had to stand. The chairs had been setup in a circular fashion.

48

When Pat first walked into the room, she stayed towards the back near the entrance. Bobbie saw her come in and, from the opposite side of the room, came to sit beside her. She told Pat emphatically that she should not be talking about this matter at all! Pat spotted Joe Soll and decided to move over by him where she felt she could draw solace. Bobbie followed close behind and sat on the other side of Joe. She nudged him and said, "Don't let her talk" to which Joe replied, "I can't stop her from talking".

When CUB's business was complete, Janet turned the meeting over to Pat to say a few words. At that point Pat got up and made an announcement "I think everyone knows by now that The Musser Foundation has a little problem". B.J. Lifton, author and adoptee, immediately spoke up and said "It's not a 'little' problem"! She was right. Pat continued, "The Musser Foundation has been indicted for their work in reuniting families". She then mentioned the need for us to raise funds, told them that a Legal Defense Fund had been established and that envelopes were available on the book table. Many people contributed during the conference which was an enormous encouragement to us.

As Pat began to read the newspaper article listing the charges, Bobbie suddenly flared up and said "I don't want that read!" An editor of one of the magazines stood up and said "Well, I want some answers. How can I be expected to give my support if I don't know what's going on." It seemed to be apparent she was speaking on behalf of many others in the room. Sandi Grimmie, adoptee and founder of a group in DE said "I don't think there's anyone in this room who hasn't or wouldn't have done something illegal to get their records, and if you say you wouldn't, I don't think you're being honest!" Certainly strong words, but words to which many could relate to as well as agree with. She said she recalls Bobbie sitting with her arms folded, glaring at everyone as if to say "I just dare you to say anything!"

Pat offered copies of the article to anyone who wanted to read it "and it is a matter of public record", she said. Hands went up all over the room and the copies were distributed, in spite of Bobbie's objections. An adoptee/birthmom activist graciously took it upon herself to get extra copies made and placed them on the book table.

Three Michigan birthmothers had come to the conference hoping to meet with me. In fact we had made tentative lunch arrangements. Our organization had been the catalyst for their completed searches. Val, Jan, and Debbie were terrific moral support for Pat & Mom. There were a few leaders of other organizations who offered Mom and Pat assistance, but for fear of repercussions from the government, their names are not being mentioned.

49

Later that evening, Pat was approached by a birthmother who wanted to talk to her privately. She informed Pat that she had a $10,000 CD that was ready to roll over and wanted to offer it to me as a loan if it would help the immediate situation. She suggested that it would help us buy time to build the legal defense fund and we could repay her later or as the money came in. Pat was in awe of her generous offer, and when she called to tell me about the offer, I was also in awe. I called and spoke with this very dear and loving woman later in the evening and told her that I was deeply touched by her offer, but would like to keep it as an ace in the hole should the defense fund not materialize. The fund did materialize and the generous loan was unnecessary, but I shall always remember this very special person for such a special thought.

An uncomfortable undercurrent permeated the entire conference. Many attendees expressed anger that the matter of the indictment was not being "brought to the table and dealt with" but, rather, swept under the rug. Why would the AAC leaders want to ignore the indictment of "two of their own" - myself, a former Board member who had served four years, spent many volunteer hours working on behalf of the organization; someone who supported the AAC as a Lifetime member as well as monetarily by supporting regional and national conferences and donated time as a speaker and workshop leader; an activist leader in the adoption reform movement for 17 years! Why?

Why would the AAC leaders ignore Bobbie, with whom they had done a considerable amount of business; who helped them bring about many reunions, and provided at least two of them with personal income. Why? Why were they pretending to have "clean hands"? What was their motive or intent? Were they distancing themselves out of fear for their own skins?

Was this some clever political move? Wouldn't it have been better to rally around and band together to fight "city hall" than to jump ship? Or were they just too wounded by their own personal adoption experience to be able to reach out to other wounded souls?

Their legislative chairperson had been a civil rights activist during the 60's and was quite familiar with the in's and out's of "stirring the pot". In fact, he wrote a booklet entitled **Adoption Revolution**. While attending the March on Washington in 1989, he scheduled various "how to" sessions with groups willing to cover his expenses. When I returned to Florida, he called to see if we wanted him to give a presentation to our small group. We did. We agreed upon a date and a few months later, he came to Florida. He stayed in my home for a few days; we 'broke bread' together. Now five years later, he was among the **silent ones** who evidently did not want to become involved or offer any kind of support. Not a single word. Huh? I don't get it!

Rumors abounded. Clusters of people gathered everywhere, whispering in hushed tones. New attendees had no idea what was happening and, since no one was "talking," they remained in the dark. Many expressed disillusionment. The AAC leaders, known for their infamous clique, were doing what they did best - socializing with each other and ignoring their constituency, as well as ignoring any major problems. It's what they seemed to do best.

The silence from the "leadership" was deafening throughout the entire duration of the conference and has remained so to the present day. Bobbie, in her own unique way, was attempting to keep a lid on everything. Mother expressed surprise that only one of the Board Members made an attempt to greet her (the Canadian representative). She could not comprehend their attitude in light of the fact that this was her first conference, and the fact that her daughter had been an active member of the AAC since its inception in 1979. They did their best to ignore her and they succeeded. Imagine ignoring an 81 year old lady - no matter what you think of her kid!

Following is the article that was presented on my behalf by my friend, Lee Campbell.

The Real Story

On Saturday, March 27, 1993, I learned by reading a brief article in my local paper that I had been "indicted by a federal grand jury for allegedly obtaining confidential information". You can imagine my surprise. Like many in this movement, I am, have always been, and will continue to be committed to reuniting families. That has always been the primary goal of The Musser Foundation.

It appears that I will now have to refocus my energies for awhile. In the days ahead we may each be called upon to give and receive emotional support to one another. I know we are capable if only we are willing. A note I received from one of our support groups said, "You will never have to walk alone. We are here!" It was a reminder that deeply touched my heart.

Now let's discuss what's really happening. The U.S. Government is now aware of our passion and drive, and are attempting to subvert our search and reunions of family members. Does this mean that they will be willing to open the records? Of course not! What will they do instead?

They will setup a process whereby you MUST petition the courts through an attorney costing you several hundred dollars with no guarantee of results! Or they will "authorize" their "agents," the adoption agencies, to be your intermediary at a "nominal" cost. Keep in mind that they are sitting there with all YOUR INFORMATION! The entire search and reunion process will be controlled by them - which is what they like best! You will be maintained in your role of "child" - unable to make your own choices.

When the indomitable state saw fit to separate you permanently from your own flesh and blood, it was an act that was unconscionable. The heartache and pain of people from every walk of life cross our desks every day.

I am reminded of 28 year old adoptee, Jill McCallister, whose two little boys recently died due to a rare genetic disease. Jill was not able to obtain any medical information until it was too late. And Nellie Tucker, an 82 year old birthmother who was searching for her 63 year old son. She later married the birthfather and they had 12 more children (all full siblings), but she had never gotten over the loss of her firstborn child. Nellie never had the opportunity to meet her son - she died shortly before he was located. Adoptive parents, too, are calling, wanting to help their teenagers answer the age-old question of "Who Am I"?

Every government agency in this country - the social welfare agencies, the courts, vital statistic offices, hospitals, etc. should be establishing Bureaus of Reconciliation - an idea suggested many years ago by Jean Paton, 85 year old Mother of the Movement. It should be funded by our state governments since they passed the laws that created the permanent separation in the first place.

You would think they would come out in throngs when they hear your pain and see your loss. You would think they would want to help you begin to heal - but NO - they want only to "protect" and "control." Don't they realize that our hearts and souls are in those records - and that those records actually belong to us, the people whose lives have been affected so dramatically! Rather than helping you, they want to keep you enslaved - to maintain control and keep you dependent.

It is time for us to RISE UP as never before! They are attempting to silence my voice, but YOU'VE GOT A VOICE! Do not become discouraged and don't give up the fight! This may very well be the golden opportunity we've been waiting for - "a blessing in disguise!" When the ALARM Network was established in 1987, we had as our goal "To Be Free by '93". Maybe this is the year we can begin to claim our freedom!

And now - what can you do? Let's begin simply by supporting each other. When one of us falls and stumbles, let's be there to pick each other up so that the wounds will not become permanent scars.

same fight and want the same result.

Here are some specific things you can do immediately to become involved:

- Write a letter to the Editor of the *Cleveland Plain Dealer*, 1801 Superior Ave. Cleveland, OH 44114 and the *Ft. Myers News-Press*, PO Box 10, Ft. Myers, FL 33901; (these two papers 'broke' the story);

- Join the March on Washington sponsored by the Council for Equal Rights in Adoption;

- Purchase the booklet *"ADOPTION REVOLUTION"* by John Goldberg;

- Write to the *New Yorker Magazine* and express your outrage over the article defaming Concerned United Birthparents;

- Support the Musser Foundation Legal Defense Fund;

- Get involved with your local support group and stay involved at some level;

- Call the White House Switchboard at 202-456-1414 and let President Clinton, Hillary, and Donna Shalala, Health & Human Services Director, know that adoption rights are long past due. Hillary's fax # is 202-456-6244. Donna Shalala's office # is 202-690-7000 and her fax is 202-690-7203. Many believe that our new administration cares deeply about people. Let's give them the opportunity to prove it;

- Light a candle for your missing loved one or in honor of your found loved one on April 23rd. The flickers from many flames will be pictured in my mind as I prepare to "face the music."

- Finally, remember and keep in mind that we are dealing with man-made laws. I am truly convinced that God never intended for us to be separated from our kin. There is a scripture verse that states:

"I have seen their affliction and have heard their cries"

God has heard and He is responding. My love to all of you.
Sandy Musser

When Mom and Pat returned home from the conference, we decided it was time to send out a fundraising letter. My arraignment was only a few weeks away so we needed to start raising funds immediately. My attorney said he needed half of his fee by May 15th and the other half before trial began.

The following letter went out to all the people we had helped reunite as well as support groups around the country. Since I had never been in a position of needing to "beg" for money, especially on my own behalf, it was a difficult letter for me to write.

Dear Family & Friends:

I wish this could be a personal letter to each and every one of you. But because of the severity and urgency of the situation, I find it necessary to contact you in this manner.

On Saturday, March 27, 1993 I learned by reading a brief article in our local paper that I had been "indicted by a federal grand jury for allegedly obtaining confidential information". You can imagine my surprise. As you know I am, have always been and will continue to be committed to reuniting families. That has always been the primary goal of The Musser Foundation.

Enclosed are newspaper articles from our local paper and a two-page statement that was recently presented at the National American Adoption Congress conference in Cleveland, OH. After reading the article and statement, you will understand my need to come to you and ask for a small donation for the Musser Legal Defense Fund.

Asking for money has never been a strong suit of mine, but if I am to obtain the services of an attorney I must start now. The attorneys I've contacted are quoting between $10,000 to $15,000. After this case is over, we plan to take this issue to the Supreme Court. Sealed adoption records are immoral, illegal and unconstitutional.

Over the past four years The Musser Foundation, in addition to reuniting hundreds of families, has been active with the following projects:

- We've printed volumes of educational material for free distribution;

- Donated substantial funds to support Family Preservation efforts;

- Accepted hardship cases, free of charge to the person searching, though we paid the investigator(s) for the search;

- Contributed a fax machine to one of our sister organizations;

- Published a book entitled "Chasing Rainbows" authored by a 62 year old adoptee / birthmother;

- Supported several adoption reform organizations with membership fees and other special projects;

- Lobbied at the grassroots level around the county to open sealed adoption records;

- Recently began work on a video project entitled "The Reunion Story / Breaking the Adoption Seal".

Now more than ever, we need both your financial and emotional support. An envelope is enclosed for your convenience. If you have any questions, please feel free to call the office. And please keep me in your prayers during these next several months.

With a humble heart,
Sandy Musser

The response was immediate and gave us renewed hope. We were in total awe of the fantastic feedback. Most people expressed shock that this was happening to us. Many of them said it didn't matter whether we were guilty or not guilty; they would have gladly broken the law themselves to obtain information. Several sent us copies of letters they had written to the court, the probation officer and the media on our behalf.

About 10 days after the conference, I received a surprise fax in the office. It was from a former high school classmate who was now living in CA. A birthmother friend of his had attended the conference in OH and when she returned to CA, she proceeded to tell him about the indictment. Doug couldn't believe it when she mentioned my name.

Doug was also a close friend of the birthfather. He and Jane are now working with adoptees, birthparents and pre/post adoptive parents through their organization known as Adoption Synergy Associates.

The time for my arraignment was drawing near, and the closer it got, the more apprehensive I was beginning to feel. A brand new scary experience for a small-town girl.

"Although volume upon volume is written to prove slavery a very good thing, we never hear of the man who wishes to make the good of it by being a slave himself."

Abraham Lincoln

• • • • • • • • • •

"There are those who say to you - we are rushing this issue of Civil Rights. I say we are 172 years too late. There are those who say - this issue of Civil Rights is an infringement on states' rights. The time has come for the Democratic party to get out of the shadow of states' rights and walk forthrightly into the bright sunshine of Human Rights..."

Hubert H. Humphrey
1948 Democratic
Convention

AKRON BOUND

My arraignment was scheduled for April 23rd. I remember wondering what was going to happen at "my arraignment". I wasn't even sure what the word meant and so I went to Webster to find out - "to call before a law court to answer charges".

I called to make flight arrangements for the first of four trips to Akron. "It will be cheaper for you on a Tuesday or Wednesday" my travel agent Martha said. Since the arraignment was being held on Friday, I decided to fly up on Wednesday evening. I then contacted the Akron Chamber of Commerce to inquire about a place to stay. Bed & Breakfasts' have always been more interesting to me than hotels or motels. They generally provide a warm and 'homey' feeling and I knew that's what I'd be needing! The Chamber gave me a few referrals and I chose one which turned out to be close to the airport. Mrs. Clay, the owner of the B&B, offered to pick me up at the airport for a small charge.

A young woman from California had decided to come to the arraignment to show her support. She had contracted with us to do her adoption case and when she heard about our legal problems, she offered to do whatever she could do help out. One of the ways she offered was to document the event by videotaping it since she and her husband owned a video company. Since I barely knew Michelle, I was awed that she was willing to travel all the way from California in order to show her support. She recently sent me a letter recalling that period of time:

> *"Before I knew you, I had of course been searching for years. Not just for my birth family, but for something important -some way to define my life. Just having a job never seemed enough. I always wondered at the purpose of life if all you do is work, make money, love a few people on the way and die.*

Being adopted and the difficulties involved in searching were always painful and frustrating to me, but when I made the phone call to you and discovered that the government was indicting you and considering you a FELON for helping people on their paths to discovering the truth, I was furious!

In the year that has passed since then, that anger has given me purpose and direction. I finally found my voice and know that I do have power. I'm angry with the system and I want it changed - I think that my ultimate goal would be that no birthparent or adoptee should ever again have to go through what I did to find their family. It's immoral and unconstitutional that the system punishes us by withholding knowledge about our lives and then arrests us when we try to discover the truth.

When I decided to go to your arraignment, I was so scared. I had never traveled anywhere by myself. Never rented my own car, or checked myself into a hotel. But I was appalled that after all you had done for others that you were going to be going through that ordeal alone - I didn't know how my being there could help, but I knew I had to be there.

Since then I've traveled all over the country by myself. I don't know how much of a difference I'm making but every time someone says to me 'I didn't even know there were support groups or search specialists', I know I've helped in a small way to change lives and that's the most rewarding feeling I could ever have. My parents and friends have all said "you've found your family, why do you keep doing this?" Well, after searching for over 10 years and knowing what I do, how could I not help people who need help. I got that from you, and words could never thank you enough."

Michelle not only came to the arraignment, but she also got involved with the media and did substantial public relations work on my behalf. The 23rd of April came very quickly. I did not have a clue as to what an arraignment was about or what I would be facing. Though my husband had volunteered to go along for moral support, I made the decision to "go it alone". He tends to have a hyper personality and I was afraid that his presence might make me more nervous than I already was.

People who had attended the conference and heard the reading of "The Real Story" had written or called to let me know that their candles would be burning brightly as I embarked upon this new unwelcome venture. Much of my time was spent thinking about those flickering candles and envisioning myself enveloped in the warmth they radiated.

Mrs. Clay was waiting outside baggage claim when I arrived. She had asked me to send a picture so she'd know what I looked liked and we managed to find each other with little effort. On the way to her Bed & Breakfast, we discussed how she had decided to establish a B&B. The home I had owned in New Jersey was a three-story Victorian and I always thought it would make a terrific Bed & Breakfast. Mrs. Clay said she got the idea after she retired from teaching and her husband passed away. She did some remodeling, converted the upstairs, and joined a Bed & Breakfast Network. It became the place I "hung my hat" and gathered with friends during my trying ordeal.

The following evening my attorney and I met for the first time. I had brought all the paperwork I thought he might want or need to look at. It included all The Musser Foundation financial records including cancelled checks and bank statements, IRS tax returns, our FL Incorporation papers, our requests for tax-exempt status (one request which had been turned down, and one that was pending); also articles that dated back to the late 70's in order to show the amount of time I had personally invested in the area of reform.

As we spoke, he impressed me as being an 'easy-going' person, unhurried, easy to talk with, and I felt we had an acceptable rapport. He took general basic personal background information: age, date of birth, place of birth, how I became involved in the reform work, and my perception of the events leading up to the charges.

He said we would wait to receive the Discovery Papers before deciding how to proceed and that as soon as he received them from the government, he would fax them to me. We discussed whether or not I would testify on my own behalf, since his last five cases were won without putting the defendant on the stand. But I wanted to be able to go on the stand. I was proud of what The Musser Foundation had accomplished and felt confident that I could explain the good work our organization was doing, how important it was and that we hadn't done anything wrong. Sealed records were wrong!

I asked him if there was any problem with talking to the media. He said he didn't have any problem with it. While the media can make or break a case, they can also bring an awareness to a subject which has never before been exposed. It was our hope that we could use the media to our benefit.

He then took considerable time to define the various charges against me by pointing them out in the statutes. He said the conspiracy charge would be the one most difficult for the prosecution to prove, but it was also the conspiracy charge that was the basis of all the others. If the prosecution could prove there was a conspiracy, then it was just as though I had personally committed the actual acts which my codefendant had committed and admitted to: i.e. using various impersonations and ruses when calling courthouses, agencies, vital statistic offices, social security administration, etc. I had not committed any of those acts, nor was I aware of exactly how my codefendant was getting the information. By the same token, it did not matter to me as long as families were being reunited.

I explained to Mr. Keith that I have always believed that acts of civil disobedience are necessary if a law conflicts with one's moral beliefs (i.e. conscientious objectors, etc.). It was a well-known fact among most of the adoption reform leadership that I was willing to go to jail for the cause. It was something I had verbalized from time to time. So it makes sense that if I had known what my codefendant was doing in order to obtain information in the work of reuniting loved ones, I would have done the searches myself. I subcontracted the majority of the cases simply because I didn't know how to do them, nor did I know how they were getting done! I was only grateful that they were.

As someone responsible for overseeing a national organization, cover tremendous overhead and make sure that the organization remained solvent, it wouldn't have made much sense to expend money that wouldn't have had to be expended. After spending about an hour and a half together, Mr. Keith said he would meet me at the courthouse at 8:30 am and the arraignment would only take about 15 minutes! He was right.

When I arrived back at the B&B, Mrs. Clay said I had a few calls. One was from Michelle. She called to tell me she was staying at a Holiday Inn on the other side of town. When I returned her call, she was already in bed, tired from the long flight. We agreed to meet at the courthouse cafeteria at 8:00 for a quick cup of coffee before proceedings.

The other call was from a birthmother I had met 10 years before. I was so excited to hear from Bev and anxious to get together with her. She said she lived close to the B&B and wanted to know if I had dinner yet. I hadn't so we met at a little Italian restaurant right up the street from the B&B and it became a favorite eatery. In fact, our regular waitress was an adoptee who eagerly followed the story as it unfolded.

As I dressed for court the next morning, I began to get the jitters. I imagine it was 'fear of the unknown'. When I arrived at the courthouse, Michelle, Bev, Carol, Becky and Jeannette (my original search contact), were already there. Their presence was comforting. It meant so much to me to simply know they were there pulling for me. We chatted briefly. Michelle said she was informed of the fact that she would not be allowed to do any videotaping in the courtroom. It was "against the rules" - a federal law - no cameras allowed!

My attorney arrived at about 8:25 and I joined him. He provided me with a bird's eye view of what was going to take place in court, and assured me it would be over very quickly. It was.

It was time to board the elevator and stand before the judge. I was surprised that the jitters I had felt earlier had subsided and I was feeling more calm and confident. We walked into a small courtroom; one much smaller than I had imagined. Mr. Keith said to stay by his side and led me towards the front of the room. There was a well-dressed man to my immediate left who I correctly presumed to be the prosecuting attorney, Mr. Getz. I recall thinking that he was so smartly dressed that he could have stepped out of a men's fashion magazine.

The Judge asked my name and then asked Mr. Getz to read the charges. When he was through, the judge asked if I understood the charges and I replied "Yes, Your Honor". "And how do you plead"? In a clear, emphatic voice, I said "NOT GUILTY Your Honor"! He said that I would be released on a $10,000 unsecured bond in my own recognizance and that I could only travel between FL and OH without prior permission. Since my husband had won a free trip to Hawaii for his sales performance with his company, my attorney requested permission for me to travel at the end of May. Permission was granted.

A plump, ruddy-faced, balding U.S. Marshall, who looked to be in his mid-60's, said to follow him to the fifth floor where they would "book" me. Booking involved being fingerprinted, photographed and assigned an 8-digit ID number. My attorney said he'd see me later and left; my friends said they'd wait for me in the cafeteria. I followed behind the U.S. Marshall and tried to remain 'cool' and calm.

We entered a large room with several desks. When we got to his desk, which was in the middle of the room, he told me to sit down. He proceeded to ask me several routine questions - name, address, phone number, social security #, husband's name, profession, children's names, addresses, professions, siblings names, addresses, professions, parents' names and addresses, (father deceased). I had given my name as Sandy Musser and my husband's as Norman Smith. This seemed to cause some confusion for him, so I explained that I use my maiden name in my adoption reform work, but that my 'legal' name is Sandra Musser-Smith.

He continued with the questioning. When he got to the information concerning my brother's profession (Retired Air Force General), he told me that he, too, was retired from the Air Force. Though I've always been quite proud of my brother and his accomplishments, I've also had ambivalent feelings toward the military (i.e. securing peace while killing others). He told me where he had served and wondered if their paths may have crossed. I mentioned that Stan had been on The Thunderbird Team in the late '60's and early 70's, and had served all over the world, including Viet Nam.

By now we had graduated to the flip side of the two-sided form. What other employment had I had? "Well, I've been a school secretary and a waitress." Where else had I lived? What places did I frequent? (I got stuck on that one!) "You know - dance halls, beer joints", he said. "No, I don't hang out in those places, though I occasionally have lunch in restaurants that have lounges (does that count?)", I commented in a

61

matter-of- fact way. Dance Halls?? Sounds like a 30's term ! Maybe the form needs to be updated.

"Have you ever been in trouble before?" he asked. Tongue in cheek I said, "Yes, when I was 15 years old - that's what got me here!" I responded. Either he didn't understand or he didn't think it was funny. I tend to think he didn't understand, or maybe he did understand and didn't think it was funny!

He then had me follow him to a back room where I was photographed and fingerprinted. My 8- digit numbers were placed onto a board which I was instructed to hold in front of me for the "mug shot". My personalized set of numbers, which would forever classify me as a "criminal" are 51963-060. I remember thinking to myself, "This is so unreal! This can't really be happening? Soon I'll awake from this awful dream." . But it was no dream. This was real life - and a brand new experience for this little gal, born in a small farming community in upstate PA. When and where it would all end was anybody's guess.

The Marshall asked me to wait at the front counter while he put my "I.D. number" into the computer. While I was standing there with my briefcase in hand, a man who had been sitting at a desk at the back of the room staring, came walking towards me. He stopped beside me and abruptly blurted out the oldest line of all time - you got it! "What's a nice girl like you doing in a place like this?" I said "Don't you know?" He said "No, but I'll find out soon". I said "I'm sure you will". He then said he had noticed my briefcase and wondered if I was in real estate. (Are realtors the only ones who carry briefcases?) "No," I said "I reunite families and that's why I'm here". The rest of the conversation was a blur, mostly small talk, but I was annoyed since his opening comment reminded me of the investigator who had set me up with a bogus case. He, too, had made a sexist remark that was uncalled for - especially in light of the set of circumstances. It was certainly 'unprofessional', but that's the way they play their game.

A short time later, the Marshall returned and escorted me down to the first floor where I signed a copy of the unsecured bond form. I was being released in my own recognizance with the understanding I would appear for all scheduled hearings. If I didn't, I would have to pay a $10,000 fine. I would appear.

Since I wasn't leaving until Sunday, the rest of the weekend was free. I had previously been invited to do a local TV talk show, so Friday evening Michelle and I were interviewed on the Ken Jurek Show. Michelle had an opportunity to discuss her own search and I discussed various reform issues.

Saturday, Jeannette extended an invitation to Michelle and me to take a mini- tour of Akron. The first and most fascinating stop was the old Florence Crittendon Home for Unwed Mothers where Jeannette's sister had stayed several years before. It has since been converted to a conservatory. Built around the turn of the century, it is an exquisite Victorian-style building, with the architecture of the day being huge rooms, high ceilings, wide natural woodwork, hardwood floors, gas lights, etc.

But this gorgeous building had once housed hundreds of mothers who had to give away their babies. Somehow, that harsh realization and knowledge distracted from its beauty. Walking from room to room, we discussed its history but felt a deep sense of sadness. Michelle had her videotape in high gear!

The rest of the weekend was spent doing a little shopping, some reading, and thinking - a whole lot of thinking. It would be less than six weeks before I would be returning to Akron for "pretrial". I wonder what happens at a pretrial?

I had only been home about a week and a half when I received a late night call from Bobbie. We had started the defense fund the first week in April and, at the end of the month, sent an accounting to all those who had contributed. It was 11:30 in the evening and she was calling to demand half of the defense fund. She said someone had just faxed her a copy of the accounting and "everyone thinks the fund is for both of us", though she couldn't tell me who **"everyone"** was. In addition to being completely flabbergasted by her attitude, I was annoyed she was calling me so late at night. Though I had been advised by a close friend **not** to send an accounting, I sent it anyway as I felt it was important to keep the contributors informed. The accounting showed the total amount received to date and the expenses incurred up to that point. Also included was a general note of thanks with a list of all those who had made donations though not listing the amounts.

I proceeded to explain, (wondering why I even needed to!), that the fund had been established specifically for the defense of The Musser Foundation and I didn't know where she got the idea it was for her too. I said that we both had the same capability of requesting help and since a large portion of the early funds coming in had been donated by my family and close friends, why would I give her half? I then suggested that she tell anyone who thought they were donating to both of us to get in touch with me and their check would be refunded. They could then divide it the way they wanted to. I never received a request for any checks to be returned.

She continued to be obnoxious and said she was going to discuss it with her attorney. I said "fine" and hung up. I remember feeling outraged that she would somehow feel that I "owed" her something. She never ceased to amaze me with some of her outrageous comments. I wondered who would fax her a copy of the accounting at that hour of the evening and for what purpose? An enemy in the camp of supporters?

Preparing for Pre-Trial

A few days before leaving for the pre- trial hearing, I received a call from a TV station known as Broadcast News Network from upstate New York. They wanted to know if I would be willing to give them an interview after the pretrial hearing was over. But since it was a six hour drive for them from upstate New York to Akron, they asked if I would mind meeting them halfway.

I wasn't thrilled about the thought of driving three hours for an interview and that's exactly what I expressed to the reporter. Though I was committed to getting the message out, and at one time would travel almost anywhere at my own expense to do so, I no longer had that need or desire. She said she felt it was a really important story, that my side of the story needed to be heard, and that their network covered six states.

I asked if they would cover my expenses to make the trip. I had already planned to rent a car, but was simply requesting gas money. She said "Well, we're not allowed to pay for interviews". I said, "I'm not asking you to pay me for an interview. I'm asking you to pay for my gas since you want me to drive 3 hours to give you a story. I don't think that's asking too much". She said she'd get back to me.

The next day she faxed me a note that said she had spoken with her boss and she was very sorry, but they would not be able to pay for my gas. I wrote her a note back and thanked her for the invitation to do an interview, but that I wasn't interested in driving 3 hours at my own expense. There was a time early on when I would have, but those days were long gone.

She called after receiving my fax and said that she would pay me "out of pocket" if necessary. She explained that this was a story she really wanted to do and it would help to tell 'our side' of the story. Would I please agree to meet with her? Because of her persistence and willingness to cover my expenses, I agreed.

Much to my chagrin, part of this interview ended up on Dateline in September 1993. A few months later, the same reporter contacted Pat at the office to say they were working on a documentary. Were there other people Pat or I could put her in touch with? In one of my phone conversations from prison, Pat mentioned it to me. I suggested that she respond by reminding the reporter that, though they did not want to even cover my expenses for gas, they turned around and sold the story!

It reminded me of an interview I recently saw on CNBC. Tom Snyder was interviewing Sally Jesse. The discussion turned to the Baby Jessica case and the fact that the Schmidts' were being featured on a show called American Journal. Sally, an adoptive parent, immediately spoke up and said something to the effect of "Well, you know they got paid for that interview!" Tom's response was so great that had I been there, I would have given him a big hug. Though I am unable to quote him verbatim, in essence, he said "You know, you and I get paid very well for what we do - which is talk. What's wrong with people getting paid for telling their story?" That was the gist of it and he was right!

The point is this. The media makes money telling our stories. That's how they exist. The talk show hosts make million dollar salaries - from what? Our stories! Why would Sally want to deny the Schmidts a few thousand dollars for telling their story. I don't understand.

Pre-Trial Jitters and a Revelation

The last weekend of May, I was back in Akron for my pretrial. Like the arraignment, it was being held on a Friday so I flew in the day before. This time I decided to rent a car so I wouldn't need to be dependent upon others to get around.

Again Bev, Carol, Becky and Jeannette provided me with 'entertainment' while I was there. Maria joined us on a few occasions. Since I enjoyed flea markets and thrift shops, one of them was usually available to take me to the good spots.

Bev called as soon as I got in and wanted to meet me for dinner Thursday evening. She wanted to bring me up-to-date on the relationship with her daughter had she found in 1983. Though Bev and I had met several years before, we had been out-of-touch. This would give us an opportunity to catch-up with each others lives and I was looking forward to it.

Jeannette called late in the afternoon and said she and Bobbie were going to the support group meeting in Cleveland and wanted me to go along. "Bobbie thinks it would be fun for you two to walk in together"! Though Bobbie and I were still 'speaking', I certainly wasn't interested in attending a support group meeting with her. For that matter, I had no desire to attend the meeting at all. Though I had networked with the group in the past, they had not offered any support in any way to either one of us.

The entire situation was puzzling to me and I couldn't understand Bobbie's strong desire to go or to be with me. If this group was gungho in their support of what was happening to either of us, I could understand it, but that was not the case. This large Cleveland group chose to make their stand by NOT taking a stand! Weren't we fighting the same battle? Regardless, I had no desire to attend the meeting. What would be the purpose? It just didn't make any sense to me. When I expressed my feelings to Jeannette, she agreed, but reiterated that Bobbie really wanted me to go. I reminded her that I had made dinner plans with Bev and had no intention of changing my plans.

About 15 minutes later she called back to tell me that she and Bobbie had decided to meet us for dinner! "Where are you going?" "I'm not sure - you'll have to call Bev." Though I wanted to spend time alone with Bev, I didn't know how to tactfully say so without making waves and ruffling feathers - but why should I have even cared?

Since Bev was going to be late getting home from work, Jeannette, who lived close to the B&B, said she'd pick me up and Bev would meet us later at the restaurant. As we pulled into the restaurant parking lot, Bobbie, who had driven down from Cleveland, pulled in right behind us. We greeted each other as casual friends do. Considering we hadn't spoken since the crazy phone spree following the indictment, I had no idea what was happening with her part of the case. At this particular juncture, I was not aware that she was going to testify against me - though I was about to find out.

Had I been more knowledgeable about guilty pleas, plea agreements, plea bargains, etc., I probably would have realized what was going on, but this was all new territory for me; an area I had never before encountered. I was also ignorant of the fact that I was about to place myself, once again, in a vulnerable position. Blindly, I walked into what, I now believe, was another setup.

We were only in the restaurant a short time when Bev arrived. I was glad to see her because I felt the beginning of an interrogation. We had just started to discuss my "not guilty" plea when, out of the blue, Bobbie said "Well, I guess you know I have to testify against you". Though I had a strong suspicion, hearing her actually verbalize it was a weird feeling. My body felt suspended in time and for a brief moment, I questioned myself as to whether I really heard it right. But that was only the beginning of a strange evening.

"No, I didn't know. What do you mean you HAVE to testify against me? I don't understand! You called the office only a week or so ago and specifically told Pat that you weren't going to plead guilty to conspiracy because you knew there had been no conspiracy!"

"I know I did, but when I told them I didn't want to plead guilty to the conspiracy charge, they said I couldn't pick and choose. I have to plead guilty to all the counts or none."

"Bobbie" that's ridiculous! Are you telling me you can't plead guilty to the charges you're actually guilty of, and not guilty to the charges you're not guilty of? You've already said there was no conspiracy".

"No, they won't let me do that."

It was then that the light bulb in my head came on. I finally understood that, without her testimony, they had no evidence with which to prove their case against me. Since it was all circumstantial, they needed her to get on the stand and say that I knew what she was doing and how she was doing it. I didn't know. Yes, there had been several phone calls back and forth, and yes, they coincided with completed cases of ours, but there were phone calls to many others in the network with whom she did business with. She was going to be their "key witness" and though she had already been charged and admitted guilt, her sentencing was not going to take place until after my trial - thereby insuring that she put on a good performance and make the agreement worthwhile. The quality of her performance would not only determine the severity of her sentence, but it would most certainly guarantee that she would not receive any prison time.

This whole matter was getting more and more crazy and ludicrous, and part of the craziness was that I was willingly supping with my lynchman. As I was sitting there mulling it over in my mind and trying to figure it all out, I looked over at Jeannette who was sitting directly across from me. She began to repeat everything Bobbie had just said and then, as if to say 'See, Bobbie doesn't really have any other choice but to say that you knew. It's the only way she can save her skin.' Without being confronting, I thought to myself "Jeannette, this is the person who cut you right out of the middle while your husband was dying and she never even informed you she was doing so! This is the person you called 'friend'." I recall feeling very paranoid about where Jeannette was 'coming from'.

I had been told that she and Bobbie had worked together for several years - long before I ever came into the picture. But when she had taken me aside at the national conference, in 1990, and asked me why we weren't referring anymore cases to her, she was dumbfounded and shocked to learn that her friend had double-crossed her. It suddenly dawned on me that I was actually the outsider here - similar to a marital situation when a husband is caught cheating and his wife chooses to blame the other woman rather than him! Jeannette wanted to hang on to this relationship with Bobbie at any cost. Bobbie could still be of valuable use to her in more ways than one.

Bev was just sitting back listening and wondering what the heck was going on. I was thankful and grateful that she was there to witness it. I suspect that the following scenario would have taken place had I agreed to attend the meeting (and there would have been no witness!).

I reminded Bobbie of the first phone call she made to me following her indictment in which she stated that the government was really looking for "The Searcher". As I picked up my drink and took a sip, I said "You've occasionally mentioned knowing who he is and his whereabouts? Why aren't they going after him? Why me? The only thing I've done is to provide both of you with lots of work!"

In the original phone conversation following her indictment, we discussed the possibility that "The Searcher" was capable of assassination if he thought someone was going to turn him in. Maybe she had decided it was much too risky to turn him in and chose to turn on me.

At that point she reached under the table, into a little gift bag, and brought out a small doll. She said it was her "good luck charm" and that she takes the doll with her everywhere she goes. She joked (or was it?) that her little doll even had a microphone hidden in her hair. Then she did the most bizarre thing. She brought the head of the doll close to her mouth and said "If they ask you the Searcher's name, you can tell them it's D____ C____ at 5___ P___ H___, M_____ __ ___ L___." It was no sooner out of her mouth when Jeannette repeated it verbatim - just like a parrot!

My insides felt as though a bomb had just been dropped and the explosion was occurring throughout my entire body. I was aghast, shocked, confounded and blown away since I had never before heard his name mentioned. His name had never been breathed by anyone, as far as I knew. His identity had always been held in the strictest of confidence and was only known by, I was told, five or six people in the entire country. Now it was being dumped in my lap. Why??

I could not fathom why she had blurted this 'sacred' information. Why was she telling me? What was her purpose? Was it his real name or was it a made-up name? Was this part of her plea agreement - a plan of the government to protect her or get her off the hook - was it a test to see how far the information would travel? Or is it possible that she had a soft spot, and was trying to provide me with a bargaining tool in case I decided to make my own deal with the government?

I was completely taken back and stammered something like "Oh, that's it, huh? Well I still don't understand why they're not going after him if you've already told them his name and address? Why are you telling me??"

"Well," she said, "it doesn't matter now who knows. I guess they haven't caught him because they just don't have enough evidence to bring a case against him." At that moment, I was feeling rather ambiguous. Since he was a primary source of "real hope" for many people, I wasn't sure how I felt about him getting caught.

Dinner arrived and the subject was changed. I realize in retrospect that I never fully comprehended what that entire evening was all about, and I'm not sure I do to this day. When I got home, had time to think about it, and discussed it with a few friends, (without revealing his name), the conclusion was that the government undoubtedly had her bugged that evening so that she would not have to assume full responsibility when and if they landed him. (Which is unlikely to happen because I've been told he has strong political connections in the very district doing the investigations).

My own quandary, however, was the fear of being put on the stand and questioned by the prosecution about my knowledge of the underground. Up until that particular moment, I knew nothing about him. Now Bobbie had just thrown me a curve. It seemed to me that I had only two choices. Either tell them what I had just learned from Bobbie or say I didn't know. If, while I was on the stand, I spoke the name she had told me, I'd be the responsible party. If I said I didn't know, then I'd be lying on the stand - I felt as though I was between a rock and a hard place. This particular situation became one of the two primary reasons I did not go on the stand.

Bobbie had convinced the government that we were "best of friends" which is why, according to my attorney, they believed I knew everything she knew! Bobbie is not the type of person I would choose for a "best friend". However, we had a reasonably good working relationship. But as good as our relationship was, **she still would not have shared her trade secrets with me nor with anyone else for that matter. It wouldn't have made good business sense for her to do so.**

I've always taken people at face value and a handshake (they say that's old-fashioned), and I was satisfied with the verbal agreements we had made. On the other hand, what occurred with Bobbie giving Jeannette the axe might have been avoided had there been something in writing. This latest disclosure was particularly difficult for me to comprehend since I was still reeling from the personal knowledge that:

1) she was going to testify against me and say there was a conspiracy; that I knew everything she was doing and how she was doing it, and then
2) she threw me a curve when she spoke "the searcher's" name.

We finished dinner, left the restaurant and went back to the B&B. There we began to browse through the hundreds of letters which had been received in our office over the past few months. I brought them with me as "visuals" to show my attorney - to make him aware of the number of people who were desperate to find their families. It was important, in my opinion, for him to know the true mission of The Musser Foundation.

As Bobbie flipped through the letters, she began pulling out ones that she said she could do "easily". She helped herself to about a dozen of them. I remember later feeling angry at myself for not protesting - and I have no idea what happened to them. Looking back, I think I must have still been trying to "make nice" - maybe hoping she would change her mind about testifying against me. Part of me still refused to believe that another birthmother - someone who shared a pain unnatural to most - would betray the truth for her own personal means of survival. If she really considered me a "best friend", as she proudly claimed to the government, why would anyone want to hang their best friend??

She knew, I knew, everyone in our office knew, and the majority of the leadership in the movement knew that there had been no conspiracy. As I laid my head on the pillow that evening, my mind was in a dither as I tried to sort it all out.

The next morning, I arrived at the court house at 8:15. I was sitting in the cafeteria having a cup of coffee when Bobbie and Jeannette came in and joined me. We walked upstairs together and were directed into a "holding" room where we sat waiting for our attorneys to arrive. Mine arrived first. He took me into the court room and told me to have a seat. Then he disappeared.

Sitting directly across from me was Mr. Harms, who represented the Social Security Administration. Sitting up front and to the right was the court reporter. The three of us sat in silence and though I felt numb from the events of the past evening, I wanted to scream because of the unfairness of it all. Though I was able to control the urge, my resolve to be courageous was being shaken.

About 20 minutes later, my attorney emerged from a side room and said "let's go - your trial is scheduled for the middle of July." I thought to myself - that's it? This is what I came up here for? You couldn't have done this without me present? But I didn't speak up. I didn't ask questions. I didn't tell anyone how confused and mixed-up I felt. When I did try to suggest something, I felt as though it was brushed off as unimportant.

I showed him the stacks and stacks of letters from people requesting search help, but he said the judge had made it clear that adoption issues were not to be brought into this case, citing irrelevancy. "My adoption work is irrelevant and the myriad of letters hold no weight! I don't understand. That's what this is all about! That's why I'm here; that's why I'm going through this - because adoption records are sealed and people want to be reunited! How can the judge possibly say that it has no relevancy? It's totally relevant!!"

Since he was the attorney and I had hired him, I tried to leave it in his hands, but I was feeling more and more like a lamb being led to slaughter - the scapegoat required to take the fall.

The Interview at the Border

That afternoon I drove to the OH/PA "border" to give an interview to Broadcast News Network. We had agreed to meet at a Friendly's Restaurant at 3:00 pm. I went into the restaurant and looked around, but saw no one with cameras. After waiting about a half hour, I decided to call home to pass some time. While on the phone, I noticed a big burly gentlemen standing about 15 feet away with his arms folded, staring at me. My first immediate (paranoia) thought was that the government had someone follow me to see what I was up to!

As I got off the phone, he approached me and said "Are you Sandy Musser?". He then introduced himself and turned out to be a friend instead of a foe - he was from a support group in Erie, had been informed of the interview and had come to meet me. A few others from the same group were also there that day.

The BNN crew was late, but when they finally did arrive, we had a good interview. Part of that interview was used in a documentary entitled *Adoption Vigilantes* which aired on A&E in August 1994.

On Saturday, I met some CUB friends for lunch. Since they were driving from the western part of the state, we agreed to meet halfway. It was wonderful seeing them again and we spent the entire afternoon discussing old times and current events. They had put together a little book of encouraging and uplifting sayings, which I cherish. The next day, I flew back home.

The 1993 March on Washington

The March on Washington was held the last week in June. Joe Soll & Judy Taylor, Co-Founders of CERA had invited me to attend. They felt that, in light of what was happening, it would be good for me to be in attendance. Pat and I flew up to Washington and, while there, met with Rebecca Peterson, one of the producers of the 60 Minutes Program. We also had a pre-scheduled appointment to meet with one of the Congressman.

Since the speech I had given at the '89 March was still apropos, I decided to use it as a reminder that we were not much further along than we were then. As part of the public speak-out that day, we reenacted the need for us to tear down the walls of secrecy and as part of the reenactment, I was handcuffed and 'hauled off to jail'. Four and half months later, it was a reality. I was in prison.

Getting Geared Up for Trial

A few weeks after the pretrial, Mr. Keith called and said that the trial was scheduled to start the week of July 12th. We had decided that Pat would go along since there was a likely possibility that she would be testifying. As my right-hand assistant, she was aware of the day-to-day operation of the organization. We went ahead and made our travel arrangements for the second week in July.

In the meantime, we sent out another letter letting everyone know about the upcoming trial. Many had already given financial and emotional support and were interested in being kept up-to-date. We hoped that by giving them enough time, they could write to the court, or possibly attend the trial. We had also planned to have a small demonstration in front of the courthouse.

The day before our flight was to leave, Mr. Keith's secretary called and said the trial had been rescheduled. We couldn't believe it! I felt as though my emotions were being played with and that there was no concern for the turmoil and apprehension I was going through. I explained that I could not just make reservations from Florida to Ohio on the spur of the moment without it costing a small fortune. Though there was enough money in the defense fund to cover it, I didn't want to be careless with the monies that had been so generously donated. There seemed to be an apparent indifference toward my needs and feelings. When I expressed these thoughts, she said she understood, apologized, blamed the judge, but said it was not unusual for trial dates to be changed at the last minute.

Pat and I discussed the matter at great length and finally decided to let our reservations stand. We hoped and believed that our presence would provide the impetus needed to proceed with the trial. More than anything, we wanted to get it over with. I called my attorney back and informed him that we were coming up as planned. I also felt it would give us time to sit down and go over the case. We had not spent a whole lot of time together discussing it. Did he have enough of a handle on the subject to carry it off without reviewing it with me? I was beginning to wonder if or why my presence was even needed.

On Monday, July 12th Pat & I boarded a plane for Akron. We had already made rental car arrangements and reservations with Mrs. Clay to stay at the B&B. Since we were arriving late in the afternoon, Bev and Carol met us for dinner at the little Italian restaurant we had "adopted".

The following day, we went to my attorney's office so Pat could meet Mr. Keith in person. When he first came into the room where we were sitting, he tossed several unopened letters (except for one) on the table and said "here are some of your fan letters". They were addressed to HIM, and I recall feeling both hurt and annoyed that he had not even bothered to open them. I said "But these are addressed to you!" He just laughed off my comment. The rapport I had previously felt evaporated at that particular moment - not a good sign, since the trial had not yet begun! The only letter he had opened was the one sent by my brother. My brother's letter read:

> *Dear Mr. Keith:*
> *I have served this great country of ours for over 35 years as a member of our Armed Forces. I served two tours in Vietnam, was shot down twice and was willing to give my life for our country and our ideals. However, I am now becoming very concerned with many of the things that are happening in our country, particularly in the criminal area. I see murders, rapes, child molesting, and other serious crimes being committed and the offenders set free on some small technicality. They are then right back on the street doing the same thing all over again.*
>
> *Now my sister has been charged with conspiracy in trying to help loved ones get back together after our adoption system has put them apart forever. To me it is absolutely ludicrous for our government to spend this kind of money on a case such as this. Sandy is a very caring individual.*
>
> *It seems that our government has not faced up to open adoption and in fact is almost like a communist state when it comes to falsifying documents, changing newborn names and all the things that go along with closed adoption procedures. We must change our policy in this regard.*
>
> *I hope you are successful in getting the jury to understand this. Thank you for your help.*
>
> Stanton R. Musser, Maj
> Gen USAF (Ret)

Mr. Keith then asked Pat to share her story as to how she had become involved with The Musser Foundation. She explained that she had come into the office to speak with me about searching for her daughter she surrendered in NJ in 1955. She then began attending the support group meetings. After the reunion with her daughter, she started to volunteer in the office and finally she was asked to work full-time on a commission basis. She explained that she was hired primarily to do the bookkeeping. Later she became my right-hand assistant and did whatever needed done, in order to keep the office running smoothly.

After speaking with Pat at length, he seemed impressed with what she had to say and said he would most likely want her to testify. This meant that she would not be able to remain in the courtroom during any of the testimony. Mr. Keith had also been speaking with Hal Aigner, an adoptee reform activist of 20 years, and was planning to have him testify as a "professional". Though the government purposely and intentionally made SS#'s the central theme of the case, it was not. Sealed records was really the issue!

Mr. Keith had planned on using Hal Aigner to give testimony on my behalf. Hal had written a search book entitled *Faint Trails*, and could speak to the fact that social security numbers could be obtained from various public records and did not have to be obtained illegally. This would help to verify the fact that I would not have necessarily known that information was being obtained illegally.

The next day, we took a ride downtown so Pat could see the layout of the courthouse. Since the rally had tentatively been scheduled for the following day, we wanted to leave a message with the clerk's office that it was cancelled in case anyone called to inquire about it.

While we were standing at the counter, a young woman was sitting at a table nearby with an open file in front of her. Unknown to us at the time, she was a reporter from the Beacon Journal who happened to be going through my case file at the precise time we were talking to the clerk. She overheard our conversation, followed us out into the hallway and asked if she could speak with us. She said she was impressed with the number of letters that had been sent to the court and placed in the file. According to her, they were all positive. She mentioned she was going to be covering the case and seemed sensitive to the cause. We spoke with her briefly and an article followed within a few days.

Throughout the rest of the week, Pat and I began to make preparation for the demonstration. We took several of the letters received by The Musser Foundation to a Kinko copy center and had them laminated. We then strung them on blue ribbon and planned to hang them along the wall in front of the courthouse as part of the demonstration. We also purchased little gold bells and attached a small blue bow for each participant to wear. The liberty bell and the blue ribbon had become the symbol of freedom for triad members. It was introduced by CERA on one of the early marches. We knew the local media was going to be present, including 60 Minutes, and we wanted to provide them with as many "visuals" as possible.

Sunday, July 18th was Wendy's 39th birthday. I was feeling extremely ambivalent in light of the current circumstances. In my desire to help others find the peace I found when I found her, I was now on trial. I remember lying awake that evening thinking about how insane it all seemed - on one hand it didn't seem real because it didn't make sense, and on the other hand, it was too real - like a nightmare you think will never end. "And how's your life going, Joe?" (Wendy's birthfather).

That evening we went back to the Mr. Keith's office to meet with an attorney friend of his who was going to put me through the ropes in preparation for testimony. Pat and I were waiting for about 20 minutes while they talked in the next room. The only feeling I can recall was a feeling of exhaustion; just wanting to get this over so I could go back to the B&B and go to bed. My patience was wearing thin and I wondered what was taking them so long. Finally they came in and Mr. Keith introduced us. The interrogation began almost immediately and the questions were fired quickly. At first the questions were about my personal background, the background of The Musser Foundation, when we were founded, who else was employed, how we handled our contacts with our clients, how the fee structure worked, etc. and then the nitty-gritty:

"What was your relationship with Bobbie?"
"We had a business relationship."

"Did you have a written contract with her?"
"No, we had a verbal agreement."

"You had a verbal agreement? Why didn't you have something in writing?"
"I don't know. I'm old-fashioned when it comes to trust. I believe in a handshake - a 'gentlemen's agreement' so to speak."

"Did you know how she was obtaining the information?"
"No. But I didn't care how she was obtaining it."

"Did she ever discuss how she was obtaining the information?"
"No."

"But you knew that records were sealed."
"Yes.

"Then if you knew records were sealed, you must have known something illegal was going on?"
"Hmmmm" (and my eyes filled with tears).

At that point, the questioning stopped. The 'interrogator' left. Mr. Keith made a remark to the effect that I did not do very well. The tears

75

that had already welled up now came down like a torrential rain. I began to sob and sob. He was right. I was not doing well at all. Paranoid thoughts were going through my mind. I was thinking "My attorney is supposed to be on my side and helping me through this process, but instead he and his friend are both working for the government and trying to get me to confess. Why did they wait until the day before the trial to give me a taste of the courtroom semantics?" As I cried I said, "I can't go on the stand. Please don't put me on the stand."

Then I made an outrageous (?) statement. While crying hysterically, I said "There are two things wrong in this world - one is the government and the other is men!" (In my thinking, they were synonymous). Mr. Keith appeared shocked and glanced at Pat. Pat, too, looked startled and said "Sandy you need to calm down; you're stronger than this!" "Well, I sure don't feel very strong!" Mr. Keith then urged, "Look, Sandy, why don't you go back to the B&B, get some rest and I'll call you tomorrow". That evening, though totally exhausted, I slept very little. My mind was going a mile a minute and I was unable to fall asleep.

The next day Mr. Keith called to confirm that the trial would be starting on Tuesday, July 20th (the following day). From this point on, I have very little recall of the events and have asked my friends, who attended the trial, to help me reconstruct the subsequent week. I have recollections and glimpses, but for the most part, it was a blur.

"Our mission is at once the oldest and the most basic of this country - to right wrong, to do justice, to serve man… 'All men are created equal' - Those words are promised to every citizen that he shall share in the dignity of man.

This dignity cannot be found in a man's possessions. It cannot be found in his power or in his position. It really rests on his right to be treated as a man equal in opportunity to all others… Their cause must be our cause too… all of us must overcome the crippling legacy of bigotry and injustice and we shall overcome …"

Lyndon Johnson's
Introduction to the
Voting Rights Acts

STANDING TRIAL

Judy & Dave Taylor arrived early in the evening on Monday. Judy is a birthmother and Co-Founder of CERA. Dave is her supportive spouse who is also committed to the adoption reform work. Together, they make a dynamic duo. They came to Ohio to buoy me up, and words cannot express how much their presence meant to me. We spent a considerable amount of time preparing for the demonstration which would be held on Wednesday, July 21st in front of the courthouse. They brought lots of signs, which had been used on the CERA marches, proclaiming bold messages like: DOGS HAVE PEDIGREES, ADOPTEES HAVE SEALED RECORDS; STOP SEPARATING FAMILIES; ADOPTEES HAVE THE RIGHT TO KNOW; BIRTHPARENTS CARE FOREVER; BABY BROKERS BELONG BEHIND BARS; STOP ABUSIVE ADOPTION LAWS.

When my attorney and I met early Tuesday morning, July 20th, he informed me that the consensus of the court and the prosecution was that jury selection should be done "in secret". I could hardly believe my ears! The reasoning was because of the presence of the media." One of the reporters might mention someone's adoptive status in an article and it could pose a problem for that individual. Of course, Sandy, it's your call, but…" "Uh-huh, I think I get the picture. I don't HAVE to go along with this plan, but if I don't, things may not go as smooth or what - the Judge won't be too happy with me?" He shrugged his shoulders and I said "OK, whatever you think-you're the attorney". I just shook my head - I couldn't believe it. Jury selection was going to be done in secret! SECRECY - the very thing we're against. Secrecy always creates problems. What's wrong with openness?

It's secrecy that has presented all the problems in adoption - for adoptees, birthparents, adoptive parents and extended families. And now my own jury selection is being done in secret! Absolutely mind-boggling. Ludicrous. Inside I was feeling outrage, while at the same time I was attempting to maintain a cool composure.

We went to the 4th or 5th floor of the courthouse and into a large room filled with a pool of potential jurors. The judge presented a small talk thanking them for responding to their civic duty. After introducing Mr. Getz, Mr. Keith, and myself, he explained that the trial would probably last a few days. They were informed that, because of the special nature (?) of this case, they were being asked to fill out an extensive form. The form included several questions pertaining to adoption.

A few hours later, the Judge, Mr. Getz, Mr. Keith, a court reporter and myself went into a Board room. The Judge sat at the "head" of the table, I sat to his right, Mr. Getz sat to his left and Mr. Keith sat on my right. The potential jurors were brought in one by one and questioned by the Big Three based upon the answers they gave on the form. The judge had the stack of forms in front of him and directed the procedure. Several of the prospective jurors, when quizzed about their feelings concerning adoption, specifically mentioned the DeBoer case. I took note of the fact that when it was referred to, it was always "the DeBoer case", not the Schmidt-DeBoer case or the Schmidt case. My case was directly on the heels of this now famous case and there is no doubt in my mind that Baby Jessica's return to her birthparents had a negative effect upon the outcome of mine. But I wouldn't have had it any other way.

There were two male prospective jurors who said they were adopted and had completed their searches. One expressed indifference toward the relationship and the other, the youngest of 15, said he has a good relationship with his birth family. No one admitted to being a birthparent though one woman and one man said their sisters had given up a child for adoption. Several of them said there were adopted children in their extended families.

Though I was 'included in this process and supposedly had a voice in the selection, it was done very quickly with little input from me. I had originally made the suggestion that we choose mostly women, but Mr. Keith said that men are usually more empathetic when it comes to judging women. I wanted people of color and nationality. Generally, I believe they have a better understanding and comprehension of the need for family ties and family connections than the average white Anglo-Saxon.

Though I had little input, I did make some brief notes as the interviews were taking place. The interview process took the better part of the day on Tuesday. There were 37 prospective jurors. The first three jurors interviewed were selected. Two of them were older gentlemen, one whose daughter had been a victim. The third was a young female teacher. I had made a notation of "ok" for all three. The fourth was also a young woman, but I had "no" marked next to her name. The fifth was a woman in her mid-40's who said her father's sister was adopted. At this point in the selection process, I lost track because it was moving so quickly. I picked up again at juror eight who was a single man and, I believe, editor of a college newspaper. The next was a burly man who was a truck driver. I had marked "ok" next to his name. The next gentleman was a nice looking man in his early 40's who said his son was a cop. Though I liked his demeanor, I had "no" marked next to his name. Juror #10 was also an older gentleman whose demeanor I liked and had marked ok. Juror #11 was a woman whose sister-in-law had adopted her grandchildren - an "in-family adoption". She seemed particularly sensitive to children remaining with their families and, of course, had thumbs up from me! The last was a college student who was pursuing a teaching degree. All in all, there were 8 men and 4 women.

The Trial Begins

Once the jury was selected, the trial began at approximately 3:30 PM with Mr. Getz and Mr. Keith giving their opening statements. They each spoke for about 20 minutes.

There were several blatant untruths in the prosecutor's opening statement: The first one (quoting from the transcript) was that "the defendant contacted Bobbie Moskowitz some time in 1988 or '89 and solicited her services as one of the Musser Foundation searchers or investigators." As stated in the Awakening chapter, Jeannette was the person I had originally sub-contacted to do searches, and was completely unaware, at that time, that Bobbie was her primary source.

The second untruth was "They were close confidants. They were in almost daily contact even after the indictment was returned." If the government had checked the phone records carefully (and I'm sure they did), they would have known that all the calls following the indictment were from Bobbie to me. I never considered us "close confidants", though she had obviously convinced the government that we were. I considered her a business associate.

The third untruth was "The defendant proposed that for each search that Bobbie would conduct only to get a social security number, both would be paid $100." The truth is that I did not even know a SS# could be obtained until she suggested it to me and even then, she did not say where or how she was obtaining the numbers. The last, while a half-truth, was the most blatant because of the way the story was twisted - again, I'm sure, with the help of the government.

79

Quoting from the transcript of Mr. Getz' opening statement - "She even participated in some of the phony phone calls. One in particular you'll hear about which involved an attempt to obtain a patient's medical records from a hospital". NOTE: The transcript quotes are verbatim, including whatever grammatical errors were made by the court reporter. Mr. Getz is questioning Barbara Moskowitz. This particular testimony begins on page 191 of the transcript. The responses are marked with an asterisk.

"Who is Dr. Franklin"
*"He's the fictitious doctor or she's a fictitious doctor. It was a male for a long time, then it was a female."

"And is that a name that you used?"
*"Yes."

"How often did you use the Dr. Franklin name?"
*"A lot."

"And for what purpose would you use that name?"
*"Only for the purpose of filling in needed information to help locate a birthmother. We were never interested in any medical information, anything in the medical chart. We just needed one piece of information to go with, part of a name, or fill in a middle name or birth date."

"Was it used to obtain information from hospitals and medical records centers?"
*"It was used to obtain information that sometimes you didn't even have to go into the medical record. You could just get the information off an admission card."

"Do you recall a contact with Bellevue Hospital where that name was used?"
*"Yes."

"And first of all why do you recall that particular contact?"
*"Well, I wouldn't have recalled it. It was brought back to my attention and then I did recall it. I had made a call there and at the time I wasn't aware that they were figuring out what was going on. And I felt like I was just inches away from getting that information and I had called Sandy in Florida today (?) and I said that we were I was just inches away from getting the information but the only way we can get

it is if we had a call back number and I never ever gave my number out."

"Had you been providing call back numbers to the hospital?"
*"No."

"But they were requiring that you give them one?"
*"They said yeah oh we have it right here but we have to call you back."

"And did you have a conversation then with Sandy about it?"
*"Yes, I did."

"What was the substance of that conversation?"
*"I called her and I said Sandy I'm just inches away from getting that information, but they wouldn't give it to me unless they can call me back. She said well give them my 800 number. And I said Sandy you know aren't you afraid. She said, you know, she laughed and she said, hey, you know, if I go to jail, I'll just write my book."

"What did you do then?"
*"I did it. I gave them that number."

"What was that number?"
*"1 800 477 and I had to transpose the word "seek" into numbers."

"And why did you do that?"
*"Because I didn't want to tell them 1-800- 477-SEEK."

"Why not?"
*"Because it would seem pretty strange to them."

"Could you obtain the information?"
*"Did I obtain the information, no."

"What happened?"
*"Sandy had just gotten a new phone system and she was supposed to be able to hook me up three way and when the call came in, we couldn't get it to work so we never finished that case. As far as I know that case has never been finished."

There is a scripture that says "Come let us reason together". Now let's really think about this. Would 'Dr. Franklin', who is calling a hospital about an emergency, NOT have a call back number ready - or on the other hand, would Dr. Franklin call the hospital back and say "Oh, this is Dr. Franklin calling you back with a call back number - you know, for that emergency call!" Very unlikely.

The true scenario, as it occurred, will help to explain how easy it was for the government to take the story concerning the hospital call and, with a few twists and turns, make it very convincing. The phone call DID occur, but it happened in the following manner:

Bobbie called and said she was close to getting information, but they wanted a call back number so she said she went ahead and gave them our 800#. "When it comes through, they'll ask for Dr. Franklin -just patch it into me." That was the first time I had heard about "Dr. Franklin". I got off the phone and told Pat what she said. Pat, knowing me so well, said "I know you're uncomfortable with it, aren't you? Why would she even give them our 800#?"

Within a few minutes, the call came through. When the person on the other end asked for Dr. Franklin, I said "hang on" and then immediately hung up. I called Bobbie back, told her I 'lost' the call, explaining that we had a new phone system and I was still not familiar with the workings of it. As far as I was concerned, that was the end of it.

Following Mr. Keith's opening statement, a short recess was taken at 4:10 and convened at 4:25. Mr. Flavin was called as the first witness for the prosecution.

I remember feeling dazed as the trial ensued. It was like a dream - a bad one. Voices in my head were saying "But Sandy all you had to do was plead guilty and you wouldn't have had to go through this. Even if you didn't do it, people have told you that the government is easier on you when you 'cooperate' or do what they want you to."

As the testimony began, I completely tuned out and began to write on the yellow pad George had given me. Throughout the trial, I made notes of things that were going on around me and a few conversations I had during the breaks. These are some of the notes I jotted as the trial got started:

"Why am I here and what are we doing. 9 out of 10 mass/serial murders in the past 20 years were committed by men who were separated by adoption. The anger, frustration and pain of the loss is so great that people around the country are lashing out at the system that causes and perpetuates the separation.

We were treading on the government territory (re: investigations) both literally and figuratively and we were being much too successful."

Since I recall so little of the actual trial, and for the purpose of accuracy, I will be quoting directly from the transcript.

Beginning on page 32 and ending on page 44, Mr. Getz, the prosecutor is questioning Mr. Flavin, one of their 'star' witnesses.

"Are you employed at this time, Mr. Flavin?"
*"No, I'm not. I'm retired."

"What are you retired from?"
*"From the NY State Department of Health."

"How long have you been retired?"
*"Just a little over two years." (This was Mr. Flavin's last case. The investigation of The Musser Foundation ended in January 1991. He retired March 27, 1991, and the indictment came out in the paper March 27, 1993.)

"What did you do for the NY State Dept. of Health?"
*"At the time that I retired I was a Health Department Investigator Two. I was in charge of the investigation unit of the office of counsel.

"And can you explain a little bit about what that office is?"
*"This was an office that was set up at the commissioner's request to aid the office of counsel attorneys in completing investigations, case preparation for hearings and trial and also to conduct investigations requested by the commissioner of health and the chief counsel of the department."

"And how many years were you employed by the NY State Dept. of Health?"
*"26."

"Could you briefly explain what your particular duties were and your last position with that department?
*"Well actually it was anything that the department or the commissioner or the chief counsel requested. My last assignment was to investigate allegations that our vital records security had been breached."

"And what kind of vital records are maintained by the Department of Health?"
*"All right. The NY State Dept. of Health is the keeper of the records for all the vital records for the State of New York. That starts with birth certificates, certificate of birth, marriage license, records of divorce, and death records."

"And are any of those records maintained in confidentiality?"

*"Well, yes. All of those records are maintained in confidentiality. In order for any of those records to be released to an individual, they must have some interest in the document."

"Now you testified that you were asked to conduct some kind of an investigation regarding leaks of information from the vital records unit?"

*"Yes. The department became concerned that several instances of unusual telephone calls, unusual activity on the part of outside individuals attempting to obtain information from records."

"And did you in fact become involved in the investigation into that activity?"

*"Yes, I did."

"And how long were you involved in that investigation?

*"I believe my assignment was the latter part of 1989, and I continued until my retirement which was March 27, 1991."

(Exactly 2 years to the day the indictment was handed down! Was there a statute of limitations? How come we were allowed to continue our work so long after the investigation stopped if we were committing such a terrible crime?)

"Are you familiar at all with the defendant Sandy Musser or with the Musser Foundation?"

*"I'm not personally familiar with Mrs. Musser, but I am aware of her presence and her activities."

"When did you first become aware of her activities?"

*"Oh, on April 10, 1990 I came home from work and my wife indicated to me that there had been a segment on a television program called the Home Show depicting the— a woman and a daughter being reunited. This was a daughter that had been placed for adoption. Mrs. Musser took part in the program, and indicated that she did searches for birthparents who had given up children or children who were seeking their birthparents. And at the end of the program Mrs. Musser said if you need more information, please call the station and get the telephone number."

"What was your interest in that particular television show at that time?"

*"Well, we were, well in that particular television show I had no interest in it until it showed and then one of Miss Musser's statement was that the investigator in that particular case was one of their better investigators out of the Cleveland, Ohio area."

"And did that have some connection to your investigation?
*"Yes it did. We had been aware of the operation of a female individual — we referred to them as searchers — in the Cleveland area for some time. In fact, we became aware of this activity through the attorney general's office of the State of New York. They had conducted an investigation and had concluded that this searcher from the Cleveland, Ohio area had in fact been working in the State of New York.

"And who was that searcher that the defendant had indicated was—
*"Originally the name that they had was B. Howard. We later determined that it was B. Moskowitz."

"Now you say that at the end of the television show there was a telephone number that was given?
*"No, they said to contact the station and obtain a telephone number which I did the following day."

"And do you recall what the telephone number was?"
*"It was an 800 number. I'm not— I can't recall the specific number."

"And what did you do at that time?"
*"On the 11th we had a meeting with our vital records people and with my boss, and it was determined that I would call Musser Foundation, obtain information relating to their activities."

"Did you have any kind of an investigative strategy put together?
*"Not at the time I made the call. We weren't sure of what the activities were and how this would fit in with our investigation. But after my conversation with Miss Musser we did develop a strategy for the investigation."

"Did you in fact make a call to that telephone number that was given?"
*"Yes I did."

"May I approach the witness, your Honor.
The Court: Yes.

"I've handed you what's been marked as Government Exhibit number 4. Do you recognize that?"
*"Yes, I do."

"Can you identify what that is?"
*"Yes, this is a tape of the telephone conversation that I had with Sandy Musser on April 11, 1990."

"Did you produce that recording of that conversation?"
*"Yes, I did."

"Have you reviewed that recording since that time for accuracy and completeness?
*"Yes I have."

"And is that an accurate and complete depiction of that conversation?"
*"Yes, it is.

"Did you have any written transcripts prepared from that taped conversation?"
*"Yes, a transcript was made."

"And have you had an opportunity to review that transcript for accuracy?"
*"Yes I have, and it is accurate."

"Okay. Your Honor, at this time I would ask permission to broadcast or publish the tape to the jury and also to pass out copies of the transcript.

The Court: You've seen it Mr. Keith and heard it?
*"Yes, your Honor. We have had the opportunity to review it.

The Court: You may. Ladies and gentlemen, the use of transcripts — let me indicate to you the transcripts normally are made for your assistance in listening to the tapes. You must remember please that the evidence in this case is the tape that you hear, not the transcript that you read. So if there is any difference to your ear, the transcript governs — tape governs, excuse me if I said it the other way. The tape governs. Okay, Mr. Getz.

"Thank you, your Honor.

(Tape played)

As the tape began to play, I felt my self/spirit/mind (whatever you choose to call it) separate from my body and felt as though I were hovering over the proceedings and watching someone else's trial. I was aware of exactly what the tapes said. They were part of the Discovery" that Mr. Keith had received from the government and forwarded to me soon after the arraignment.

Since Mr. Flavin had contacted our office on many occasions, I had several conversations with him - all of which he had taped (unbeknown to me, of course). In our first and second phone conversations, I made a few remarks that, in retrospect, were apparently very damaging. In response to a comment Mr. Flavin made that he had always been told that this information was sacrosanct and very confidential, I said "Well, it is, but what we have managed to do is beat the system." The other was in response to his remark "Can I get into trouble by hiring you guys? I don't want to go to jail. Laughing, I replied, "I don't think so. If anybody goes to jail, it will be me!" In a friendly tone, he said - "If things go bad, you'll go to jail? I appreciate your concern. Will you put that in writing for me? Again laughing, I said "I've already volunteered." We continued this bantering for several more minutes. "Have you ever been in a New York State prison? They're not good at all." "No, but I'm in Florida so hopefully, it would be a Florida prison." "You have those good Federal prisons down there that are low security with the putting greens. I heard about them."

The Fictitious Scenario

Picking up on page 39 of the transcript. The following is testimony by Mr. Flavin concerning the fictitious scenario he created.

"What occurred next in your investigation, Mr. Flavin?"
*"The next thing that occurred was at that point we met as I said with my boss, with my partner, and with the people from vital records. And we determined that we would set up a fictitious scenario. I had answered one of your questions before did you have something prepared before you called the Musser Foundation. My response was no I didn't. This may give you the impression that I did have, but what I said on the tape about my daughter was spontaneous. It was something that was just in response to Mrs. Musser's questions so that we did not set up the scenario until after this conversation."

87

"Can you explain the kind of scenario that you set up?

*"Yes. We started by sitting in the office and making up this scenario. We gave the girl that I was looking for the name of baby girl Skinner with a mother Geraldine Skinner and an address, the mother's address of 144 Broadway, Rensselaer, New York. With this information I went and had meetings with the administrator of the Tioga General Hospital in Waverly, New York, with the local registrar for that area in the town of Barton, and with the clerk of the Family Court in Waverly, New York and requested their assistance in this investigation which they volunteered. When I got back to my office we then determined what information we would put on the amended certificate of birth and possibly at this time I might explain the difference between the birth certificate and an amended certificate."

"Would you please?"

*"Okay. When a child is born in the State of New York a certificate of birth is issued. If it's in a hospital, it's issued by the hospital. If it's a home birth, the parents record this information. This information is then given to the local registrar which might be a village, a town, or a county clerk, or with the department of health directly. If the registrar receives this information, they immediately make a copy for their own records, and they send the original to the New York State Dept. of Health where it's maintained forever.

If the child is subsequently adopted, this is done through the court of jurisdiction which in the State of New York is either family court or surrogate court. At the time of the adoption, the court of jurisdiction completes papers relating to the adoption.

These papers include the original name of the child, the name of the birthparents, and also the names of the adoptive parent and the new name for the child if the child has been renamed. The court then sends a copy of this information to the department of health. When the department receives it, they produce what we call an amended certificate which contains the new information. It would contain the new name for the child, of course, the place of birth, the date of birth remains the same, and the names of the adoptive parents. Some registrars or some registration districts have a little different form. And they also include some additional information about the adoptive parents, employer, or sometimes social security number.

At the time that the amended certificate is produced, a copy is sent to the local registrar with the instructions that this supersedes the original birth certificate, and the original birth certificate must be sealed. And they usually do this by physically pasting the amended certificate over the original certificate. In the Department of Health, the records that were obtained by the — from the court of jurisdiction are placed in an envelope along with the amended certificate and the original birth certificate, and they are sealed, physically sealed with tape.

The court of jurisdiction is furnished with a copy of the amended certificate and by court order these records are sealed. Now also in the State of New York, we keep a computer record of all birth certificates so that when the records are sealed, the image that would appear on the screen if someone were searching for that birth certificate, instead of the birth certificate coming up, the operator would be faced with a code. And each code means different things.

One in nine (?) means it's an amended certificate. 20 might mean a change of name and all the way through so that if a request is made for that information, the computer operator automatically knows that this information cannot be given out there. That is sealed information and no one can obtain that information."

"Now, turning your attention to Government Exhibit 3 which is before you, did you find that exhibit?
*"Yes."

"Can you identify what that is?"
*"Yes, this is the information that we determined we would include in the fictitious scenario along with a fictitious certificate of birth and a fictitious certificate of live birth containing the information that we had decided would be made available on an as requested basis. This was the same material that we had discussed with the registrar of the hospital administrator and the clerk of court, to the local registrar, and to the administrator of the hospital."

"And did you prepare this information?"
*"Yes I did."

"And that would be for which exhibits that are before you, besides Exhibit 3?"
*"3-A and 3-B which contain the same material except a name on the cover letter is different."

"And what is— who is the cover letter in 3-A sent to or addressed to?"
*"All right. 3-A is Primrose Schafer who is the clerk at the Tioga County Surrogate Court in Owego."

"And what about Government Exhibit 3-B; that is addressed to whom?"

*"That is to Frederick Kaufman who was the administrator of Tioga General Hospital in Waverly."

"Your Honor, permission to publish the contents of the Exhibit 3 for the jury. I have some enlargements."

The Court: Any objection, counsel?

*"No, your Honor.

The Court: Go right ahead. May I suggest then that you may wish to stop for the afternoon on that production, Mr. Getz, so that we don't destroy the efficacy of your client's testimony by interrupting it any more?

"At the conclusion?"

The Court: Or is there a better place that you can think to stop?

"This would be fine at this point"

The Court: At this point. Do you want to show this first?

"Well, I was going to have the witness explain some of the information obtained. May take a little bit of time."

The Court: All right. We'll stop here then.

ADJOURNED AT 4:57 PM

That evening, I was extremely restless and anxious. Though I laid on the bed and tried to go to sleep, I didn't sleep at all. Finally, around 4:00 am. I got up and felt compelled to write a note to my attorney. With a feeling of frenzy, I began to pour out an abusive past, the losses I had suffered, and the manic-depressive illness which affected members of my family.

On the way to the courthouse, I asked Pat if she would read what I had written and copy as much of it as she could. The heading was **Personal Thoughts at 4:00 am**. Some of what I wrote follows:

I'm not holding up as well as I thought I was going to. Manic Depression runs in the family. I've had a few minor bouts with it. I asked my Dr. for medicine in March when the story broke and he said "you don't need it." Right now, I'm feeling as though I do." I went on to explain my general dislike for men and listed the reasons why. That would need another book, which I will not go into here. At the end of the note, I had written 'I'm simply trying to survive and for some reason, **the fear of jail does not scare me as much as having to relive all this pain which is being dredged up within me as a result of this trial**.' As I look back upon that writing now, I realize what a profound and telling statement that was.

We had to be at court at 8:00 AM and I was ready in plenty of time. Several of us had planned to meet at the courthouse early since the demonstration had been planned for that day. When Pat and I arrived, Judy and Dave were already there distributing the signs and pins to the demonstrators. Adoptees and birthparents from a New York group had come to offer support and be part of the demonstration.

We had strung about 75-100 laminated letters on a blue ribbon and were attempting to tape them to the concrete wall. Suddenly a uniformed officer came out from the courthouse and said we could not hang them on the wall because it was considered "defacing property". We were allowed to lay them in front of the wall, but not on it! A film crew was there from 60 Minutes and, after taking lots of pictures of the demonstrators, they asked me to walk into the courthouse with my briefcase in hand. Again, the uniformed officer appeared and with his hand up, like he was stopping traffic, he said "No filming on government property!" No filming on government property! Didn't the taxpayers pay for this beautiful complex?? It felt very oppressive - as though we were in a communist country.

It was time for me to meet George in the cafeteria. I had brought the note I had written and handed it to him. The only thing I said was "I want you to read this." He immediately put it in his inside coat pocket. Though it seemed important to me that he read it right away, his main concern right at that moment was (I think) defending me. Nevertheless, I was feeling empty, detached, forlorn, alone and helpless.

When we took our places in the courtroom, I was shocked to see two members of the AAC Board sitting in the front row! I wondered what in the world they were doing there. What was their purpose for coming? Certainly it wasn't to offer support. That was a bit too late. Was it supposed to be a form of intimidation when and if I got on the stand to testify? Were they getting nervous about what I might say? Or did they come to testify against me? Am I being or have I been setup by my own people? I believed so.

When the trial resumed Mr. Getz was continuing direct examination of Mr. Flavin. A few excerpts from page 62 of the transcript follow:

"Were there any other search scenarios or any other strategies that you developed besides the one involving your fictitious daughter?
*"Yes, we had a second scenario. My partner Stephanie Vanderpool has a daughter Vikki Salamida, and we determined that we could have Vikki Salamida send a completed application to the Musser Foundation asking that they locate and identify her birth mother."

"And what in relation to that part of the investigation did you do?"
*"I was responsible for completing the application; the application was typewritten.

Beginning on Page 64 to 71, Mr. Keith is cross-examining Mr. Flavin. The responses are marked with asterisks:

"Mr. Flavin, may I ask how old are you?
*"64"

"What was your final salary with the State of New York Department of Health?
*"Oh, approximately $45,000 a year, give or take a few bucks." (I had asked my attorney to ask that question so I could prove, at least to myself, that Mr. Flavin made more money in one year than the Musser Foundation grossed the first two years of operation).

"Tell us if you would again, sir, your investigation begins in essence in, I guess, March of 1989; is that correct, or is it March of 1990?
*"In the latter part of '89 sir."

"Latter part of '89?
*"Yes."

"And what triggered the beginning of that investigation?
*"Various things. If I might explain, in the State of New York we have many, many, many registrars who have, who are the keepers of these records, as well as the state health department. We were receiving reports back from the local registrars and from our vital records unit that they were receiving unusual telephone calls, telephone calls from people who identified themselves as being from judges' offices, from our own vital records unit, from social service departments, and they

were requesting information that if they were from these department or entities they would have known that the information was sealed by the courts and was not available to them.

These reports filtered down to the office of counsel. The counsel discussed it with us. The counsel discussed it with the commissioner of health. The commissioner was very concerned. And I was given the assignment of, one, determining whether our security had been breached, two, if it had been breached, identifying the perpetrators, and three, if the perpetrators were identified, to prosecute.

"So you began this investigation looking eventually to proceed through a prosecution; is that correct?
*"That's correct".

"Okay. Up until after I believe April the 10th is the date or April the 11th you first called the Musser Foundation in Florida; is that correct, that's 1990?"
*"April 11th of 1990, I believe, sir."

"And you had no awareness before April 10 of the Musser Foundation?"
*"That's correct."

"But you had awareness of a Betty Levine who was making some phone calls?"
*"At that time I'm not sure whether the name Betty Levine had arisen. It has arisen many times during the investigation. I'm not sure of the date when it first came to my attention."

"Well, what if anything had your investigation revealed up until after the 10th?"
*"Prior to April the 10th, as I have stated, I had a meeting with the director of investigations of New York State Attorney General's Office who had been conducting an investigation in the Erie County, New York area relating to with what he referred to was a searcher and the allegation of a breach of our security." During that investigation certain money orders were sent from the — it was the adopted child who was seeking the mother. And the adopted child had sent $2500 in money orders to a B. Howard at an address in Cleveland. Further investigation determined that B. Howard was actually B. Moskowitz."

"So this much you knew as of April 10th?"
*"Before."

"Before April 10th?"
*"Yes, sir."

"Did you have a post office box for Bobbie Moskowitz or did you have a street address?"
*"I believe we had both."

"You had both. Did you have a telephone number for that street address?"
*"Yes we did."

"Okay. So, you had the person that you were involved with, if you are aware, engaged Barbara Moskowitz to do a search?"
*"I don't believe the person directly hired Bobbie Moskowitz. It was through, I believe, three intermediaries in the Erie County area."

"Were any of those intermediaries the Musser Foundation?"
*"No."

"Okay, had the search been completed?"
*"The attorney general's search?"

"No the search for the individual that paid the $2500?"
*"Yes it had."

"You in fact title your memorandums in your investigating as the searcher; do you not?"
*"Yes."

"Why is that?"
*"It was a common term that we determined would identify these people that we were seeking or the people who were seeking the information."

"Do you believe there was more than one searcher?"
*"Yes."

"Have you availed yourself of knowledge of the adoption reunification movement? In other words, have you educated yourself about it?"
*"Not that title, no, sir."

"Are you aware there are various groups in the State of New York which are either moving to unseal publicly closed records or in the alternative to help people reunite families?"

*"I know that there are groups that are helping to reunite families. I'm not personally aware that any of those groups are seeking to have — I should say I'm not aware that any of these groups have approached the courts or that there's any legal action in the State of New York to change the laws relating to sealed records."

"By action, I mean political action. Once again, your answer is you're not aware?"

*"I'm not personally aware of that; no, sir."

"Mr. Flavin, as a result of your investigation obviously you found Barbara Moskowitz as a searcher. Did you find any of the other searchers?"

*"Yes."

"Were any of them also located in the Cleveland area if you know?"

*"We, I expect from the personal knowledge that there was another person in the Cleveland area somehow affiliated with the searcher or possibly was a searcher."

"Could you tell whether or not Barbara Moskowitz and that other person were in fact the same person?"

*"I would believe not."

"Now, Mr. Flavin, I think that you're aware that there are certain records in the State of New York that are in fact publicly available; is that correct?"

*"That's correct"

"For instance, the New York City, I believe - and correct me if I'm wrong— is 42nd Street Library contain the birth records; is that correct?"

*"Well, they may not contain them at the present time — if I may explain."

"Certainly."

*"The New York City Department of Health is the keeper of the records for the five boroughs of New York City. They're developed over the years a habit of at the end of the year, well what we refer to as flush the records and furnishing the public library, the New York City public

library of a print out of all of the birth records that took place during that year. These records unfortunately contained also the amended records. And I believe that was the reason why there is a lesser fee charged by The Musser Foundation for the New York City searches because even though —"

"Did you discuss that with anyone at the Musser Foundation or are you remembering extemporaneously?"

*"No, in the taped conversation you will see that Mrs. Musser alluded to the fact that she asked me whether I was upstate or in the New York City area. And that there was a different rate for the New York City area than upstate. Even though the information in the original record is changed when there's an adoption, the certificate number remains the same.

In the New York City library, if someone has the patience and you know what year someone was born, you can merely physically go down the right hand column of those records until you come to that birth certificate number. Reading to the left, you will find the new names. Now, our department has notified the New York City Department of Health that this is in violation of the Domestic Relations Law of the State of New York, and this situation should cease."

"But up until — as far as you know, until the present any individual could walk in and literally if they had the patience go through those records and find someone; is that correct?"

*"I believe so, yes."

A lot of discussion about Bobbie's telephone records being subpoenaed followed. (Picking up on page 76-92)

"You've told us that you received some records from the New York State Attorney General's office."

*"Yes, sir."

"And you also seem to be telling us that there were other records that you had obtained?"

*"I'm telling you, yes."

"And where were those obtained from?"

*"They were obtained from AT&T in Atlanta, GA."

"Those are other records?"

*"Yes sir."

"And how did you cause those to be given to you?"
*"We subpoenaed them from AT&T."

"And who issued that subpoena?"
*"The commissioner of health, and I believe, yes, the chief counsel of the State of New York signed the subpoena.

"Chief counsel for the State of New York. Would that be the attorney general?"
*"No sir. Peter Mylek (sic) is the chief counsel for the state health department."

"Chief Counsel for the state health department for the State of New York?"
*"Yes."

"Do you know when that subpoena was issued?"
*"There were a series of subpoenas issued. I'm not sure of the date."

"Would it have been before or after April the 11th of 1990?"
*"I can't honestly answer that question. It would have been around that time."

"And how about the record that the attorney general's office had obtained? When did you have those; if you know?"
*"Prior to April of 1990.

"When did you become aware once, or when did you first make contact with some agency of the federal government with regard to this matter?"
*"It was somewhere around this time. I don't know the exact date. That was in early 1990."

"Would it have been before or after you cooked up a false scenario including false social security numbers for baby girl Skinner?"
*"I can't honestly say."

"Were there other scenarios that you set up other than the one for yourself and the one for Vikki Salamida?"
*"Not in the same way, no. But there was another scenario set up where we were receiving telephone calls asking for information about a

97

particular individual. And again, I had arranged for the vital records unit to transfer those calls to me, and we had set up a fictitious response to those inquiries.

"In essence, sir, you set up a scenario with regard to baby girl Skinner, and you sent these people out to look for somebody who actually does not exist; is that correct?
*"That's correct."

"You know that they're never ever going to be successful because I would guess, sir that you checked to make sure that these people did not actually really exist; is that right?"
*"We had no records of their existence."

"But you check your records to make sure of that?"
*"Yes, sir."

"Okay. You then send it out and through a series of telephone calls you attempt to then push or prompt this search, don't you?"
*"Yes."

"And at some point you obviously are aware that what you're trying to do is to establish the use of social security numbers, is that correct?"
*"That's correct."

"Because by the 9th of July, the 12th of July, whatever it is, when you're masquerading as Leo Rivers you're giving out different social security numbers, I think you change it from the first call to the second by one digit; is that correct?"
*"I believe it was one digit. I did change it the second time."

"Was 11856 the first time and it was 12856 the second time?"
*"The records will speak for themselves. I don't recall those exact numbers. I don't — they're different."

"Once again, you're trying to prompt a wild goose chase?"
*"I'm trying to trace the information we give to this individual to the social security records. I would not call it a wild goose chase."

"You certainly don't intend for them to be successful. You intend for them simply to search fruitlessly?"
*"We intended for them to search to see if they could identify my daughter."

"Now you indicate that you received a Musser Foundation information packet on April the 21st of 1990; is that correct?"
*"Around that date; yes, sir."

"And that was sent at your request?"
*"That's correct."

"Once again, you have no real intention, I mean, there is no adoption in your family or no search that would be related to you personally, is there?"
*"That's correct."

"And then on July the 24th or thereabouts apparently you receive an agent-client agreement that's returned to you; is that correct?"
*"I received an agent-client agreement. I don't recall the exact date."

"And once again that's not for the purpose of any meaningful or productive activity other than for you to once again put together evidence for prosecution?"
*"Yes, it would have been productive for us, but not for anybody else, I guess."

"That's right. Now, we've heard the tapes of several phone calls that you had with Sandy Musser; is that right?"
*"Yes, sir."

"Were there other conversations that were had?"
*"With Sandy Musser?"

"That's correct."
*"I did receive a final telephone call from the Musser Foundation — I don't know the exact date —that the gist of the conversation was Tom, we've exhausted all possible leads, we've come to a dead end. Our investigator is closing the case. We do have new investigators. If you can furnish us with any further information, we will consider continuing or starting a new investigation."

"There was no demand for money even though they had not been able to provide the information?"
*"No. The only demand for money was when they called me and said Tom, we've located your daughter, we're calling you so you can get the $500 ready (mistake made by court reporter). We'll be calling

99

you in a couple of days." (That call was made by Doris since I was away).

"That's correct. There was a notification to you that they believed they were going to be successful in letting you know to be prepared for that transaction; is that correct?"
*"That's correct."

"Okay. But at the end of it when no information was forthcoming, there was no request for funds, was there?"
*"No, sir."

"During the course of those telephone conversations you had asked on a couple of occasions very obliquely if you understand what that means?"
*"Yes."

"How this was to be conducted; is that correct?"
*"That's correct."

"The only time you were given any real indication of that was by the investigator Bobbie who you spoke with in a three-way conversation, having to do with her talking to a mailman; is that correct?"
*"I'm not sure I understand the question."

"In other words, you asked repeatedly how are you doing this search or I can't quote you correctly, but you inquire at one point in the middle of the conversation you talked about getting some hospital records for instance. And the only real statement about where this information might come from was somebody said we called a mailman who had been there at the time. He was retired. He didn't remember any family of that name; is that correct?"
*"There was a comment made by the person we believe to be Bobbie Moskowitz after I had given her the first set of social security numbers. She called me back and said those numbers go nowhere. I believe those were her exact words."

"That was a conversation between you and she without Sandy Musser being on the line; is that correct?"
*"That's correct."

"Okay. You obviously have some experience at this in the past, would you agree with that, in terms of setting up a scenario and carrying in through to invite someone to be involved.

*"Not is this particular format, but we, yes, we have—I've been an investigator since 1953 so I've done almost every investigative procedure."

"Well, certainly as Leo Rivers you were able to when what you later find out to be Bobbie Moskowitz calls you were able to hesitate. She called, she asked to see something. You say wait a minute, wait a minute, let me go get that file. You don't, you aren't so implausible that you immediately have it in the front of you and go forth with it. Those are little flourishes, are they not?"
*"I believe so, yes."

"In any event, one of the things that you attempt to do as part of this is to get Sandy Musser to tell you about where this information is coming from or who it's being gained from; is that right?"
*"Absolutely."

"And I don't believe from your conversation with her that you can ever tell us whether or not she immediately knows, can you?
*"She who, sir?"

"Excuse me."
*"She who?"

"Sandy Musser, once again you attempt to get Sandy Musser to tell you where this information may be sought or where it comes from; is that correct?"
*"Yes, that's correct."

"And you at one point flatter her. You say things like your picture, are you as pretty as your daughter, I mean, you've very personal about all this?"
*"Yes; I have an easy way." (The comment most of us in the courtroom heard was "Yes, I guess I'm just easy that way". Whichever it was, the courtroom let out a moaning sound after Mr. Flavin made the comment and were quickly reprimanded by the Judge.)

"And through the course of it all, you are not able, she apparently does not tell you anything about where that information comes from other than from Bobbie; is that right?
*"That's correct"

"And so to your personal knowledge from those conversation she

101

does not know where that information is being sought or where it might come from?"

Mr. Getz: Objection, your Honor.

The Court: In that form, yes, Mr. Keith.

"Based on the conversations that you had with Sandy Musser and your attempts to cause her to tell you about these searches and where the information comes from. You cannot say whether or not she knew where the information was being sought or where it would come from; is that correct, sir?"
*"In at least one of my conversations with Sandy Musser we discussed the legality of the obtaining — "

"No, sir. That is not the question."
*"Please rephrase it to me."

"The question is you had provided her with a scenario — I'll back up and set it up, okay. You provided her with a scenario?"
*"Yes, but I spoke to her before that time."

"I understand that."
*"Yes, sir."

"And you started from the first conversation you had with her, you said that there was a girl during the Korean war when you had been in service who had given up a baby, and you began to lay the foundation for baby girl Skinner?"
*"I did not say Korean war. I said when I was stationed in Korea."

"I'm sorry, sir. In any event, you then set up a scenario for baby girl Skinner; is that correct?"
*"That's correct."

"And as you proceed through that scenario on several occasions you want to talk with Sandy Musser about where that information comes from; is that correct?"
*"Yes."

"And with regard to the specific areas of inquiry or the specific searches that are made, you never get any answer; is that correct?"
*"Not after I submitted the scenario; that's correct."

102

"Okay. Now there is some conversation that some of those records are sealed and some of them are difficult to get; is that correct?"
*"Yes."

"And she certainly has a bravado attitude that she believes that people should be able to do this and should be able to find these things out; is that right?"
*"Oh, yes. She was very open about that."

"That's correct. But she does not ever tell you that she specifically is violating the law or knows that she is, does she?"
*"She intimated that, but she did not specifically say that."

"Certainly you would have liked her to have said that; would you not?"
*"Oh, yes."

(JUMPING TO PAGE 87 DUE TO REPETITION)

"Couple more things, Mr. Flavin. And I may have confused this. You were aware of Bobbie Moskowitz before April the 10th of 1990; is that correct?"
*"Yes."

"You were aware of her activities?"
*"In one specific case, yes."

"Other than that specific case, and her activities with the Musser Foundation that you've told us about, were there any other activities with any third parties that you were aware of?"
*"Between Bobbie Moskowitz and third parties?"

"In other words, the first party would have been the lady you tell us about from Erie County who apparently was an adoptee?"
*"Yes."

"The Musser Foundation would have been another party. Were there any parties outside of those two that she had contacts with that you're aware of from your investigation?"
*"Yes, Bobbie Moskowitz had telephone contact with many what we call search units throughout the United States."

"What are search units?"

*"Searchers, individuals who do searches. And we also have the telephone records of those searchers calling Bobbie Moskowitz."

"Okay. And are you aware of the nature of that contact, if you know?"

*"I've not been privy to any of those telephone conversations; no, sir."

"Okay, how many others searchers would she have been in contact with?"

*"I don't know the exact number. I know that we're aware of a ballpark figure 15, maybe more, few more." (The number was closer to 40.)

"Would you recall what states those were in?"

*"California, Texas, New Jersey, I believe, Arizona. The others — there were at least two in California, one major one in Texas."

"Did you speak to any of those individuals?"

*"No, I did not."

"You became aware eventually that Bobbie Moskowitz was using her ability to access social security offices as part of her searching; is that right?"

*"That is our conclusion; yes, sir."

"And you obviously at least at some point have been privy to the social security records that showed the dates that certain computer searches were made, and they show the time?

*"They show the date and the time; yes, sir."

"And they also show the social security number?

*"Well, the searches were done in various ways— by name, by social security number, sometimes names of the adoptive parent, and sometimes names of the birth child."

"Are you aware of what a person has to be able to say to social security to get them to do that for you over the phone?"

*"In conversations with the representatives of the federal government and basically having a smattering of knowledge relating to the law, you, would have to impersonate some sort of official."

"Would you know which official or what officials?"

*"Not specifically what official."

"And how would you ask for that information? In other words, if you call the bureau of motor vehicles, you say I'd like a driver's license printout for either a name and date of birth or social security number or something, and what they will respond to this, because they're used to the public. What do you have to say to social security to get them to produce information?"
*"The only information I had relating to that would have come second hand. I don't have any personal knowledge."

"You don't know of that yourself?"
*"Yes."

"Okay. Had there been an investigation of people looking through birth records back in 1986 in the State of New York if you are aware?"
*"1986?"

"Yes."
*"I'm not really sure when this investigation was conducted by the attorney general. I—to the best of my recollection it was '87, and possibly early part of '88. But in the back of my mind I believe '87 and that's the only one I was aware of. Oh, I'm sorry. There was another investigation in Onondoga County done by the Onondoga County district attorney at approximately the same time as the Erie County investigation was being conducted."

"Now the Erie County investigation then leads into this investigation?"
*"Well, no. We had been assigned the investigation and as part of your investigation we determined that they — that the attorney general had already conducted an investigation. The chief of investigation for the attorney general office is an investigator that I hired in the state service many years ago. So we have a very close relationship."

"Who else made phone calls to Sandy Musser other than — you do you have a number of investigators?"
*"Oh, no, no one. Vikki Salamida, I believe, made a telephone call to Sandy Musser."

"Anyone else from your office?"
*"Not to my knowledge, no."

"Who else from your office, you at one point impersonated, I guess, although obviously had a right to, Leo Rivers. Who else would you have impersonated throughout the course of this investigation?

*"To the best of my recollection Leo Rivers was the only name that I took because Leo Rivers is actually the senior clerk of the vital records unit. And he would be the person, the logical person, to control this information."

"In order to control your investigation, you actually instructed those folks where you worked that if some certain phone calls came through, they were to be diverted to you as opposed to Mr. Rivers; is that right?"

*"Yes, the poor devil was sequestered and was having a hard time with receiving other telephone calls that he would normally receive, yes."

"That's right, because you once again wanted to be able to control these conversations as opposed to letting him do it and having a real conversation. You want to be able to control the flow of the information; is that right?"

*"That's correct."

"Thank you, your Honor. I have no other questions."

A recess was taken from 10:30 - 10:45.

While I was standing outside the door of the courtroom waiting for the case to resume, the reporter from the Beacon came by and said "This has really got to be tough on you." In a cynical, but quiet manner, I responded "They hung Jesus on the cross and He wasn't guilty either." She didn't seem to know how to respond and knew by my tone of voice that I didn't feel like talking. At the same time, , one of the AAC Board 'observers' came over and asked me how I was holding up. I wondered why she had waited four months to ask that question? I said "Not as well as expected. It's so unbelievable, but maybe in the long run, it'll be a good thing". She said "How could it be a good thing?"

"Well, maybe now they'll see the need for open records."

"What difference is it going to make? Look how few people are outside picketing."

"Yes, and you're not one of them!"

She appeared agitated and said she was there as an individual to observe, and that was her choice. The trial was resuming so the conversation ended.

High Hopes, But Another Set-Up

The next person to be called to the stand by the prosecution was a young woman by the name of Vicki Salamida. As soon as I heard her name, I knew that she, too, was part of the setup. It turns out that her mother was Mr. Flavin's "partner" during the investigation.

She had written and asked us to locate her mother and said that since she had never been adopted, she had access to her mother's maiden name. We sent her the form to fill out, which she returned, though she neglected to send a deposit. Since she sounded young on the phone, we thought maybe she couldn't afford it.

We went ahead and turned it over to one of our investigators (not Bobbie), who was able to locate Vicki's mother in a relatively short period of time. In fact, he sent us a printout with all the information on it. The printout showed that Vicki's mother worked for the NY State Department of Health as an investigator. Now that should have been a clue, but instead, we naively thought we had found a birthmother who would be willing and able to assist us in completing our NY cases! Doing some further investigation ourselves, we even learned the "code" name she used in her work.

We called Vicki to let her know that the search had been completed. She said she was unable to pay for her search. Whenever someone said they were unable to pay, we tried to work out whatever arrangements we could to assist them - either monthly payments or lowering the price and covering our own expenses.

When neither of those arrangements were appropriate or agreeable to Vicki, we decided to send her mother a brochure hoping she would respond and want to meet her daughter. If she did, we would then inform her that her daughter was looking for her and put them in touch with one another, with no charge to either party. We had done that on a few other occasions so it wasn't something we had just dreamed up for this situation. Many of our cases were done pro bono for the person searching, even though The Musser Foundation had to pay the investigators. We believed that was part of our mission.

Since Vicki was also a setup, this, of course, backfired and we were accused of trying to collect at both ends. No money ever exchanged hands for this case, though we did pay the investigator to get it done. We were really hoping this mother would be thrilled to find her daughter and want to use her position with the NY State Dept. of Health to assist us. I guess you'd say we had **HIGH HOPES!**

In her opening testimony, Vicki said that she works for the New York State Police and also the Albany Medical Center. She went on to explain that Mr. Flavin contrived the letter for her to send to The Musser Foundation and then claimed that we made several phone calls to her. She also said that we sent her two packets of information.

Regarding the phone calls - "bugging" people for payment was not our style and in checking our phone bills for that time period, her number only appears twice. She, however, contacted us on several occasions (with her tape recorder going). Concerning the second packet of information - she became verbally sarcastic on the phone claiming she was still waiting to receive her information. After hearing her testimony, the "Mail Fraud" charge became clearer. There had been four counts of "Mail Fraud" which simply meant the mailing of literature and material in carrying out your mission; or in their words, carrying out the "criminal activity." Ms. Salamida and Mr. Flavin had both made continual inquiries claiming they had not received our information packet of material, thereby inducing us to send them more! That explains the reason they had both received two brochures with different postmarks. Our brochures were much too expensive for us to waste them by sending them out repeatedly or indiscriminately.

Ah, our state and federal investigators will do whatever it takes to hang us. It's rather scary, don't you think? And that's exactly what they try to instill - **FEAR!** That's the name of their game. Until this experience, I took everyone at face value. The trust I once had in people has been destroyed. My rose-colored glasses are gone. I'm still shocked over the fact that the U.S. Government would go to the lengths they did in order to halt adoption reunions. But it proves what a threat we've become. It should be a clear sign to all of us that our country does not believe in family, no matter how much they tout it.

Following Ms. Salamida's testimony, there was a lunch recess.

Mr. Harms, a special agent with the office of the Inspector General for the U.S. Department of Health and Human Services was the prosecution's next star witness. When asked about his job description, he said he was responsible for investigating fraud, waste, and abuse in the 300 or so programs administered by the Department of HHS; one of those programs is social security administration.

There are 1300 social security field offices of various sizes spread throughout the U.S. that have the capacity to obtain information from the main computer system located in Baltimore, Maryland.

Mr. Harms testimony is quite extensive as he proceeds to define the various types of queries available from social security. In fact, anyone interested in learning the terminology and lingo should seriously consider obtaining a copy of the transcript.

Beginning on page 122 of the transcript, Mr. Getz is questioning Mr. Harms:

"At some point in time did you become involved in an investigation involving unauthorized disclosures of this confidential information?"
*"Yes, I did. And I believe it would be about the first week in March of 1990 **(note: a month before the House Party Show aired)**. I had an initial contact with New York Department of Health Investigator Tom Flavin."

"What was the nature of the investigation that you commenced?
*"Investigator Flavin indicated to me that he had information that a particular individual had been in contact with the social security office in Muncie, Indiana frequency of several hundred times over a period of about a year to a year and a half. Such an inquiry to me was very puzzling. I could not understand why one person as far as I knew a private person would be calling social security that many times in such frequency in such a short period of time."

"During your investigation did you obtain dumps of these certain social security administration inquiries?"
*"Yes I did. The investigation included any contacting through an intermediary at the Great Lakes Program Service Center for the social security administration, the central computer facility in Baltimore, Maryland requesting various items of information. I was interested over a period of time of whether or not inquiries had been made on specific names that were supplied to me through the investigation. If any inquiries had been made on specific social security numbers and correspondingly, in many instances these particular inquiries were also made at the almost exact same time that the employment inquiries were made."

"What was the source of the specific names that you requested an investigation of?"
*"Source of the specific names was in addition to the fictitious person that Tom Flavin had submitted to the Musser Foundation, as well as the name of or the particular request for a search for Vikki Salamida. (Note: a different investigator did Vikki's "case". Was it one of the government's "decoys" that set the trap?) This seems like an appropriate place to make an important point for consideration. **If, in fact, a loved one (once the**

name is known) can be located simply by tapping into this terrific resource that we, as a country/ government, have created - then why not use it for the purpose of reuniting families?? Some will immediately tout the privacy laws, but if you read the privacy laws, you will find that they were initially established to protect the citizens **from government interference into our lives - NOT to protect us from simply finding and/or knowing our kin.** Also, it is my understanding that Congress recently passed legislation allowing the social security administration records to be used in locating deadbeat dads. If it is being used to make people "pay up", why not setup a separate division and use it in a positive way to reunite loved ones. I'm sure I'm only one of many who would be happy to accept such a position.

Think about it:

If your son, daughter, mother, father, sister, brother, etc. had become separated from the family for **whatever circumstantial reasons,** and one of **our** huge governmental agencies like Social Security Administration or Internal Revenue Service was able to assist you by plugging into this wealth of information that **we, the government, have created, wouldn't you want to be able to access it??**

If a small $50 fee were charged for this service, we could probably pay off our national debt!!

The Last Day of Testimony

Thursday, July 22nd was the final day of testimony. A disenchanted birthmother from Naples, FL testified for the prosecution. Though she did get to meet her daughter, she claimed that we only gave her the name and address of the adoptive father. She said that only after she complained did we finally provide her with her daughter's name and place of employment.

The next witness for the prosecution was an adoptive mother. She said that she had received a call from her son's birthmother and that she was shocked. She said that she immediately wondered where this information had been obtained.

These two witnesses only took a total of 15 minutes. A recess was called at 8:18 AM because two of the prosecution's witnesses still had not arrived. One was flying in, but not expected to arrive until 10:20. The other witness was Mr. Rollenhagen, the reporter from The Plain Dealer in Cleveland. For three hours we milled around the halls of the court playing the waiting game. My attorney was still talking to Pat and trying to decide if he was going to put her on the stand. She had missed the entire trial while waiting to be called. There was a small room where most of us had gathered. The general consensus was one of encouragement that the prosecution still had not proved their case. Dave Taylor was prompting me to write my "victory" speech.

Mr. Rollenhagen arrived and the trial resumed at 11:30 am. Mr. Rollenhagen testified about the conversation he and I had the day after the story broke. A few excerpts of his testimony follow.

Mr. Getz asked him to explain the circumstances surrounding our communication. He responded "After the Indictment was returned on Friday, I attempted to contact her. I ended up finding her phone number for the Musser Foundation in Florida."

"Did you discuss the activities involved in the charges against her in this case?"
*"Yeah. I essentially told her that she had been indicted and what the indictment was about and asked her for her response to that".

"Do you recall what her response was?"
*"Generally, well, I remember specifically asking her whether she was aware that the basic thing was that her codefendant had obtained some information, social security information. And I asked if she was aware of how that had been obtained, if she knew how her codefendant obtained that information, and she said she did not."

Mr. Keith then cross-examined Mr. Rollenhagen.

"It's your belief that the indictment was reported out on a Friday in March; is that correct."
*"Yeah."

"And you obtained a copy of that indictment; is that correct?"
*"Right."

"You then found a phone number for Sandy Musser in Florida and called and let a message?"
*"Yes."

"She called you back, you spoke with her 8:30 or 9 o'clock the next morning; is that right?"
*"Yeah."

"At that time she did not know that she had been indicted; is that correct?"

*"I think she might have been aware from a paper down in that area Fort Myers, I think may have been the nearest fairly large paper that I think she said that she had either been contacted by someone (I had not) from that paper too or perhaps there had seen a story in that paper that morning also. We had talked at one point to the paper. I didn't personally, but other people at the Plain Dealer had talked to the paper in Florida also trying to get background information about Sandy Musser and the Foundation."

"Was it somebody from your office faxed Sandy Musser a copy of the indictment?"
*"Yeah."

"Okay. At the time you talked to her she had obviously never seen it; is that correct?"
*"Yeah, she had not seen the indictment."

"Would obviously not be particularly aware of its contents?"
*"Oh, other than what I told her it contained."

"And at that point in time, she told you that she didn't know anything about the invasion of social security records; is that correct?"
*"Yeah."

"Okay. And she told you that she had not talked with Barbara Moskowitz about how these things had been done; is that correct?"
*"Correct."

"And she told you about her own experience with adoption and how she had become involved in the reform movement; is that correct?"
*"Yes."

"And she told you that what was really important to her was that people were reunited and the results of these things; is that correct?"
*"Correct."

"She did not ever tell you that she knew she had participated in a crime."
*"No."

"Is that correct? I would assume you asked her about that in rather specific terms, sir?"
*"Yeah, I asked her whether or not she knew how Moskowitz had

been obtaining the information, and she said she didn't know so I —"

"She was very candid with you about her other feelings?"
*"Yeah, it was — we talked for I'd say maybe 15 minutes or something."

"Okay. During the course of that 15 minutes she was willing to tell you about the things that were important to her and even though you're a newspaper reporter and taking it down, she's willing to tell you about what is really important to her; is that right?"
*"Yes."

The last witness to be called by the prosecution was a Director of the Medical Records Department at Bellevue Hospital in Schenectady. She claimed that she recalled receiving a call at home regarding a request for medical records in December of 1990.

"I had an employee who was working the evening shift call and say that a physician by the name of Dr. Franklin had called her stating that she was calling from the Atlanta Trauma Center; that it was an emergency and she needed some information about a birth that had occurred several years earlier.

"And why were you being called?" Mr. Getz asked.
*"Because the physician had called and demanded information, would not give a phone number to return the call, and the employee was not sure how to handle the situation."

"What did you do?"
*"It ended up being a three-party call (with the employee) and I was speaking to a person who identified herself as Dr. Franklin and I said the information she was looking for was not available at the present time, and we would need a phone number. If she could give us some sort of consent to release the information, I could call her back in the morning."

"And did she give a call back number?"
*"No she did not."

"Did you receive any further calls from this Dr. Franklin?"
*"Yes, I did."

"When was the next one?"

*"I'm not sure exactly. It was a long time ago. She did call back, I believe it was the next day demanding the same information."

"And what occurred?"
*"I asked her for her phone number so that I could call her back, and she would not give me a phone number. I did while I was waiting for her to call back at another point in time go to see if I could find any information because it was so long ago, and the records that we hold were not easy to retain at that time. And then she did call back, but I didn't give her any information other than that somebody had been there at that time. She was looking for a name and an address of somebody."

"Did you have any further contact with Dr. Franklin?"
*"Yes, she had given me — I'm not sure when she had called and she had given me an 800 number that I could call her back at. And we attempted to reach her at that 800 number and it was told to me on the phone that it was not a valid number. She called back at another point in time and gave me another 800 number that I could try to reach her at. When I used that number to call her back there, somebody else was on the line, said that she could not be patched through, but that she would call me back. And at that point in time, we attempted to call the Atlanta Trauma Center because we felt that this must be an emergency of some sort. And we didn't understand why the number we were given was not correct. And the Atlanta Trauma Center said there was no one there by the name of Dr. Franklin, and I don't remember if she called back after that."

Testimony was concluded at 11:55 and a lunch recess was taken until 1:15. During the lunch recess, there was an upbeat feeling that the prosecution had not proved their case and that I would be found not guilty. Dave Taylor again suggested I prepare a speech for the media to the effect that "justice had been served".

After lunch, the following eight minute discussion transpired between my attorney, the Judge and the prosecutor. Since I do not profess to understand legal jargon, the following is unclear to me, but may have meaning to those who are more "in tune".

Mr. Keith: Pursuant to the Federal Criminal Rules and whatever applicable case law we would move the Court to dismiss all counts at this time for insufficient prosecution to place it before the jury and insufficient evidence that any reasonable minds would find guilt and reserve argument for a later time.

The Court: May I suggest given what we've discussed you rest subject to the admission of the exhibits and if you don't mind, rather than hold the jury up, we'll rule on exhibits after we have taken care of the jury.

Mr. Getz: That's fine.

Mr. Keith: That's fine, your Honor

The Court: The prosecution has rested so we go to the admission of the exhibits, Mr. Getz.

Mr. Getz: That's correct, your Honor.

The Court: Mr. Keith.

Mr. Keith: Thank you, your Honor. At this time we would have nothing to offer.

The Court: Did you have any exhibits, Mr. Keith?

Mr. Keith: Your Honor, we would have agreed that Government Exhibit number 10 will be entered as a defense exhibit.

Mr. Getz: That's correct, Your Honor.

The Court: Defense A.

Mr. Keith: Defense A, your Honor.

The Court: Okay. Ladies and gentlemen, you have heard now all of the evidence which you will hear in relation to this case. Prearranged times have been set forth in this matter, and quite frankly it's gone a little quicker than I think any of us had thought originally. The next matter that you will consider will be the argument and charge of the Court. The previous agreement indicated that we would not be working tomorrow because of prior commitments by counsel. So we're going to excuse you this afternoon and we will not want you to come in tomorrow. We will wish you to come in at 9 o'clock on Monday morning. I think I perhaps do not have to underline for you the importance now of preserving the integrity of your judgments in relation to the case. So please don't form any opinions about the case. If you can do so, put it out of your mind while you're away from us. Don't talk with anybody

115

about the matter, don't read or listen to or hear anything about it. Remember that your decisions must be based on information which has been elicited by the testimony and by the exhibits which you will have for your consideration. We will now stand in recess therefore until 9 o'clock Monday morning. We will see you at that time. You're excused.

(Jury excused at 1:20 PM.)

The Court: Now, are there objections to the exhibits offered by the government, Mr. Keith?

Mr. Keith: Your Honor, I believe they have offered their exhibit and subexhibits 1 through 14. We would have no objection to any of those.

The Court: Are those numbers correct, Mr. Getz?"

Mr. Getz: With the exception of also 16 and 16-A in addition to those which are the — would be the tape recordings of Leo Rivers calls.

Mr. Keith: I apologize, your Honor. We would also have no objection to the original tapes.

The Court: 1 through 14-A are admitted, 16 and 16-A are admitted.

Mr. Keith: The record, I think your Honor, should reflect that we were given transcripts of tapes of telephone conversations between Barbara Moskowitz and certain social security offices, and those were not played. And I think they were part of the general Exhibit 16, but, however, should not be submitted to the jury.

Mr. Getz: That's correct.

The Court: They will not be then. May I leave that to you, Mr. Getz, to make sure you check with Mr. before that goes to the jury.

Mr. Getz: Yes, your Honor.

The Court: I would assume at the end of all the evidence you're renewing your Rule 29 motion.

Mr. Keith: That's correct your Honor.

The Court: For the purpose of the record, if I have not done so, Defense Exhibit A is also submitted.

116

Mr. Keith: Thank you, your Honor.

The Court: Did you gentlemen give me the originals of the stipulations?

Mr. Getz: No, your Honor. I don't believe the original of the factual stipulation was given to the Court. I'm sure it was executed by the parties.

Mr. Keith: I probably have it. I know I have it here somewhere, your Honor. I will this afternoon make sure that it's signed."

The Court: Okay. Do you have another copy?

Mr. Getz: Yes, your Honor.

The Court: Is there but one or is there more than one stipulation? There's more than one, I think.

Mr. Getz: There was a stipulation that only regarded the Foundation for telephone records. Those have been admitted.

The Court: Okay. Well, Mr. Keith, if you'd be so kind, I'm assuming that the stipulation will be signed. If you will give that to me Monday morning. I will read that as well as any other stipulations you have to the jury before argument if that's agreeable with counsel.

Mr. Keith: Certainly, your Honor.

The Court: Okay. Having reserved your rights to argue on Rule 29, I'll be happy to hear from you sir.

Mr. Keith: Your Honor, I think at this time I would choose not to argue. The Court has heard the evidence and I think would not be assisted by my argument.

The Court: The motions then are overruled. Does this leave us then in a position where we wish now to go to work on the charge?

Mr. Getz: Yes, your Honor.

Mr. Keith: Yes, sir.

The Court: Okay, if you'll take off your coats and join me in chambers, we'll spend the afternoon together.

117

This poem was written as I was going to trial. It's written by Robin Westbrook and titled *M.I.A.* When I went to prison, Robin subtitled it *"For Sandy"*

Shot down in some foreign land,
The final orders are read
And someone tells the family
"Missing ... Presumed Dead."
A man missing in action,
His family doesn't know
If he's dead or if he's living
Or which way they should go.

I think they would understand us,
Why we search and why we strive
For us, out there there's someone
"Missing ... Presumed Alive."
They're not missing in action,
Fought to take an enemy fort,
But rather in the actions,
Of agencies and courts.

Wounded by harsh social stigma
Kept apart by records sealed
Tortured by stifled grief,
Injured and not healed.
We're all missing in action,
And persisting in our quest
To have our questions answered
To set our hearts at rest.

Did my Mother really love me?
Is my child alive and well?
Don't ask the courts and agencies,
For they will never tell.
So we fight our own hard battles,
And don't count the war as won,
Until the missing are accounted for,
Each and everyone.

Now they're taking prisoners,
And Sandy stands alone
While we fight on to find our kin
She's brought forward to atone ...
For our poor sin of living
For our simple basic need,
For the cry that we've been sending,
That they will not hear or heed.

We're thinking of you, Sandy
And we pray to God above,
That your faith will help sustain you,
That you will feel our support and love.
For because of you, we missing
In Adoption Action cope,
With a weapon you help give us,
We call the weapon "HOPE!"

118

OVER THE EDGE

We were dismissed at 1:23 and did not need to be back until Monday. Four more days to "hang out" in Akron. I couldn't believe t. My mind felt like mush. As I try to share this part of the story, keep in mind that I can only vaguely remember bits and pieces of what actually happened over the next five to six days.

I recall taking Pat to the airport on Friday. She had decided to go back home to Florida because her son was flying down from New Jersey for vacation that same day. She felt bad about leaving, but I told her I'd be fine. Judy & Dave were planning to stay over until the verdict came in and, of course, Bev and Carol were closeby.

The week-end was a blur. We had planned a pizza get-together for Sunday afternoon, but I got detoured. I know that I was not sleeping because my mind was racing. I recall making a lot of phone calls (and the phone bill proved it!) at all hours of the night. Since Mrs. Clay still had a dial telephone, I had to call the operator to make long distance credit card calls. The purpose of my calls seemed to center around trust, first names, the importance of family ties and front porches. Even the operators were included in this monologue.

While we were at dinner on Saturday evening, Carol made a comment about making sure the house was locked up tight. She knew that Mrs. Clay was not due back from her trip until the following week. I didn't give her warning much thought since I had grown up in a town where doors were seldom locked. I took the comment rather lightly, but Judy and Dave offhandly said "Well, if you get scared, just give us a call and we'll come right over".

I don't ever recall feeling afraid of being alone in a house, but about 11:00 pm I called Dave & Judy. I told them I was feeling very uneasy, but the longer we talked, the better I felt and I assured them I'd be o.k.

Somewhere close to 2:00 am, I began to hear noises downstairs. It sounded as though someone was shuffling around in the house and I suddenly became very frightened. A feeling of panic and terror came over me. Judy and Dave had said to call them no matter what time it was - so I did and they came right over. I immediately felt relieved just knowing they were there. They sensed my restlessness, tried to convince me to go to bed and get some sleep, but it was useless.

They said they were only in bed a short time when they heard me making phone calls. Again they tried to convince me that I should go to bed, but I expressed an urgency to call and talk to my friends and family and said that they would not mind (since they were my friends and family!). Not wanting to use physical restraint, they finally gave up. The last thing I recall is Bev coming over sometime Sunday morning and asking me to "go for a ride" with her. Dave was planning on coming with us (wherever we were going), but I didn't want him riding in the same car with us (he was a man and I was feeling very distrustful of men), so he followed behind. I didn't have any shoes on and asked Bev if I needed them. She said it didn't matter, so I decided not to wear them. (A few years on the farm made me enjoy being barefooted). Though I had no idea where we were going, I trusted Bev implicitly and that seemed to be all that mattered.

When she pulled up in front of the hospital, she said there was someone she wanted me to talk to "who needed help". Dave got out of his car and joined us. We went into the hospital, got on the elevator and went up to the third or fourth floor. Bev approached the nurses station and said that she was there to see her doctor.

We then went into a small room and in a few minutes a female doctor, whose aura I did not like **AT ALL**, came in. When she sat down, I asked her what I could do help her! She was brusque, curt, abrupt and didn't seem to be a very nice person. Her 'bedside' manner was nil. Since we were not 'connecting' in any way, I was beginning to feel quite apprehensive. I got up to leave and as I did, Dave blocked the door and Bev convinced me to sit down and talk some more. The discussion came back to trust and the fact that these two people who I trusted, (Bev more than Dave), felt it was going to be best for me to remain in the hospital.

Once again, I was in a dependency position of having others make a decision for me. The decision was that I needed to stay in the hospital, but it had to be voluntarily! Therefore, it was necessary for me to sign myself in. How does an incompetent "mentally ill" person sign themself in? Though I know I must have signed a piece of paper, I have NO recollection of doing so. As I think about it now, it seemed like a birthparent deja vu experience.

Having said all that, I know full-well that I had passed the point of no return and needed to be hospitalized (or at least needed some drugs to slow down my mind). After Bev and Dave left, I have just a few memories of chatting with other patients; probably a bunch of gibberish that didn't make sense to any of us! I do recall that whenever I passed the nurses station, I explained that the most important things to remember were first names, trust, and families. Every now and then, I threw in 'front porches'.

Bev recently reminded me of a memory I had briefly forgotten. Later that first evening, I was looking for a way out. Since I was in a locked ward, it was impossible. I finally found a door that was open and went in. It was apparently a very small dark room and I had crouched down in the corner. Though I didn't know it at the time, it turned out to be the chapel. A search party had been dispatched and I was found and led back to my room. Finally the drugs took effect and I slept and slept.

I was only awakened periodically by the loud-speaker calling my name for a phone call. The phone was quite a distance from my room so there were times when I was too tired to drag myself out of bed to answer it. Because I was so far away and because we are such a close-knit family, it was difficult for them not to know what was going on.

By early Tuesday, the drugs I'd been given took effect and I was getting back to "normal" (whatever that is). Since my sister was going to be arriving, Judy and Dave decided to head back to CT. They had been faithful, devoted and unwavering friends; the type that are rare to find in this day and age. Bev, too, had gone the extra mile by coming to the hospital to visit at least once or twice a day. She also acted as a laison between my attorney and the doctor.

The closing arguments and charge to the jury were going to be heard on Thursday, July 29th. The doctor gave me an "excused absence" from the hospital, but I had a curfew.

The Final Travesty of Justice

Upon meeting with my attorney early Thursday morning, he said it was necessary for him to inform me that the prosecution was offering me an opportunity to plead guilty to a **misdemeanor charge**. I couldn't believe what I was hearing! "Are you telling me that this terrible felony crime that I was supposed to have committed suddenly becomes a misdemeanor if I'm willing to plead guilty to it?" "Well, your sentence would be a lot lighter than if you're found guilty, but I told them I didn't think you'd accept their offer." He was right! And I was glad that he, at least, had gotten to know me that well; it didn't matter what the offer was - I wasn't going to plead guilty to these ridiculous charges.

121

The closing arguments by both attorneys were brief, but the charge to the jury was not. It was 95 pages long! Now think about this. If you were on a jury and were given 95 pages to read, wouldn't you think that this person must be guilty of something? What could possibly justify a 95 page charge to the jury?? It's ludicrous and outrageous, but it's part of the judicial game. It took the Judge an hour and a half just to read it and was the most ambiguous text I've ever read. It reminded me of the old cliche "If you can't dazzle them with brilliance, baffle them with B.S.!"

During the lunch break, the *New York Times* showed up to take a picture of George and I. They didn't do an interview, though they did do a story. It seemed rather interesting to me that my attorney would not participate in the 60 Minutes interview, but was more than willing to have his picture in the *New York Times*. I'm sure there must be a good reason, but I don't know what it is.

It took the jury the entire afternoon before bringing back a verdict. Guilty on 32 counts. I was found 'not guilty' of mail fraud. To say that I was shocked would, of course, be an understatement. I never dreamed I would be found guilty. Everyone who was present at the trial felt that the prosecution had not provided any evidence to prove my guilt. I've since wondered if the individual members of the jury were annoyed that they were held over those extra days, due to my hospitalization, and the guilty verdict may have been a backlash. Knowing human nature, it's quite possible.

Word had filtered back to me from the adoption network grapevine that my illness was feigned. I wish I could act that well and if I could, then I've surely missed my calling! Bi-polar is a real disease that affects about one-third of our population.

The following day, an appointment had been scheduled for me to see the probation officer in order for them to prepare a 'pre- sentencing' report. My sister was there to pick me up at 7:30 am. As we attempted to leave, we were told that the doctor had not yet signed me out and we had to wait for her to arrive before we could leave! My sister, who is known for speaking her mind (it must be genetic!), said it was ridiculous since the doctor had been informed the night before of the scheduled appointment. She finally came strolling in around 7:50 am and took her good old time signing my release. She was giving me until noon to be back!

Fat chance! By noon, we were on an airplane back to Florida! (An escapee from the mental ward with her sister aiding and abetting.) A real conspiracy!!

A Genetic Disease (Dis-Ease)

The treatment of mental illness has come a long way in the past decade, but society's grasp of it, like adoption, is still grossly misunderstood. Because it has touched members of my family, including myself, and reared its strange head in the middle of my trial, I feel compelled to include this chapter. It is simply my own personal experience and not intended to be clinical in any way.

As a very young child, I recall over- hearing whispered stories about my paternal grandmother's "nervous breakdowns". Since I was so young, I didn't understand what the phrase meant, but it didn't sound good! Discussions of shock treatment were spoken about in hushed tones and I seemed to know better than to ask for an explanation. Since the dialogue made me feel uncomfortable, I'm not sure I wanted to know nor that I would have understood.

Mom was raised in a small town in upstate Pennsylvania called Watsontown. She met Dad in 1934 while working at an ice cream factory. They had a fast romance and married within six weeks. Mom was the oldest of seven so her "example" was very displeasing to her strict Methodist parents. What she did not know about Dad was that at the young age of 23, he already exhibited alcoholic tendencies and, being an extremely handsome man, was a womanizer as well. They remained married for ten years and divorced in 1944.

At the time of their separation, I was 5, my brother was 8 and my sister was 3. I was "the middle child"! Prior to the divorce, we lived in a small town near Watsontown called Dewart. As I recall, there were less than 300 people in our little town of Dewart. Although I was only five when we moved away, I still have a clear recollection of the fun events that took place in our small community - the Easter Egg Hunt and the 4th of July celebrations are just a few of my vivid memories. I also have total recall of the layout of our home.

When Mother decided to leave Dad, she and I went to Philadelphia where her parents were then residing. We lived with Grandma and Grandpa until she remarried in 1946. My brother and sister had remained with Dad who had moved to Gettysburg. By 1946, it became too much for Dad to handle both my brother and sister, so my sister came to live with us.

Each summer, my sister and I boarded a Greyhound Bus and went to visit our father, brother, and grandparents. Grandma had a terrific sense of humor and was a chipper person to be around. She and Grandpa managed a large apartment building in the city and when we stayed with them, we had fun riding the elevators with the other kids in the complex. Grandpa had a gruff personality, so we did our best to stay out of his way as much as possible.

My sister and I recall one summer when we were about 7 or 8. Dad had received a call from Grandpa who said that Grandma had "gone off" again and needed his help to restrain her. We all hopped in the car and sped off to York, but by the time we arrived, the ambulance was already there taking her out. Seeing Grandma in a straitjacket and carried out of her house was one of those unpleasant memories you'd rather forget. She was taken to the state hospital in Harrisburg and remained there for several months. My sister said she recalls exchanging letters with Grandma while she was in the hospital, though I have no such memory.

Dad died of cirrhosis in 1975 at the age of 63. Grandma was 85, still in good health, and attended the funeral. From outward appearances, she seemed to be handling it well. As a parent, seeing your child pass away has got to be one of life's most difficult experiences - no matter how old the "child" happens to be.

Soon after returning home from the funeral, we received a call from our stepmother that Grandma had another breakdown. It was then that I broached the subject with mother. Did she recall anything about Grandma's illness? Though Mom and Dad had been married ten years, she said she couldn't cite any incidents while they were together. But soon after their divorce became final, she said she remembered hearing that Grandma had a breakdown.

One of Dad's sisters, whom I've remained close to, remarked that she thought the divorce played a critical part since Grandma, and everyone in Dad's family, had such a strong liking for Mom. And also because there had never been a divorce in either family. The word "breakdown" would not become part of my vocabulary again until November 1980, when I would experience it firsthand with my youngest daughter, who was then 19.

My Crumbling Marriage & Spiritual Beginnings

In 1970, I became an active Christian and raised my four children in a fundamental church. I taught Sunday School for many years, eventually became a Superintendent, served on various committees and boards, and spent an unreasonable amount of time playing "church" and doing church things. Though I am now at a different place spiritually, the organized church helped me survive a very strenuous period in my life.

In 1976 I made two decisions which would alter my life forever. One was my decision to search for my daughter who I had surrendered in

1954. By making that decision, I put myself in a position of strength which enabled me to make the second decision which was to leave my marriage of 18 years. It had been a marriage fraught with physical and emotional abuse, largely due to alcoholism on the part of my husband and insecurities on my part. (I believe due to the loss of my father at an early age). It seemed I had repeated my mother's pattern, but had tried to hang on much longer than she had. (As I write this, the O.J. Simpson story has just broken and I am catapulted back in time.)

Ken and I had a tumultuous love-hate relationship, as had Mom and Dad. Many of those years are even difficult to bring to mind as we all struggled just to survive. We had married in our late teens and, by the age of 23, had four children in four years. Though survival was the primary reason for remaining in the situation, it was also the reason I finally decided to leave. There never seemed to be any way out. Shelters were non-existent and the police chose to turn their heads. Therefore, the church provided the stronghold my children and I needed and probably kept me alive; especially during those times I reached the end of my rope and didn't have enough energy to tie a knot and hang on. Our divorce took two and a half years and became final June 14, 1979. Ken remarried a few months later and moved to California.

As I "came out of the closet" and spoke publicly about my birthparent experience, it was clear that the church was not thrilled. Their displeasure, however, was quite subtle. So after 10 years of total immersion and absorption in church work, I decided to leave - though I have never relinquished my spirituality. In fact, Adoption Triangle Ministries (ATM), the first organization I founded, became an outgrowth of my decision. I had a deep sense that God had other work for me to do outside the walls of the church. In the midst of the my marital breakup, a frightening experience was on the horizon.

A New Roller Coaster Ride

In late summer of 1978, I received a call from a camp counselor telling me that they suspected my daughter was pregnant! She had been attending the same church camp for several years. What a blow! Apparently she had "confessed" to her counselor that she had missed a few periods. Sherri was one month short of 17 at the time. I was, of course, in shock, panic-stricken and all the other feelings one goes through at such a time. I now had an inkling of what my mother went through when I became pregnant at 14. What were we going to do? How are we going to make it? I was raising them alone on my meager $7,500 salary. Though I had been a young unwed mother myself, I was now experiencing the reaction most parents go through. Panic, terror, hysteria, fear, dismay, anxiety are all words that seem to express the primary sensations.

What about Open Adoption? I didn't know a whole lot about Open Adoption except what I had recently read in The Adoption Triangle. But I knew it was a far cry from the closed, sealed, secret adoption system that I had been subjected to. I had just returned from a conference in Anaheim, CA sponsored by Triadoption, so I contacted the Founder, Mary Jo Rillera, who was also a friend, and told her my dilemma. She said she knew someone in CA who already had an open adoption and might be interested in another. She'd have them get in touch with me directly. I ran the idea by Sherri and she said "Whatever you want to do, Mom". What else would I expect her to say? She was always trying to please; being pregnant hadn't changed that trait.

In the meantime, I called a special meeting of my CUB group and told them what was going on and what my preliminary plans were. They went berserk! "How could you even think of giving up this baby - it's your grandchild? Do you want to have to go through another search 18 years from now? Sandy, please don't do it! We promise to do anything we can to help -we'll stand by you and help you get through it."

I then went to speak with the mother of Sherri's boyfriend. She was insistent that her son marry Sherri and "give the baby a name". I wasn't so sure that was the answer, but when I asked Sherri if she wanted to get married, she agreed. A wedding was planned within two weeks (we used to call them "shotgun weddings") and early in September, just a few weeks before her 17th birthday, Sherri was married.

It was only a month or so later when my 19 year old son's girlfriend (a 17 year old adoptee) informed her mother that she, too, was pregnant. Her mother and I had been "church buddies" so it wasn't too difficult for her to call and let me know - other than the fact that she knew what I was going through with Sherri. Again - what to do? Suzanne made it quite clear that adoption was out of the question and not even a consideration. She said there was no way she was going to give up her baby. My son expressed a strong sense of responsibility, so in November, Jim and Suzanne had a small church wedding.

Now I know this will be extremely hard to believe, and if I hadn't actually lived through it (and survived), I probably wouldn't believe it either. Before the year was out, my 18 year old daughter, Linda, announced her pregnancy. She had no plans to marry the father, but desperately wanted to have his child. I clearly remember thinking - "which bridge would be the best one to jump off" (there were several in the area and the temptation was great)!

126

And so it was that in 1979, the Year of the Child, my three oldest grandchildren came into the world. These tremendous crises' turned out to be my greatest blessings - Jill Marie was born February 12, 1979; Jay was born April 6th and Kristi Lee was born June 5th - all two months apart. Each time I look at them, I am reminded that **there are no mistakes**! They are wonderful, beautiful, terrific kids and I thank God daily that they're part of our family - the family where they belong! I'm thankful we all pulled together - and that each of their mothers and fathers had the stamina to see it through. I'm thankful for the members of the South Jersey CUB group that encouraged me to tie a knot and hang on tight.

One of the primary reasons for sharing this part of my life is because I know this experience might give others the courage to "weather the storm". Beautiful rainbows usually follow stormy weather. If you, dear reader, find yourself in this situation, please remember my story and the moral of it. The moral is that family preservation works! My family is living proof. I can assure you that these pregnancies could not have occurred at a more inopportune time. I was still reeling from my divorce. Finances were nil. We were known as a - what's the lingo today - a dysfunctional family. (Is there such a thing as a functional one?) And three teenagers pregnant at the same time! What would you have done?? You may have chosen adoption or you may have chosen abortion, but we thank God that we chose to keep our babies.

The fourth "baby" produced that year was my book entitled *I Woild Have Searched Forever*. It was 'delivered' the middle of July '79, just in time for Wendy's 25th birthday which was July 18th. We had reunited on her 23rd birthday in 1977, but she had cut off our relationship only a few months later. Even though she had not spoken to me since August of '77, I sent her the first autographed copy of the book. I had only hoped that she would understand my need to write it.

Face to Face with Insanity

The fall of 1980 became memorable for many different reasons. In September, I was finally able to get Adoption Triangle Ministries off the ground by having flyers printed which were included with mailings of the book. Then early in October, Wendy made a surprise call ending the 3 year silence. She wanted to know if I could/would come for dinner on Saturday evening. The answer, of course, was "Yes!" and a reconciliation ensued. The story of our reconciliation was told in my second book entitled *What Kind of Love Is This?* Her call prompted me to invite her to our CUB meeting in November. She came and was, of course, the center of attention. She met a lot of birthmothers and spent time with her siblings.

Sherri was particularly anxious to meet her. My "perfect child" had spent the entire previous week helping me get ready for this big event. Sherri and her husband had split up after a year and a half of marriage, and she came back home with little Jill. Since she had never been a problem, having her back home was a pleasure. Whatever I asked her to do, she did. While she had always been the caretaker of the family, it seemed moreso after her father and I parted ways.

She had a close friend who had moved to West Virginia and whom she hadn't seen for awhile. The weekend before Thanksgiving, she decided to visit Nancy, and spend the entire week. Since her husband usually took the baby on weekends and every other holiday, she told him he could keep her for the whole week. She left for WV on Friday evening.

I was working in the kitchen early Sunday evening when I received a phone call from Nancy's mother. She said Sherri had "flipped out" - she had "lost it" and they had taken her to their local hospital. "What do you mean - lost it?" "Well, she just seemed to flip out; she was ranting and raving and not making any sense. I really think you need to get down here as soon as you can." I had been dating a man for about a year. In fact, we had met just as my divorce was becoming final in June of '79. Wayne was kind, caring, considerate and thoughtful. From the panic-stricken look on my face, he knew immediately something was wrong.

We left immediately. Since it was going to be a long drive and he didn't want me to go alone, he offered to drive. It was the longest trip I've ever taken. My stomach was in one huge knot. We were second-guessing at what could have gone wrong and had no idea what to expect. Probably some of her friends put something in a drink. Because she was so "straight", we were sure she wouldn't have taken any drugs on her own - and we knew it must be drug-related. Maybe they slipped her some LSD! What else?

After a ten hour trip, we pulled into the hospital parking lot at 3:00 am. Monday morning. We spoke to a hospital attendant who asked about her medical history. Nothing significant - nothing to speak of. He led us down the hall and into a cold stark room. She was lying flat on her back on a bed that looked like a slab and the room felt as cold as a morgue. Her face was pale and her body lifeless. I was certain she was dead. (She has since said that she, too, believed she was dead). My heart felt as though it were breaking into a million pieces, and my entire body felt so weak that I thought I was going to pass out. I touched her cold arm lightly and whispered her name. Instantly she opened her eyes and in a quiet tone said "Hi Mom". I knew without a doubt - as I had never known before - yes, there is a God. My child had just come back to life.

(She said that when I touched her arm, she immediately felt warmth and life come back into her body). I said "how are you feeling" and she mumbled something incoherently; but then clearly stated that she wanted to go home. I assured her we were there to do just that - to take her home.

The attendant said he'd like to see me in his office. He informed me that it would be best for her to stay, at least until they could "stabilize" her. Since we were 450 miles from home, it didn't seem practical or feasible to leave her there. I knew I'd be able to get her "stabilized" if I could just get her out of this hospital and back home. I assured him I would take her to a hospital in NJ. He reiterated the fact that she was being released against the advice of the hospital staff.

We got her into the car and began the long trek back home. Though Wayne and I were both exhausted, we felt we had to get her back to NJ. She wasn't responding well to any of our questions and I wasn't sure why - was it because she was tired or because she was not comprehending. I was beginning to feel very anxious and nervous. A myriad of emotions were running rampant through my psyche - panic, fright, apprehension, were all converging at once. The ride back home seemed like forever, but at least I had my daughter back - or did I?

We arrived home early in the afternoon and she still had not slept. Her mind seemed to be racing so I was sure that sleep was probably what she needed most. No matter how hard we tried to reason, cajole, or persuade, we were unable to get her to lay down. She moved around constantly and spent a great deal of time getting in and out of the bathtub. Communication was practically nil. I'd ask her a question or make a comment and get a mumbo-jumbo response. I remember thinking to myself - "how can I reach her - what can I say, or do, that will snap her out of this?" In an attempt to "bring her around", I tried using reason and comfort; when that didn't work, I began to get angry. I began to feel as though she was playing a game and aware of what she was doing. But one look at her expression and you knew it was no game!

The entire household was now in an uproar as each of us tried in our own way to "bring her back to her senses". There were brief moments of sanity, but they were just that - brief! She'd make a clear, concise statement that made total sense and you'd think "oh, she's fine" and suddenly she was gone again. There was a point where I thought death might have been easier to handle. It would be final and I could accept it more easily than this - how could I possibly accept not being able to communicate with my own daughter or to reach her - and would I ever be able to again?

As I look back upon the experience, I realize my greatest fear was not knowing if she'd ever come back to reality or how long it would take. I remembered that when Grandma went away to the hospital, she was gone for several months. But I tried to remind myself that it was during the mid 40's & early 50's.

By the second day, all of us were beginning to snap at one another in our effort to try to help Sherri. None of us had any idea what to do. I had spoken several times with my mother who was living in Florida. Mother had moved to Florida in 1962 when my children were all babies. She always had a deep religious faith and now was assuring me that she was praying. I remember telling her that I was glad she was praying because I was unable to at that point. She then said something that caught me by surprise. "I'm not praying for Sherri; I know she's going to be all right. I'm praying for you." Such insight!

It was comforting to know others were praying because my own prayers were only going as far as the ceiling and bouncing back. I was angry at God for allowing this to happen and told Him so. After I had devoted and dedicated my life to Him, this just didn't seem fair. Like any mother, I would have rather gone through the experience myself than to watch my child suffer. "Why can't it be me instead of her?" I asked. I wanted to know and understand what she was going through and feeling. Little did I realize that it wouldn't be too long before that prayer would be answered.

I sought the advice of close friends and, of course, they all had different suggestions and ideas. "Make her sleep and eat" (can you tell me how?) -"call an exorcist" (my Christian daughter demon-possessed - though there were moments when she appeared to be!)

We finally decided that we had no other choice but to take her to the emergency room of our local hospital. First they strapped her to the bed due to her strength. Then one of the doctors spent quite a bit of time trying to talk to her. After an hour or so, he finally informed us there was nothing they could do. He said that they had a unit in the hospital, but the person had to be voluntarily admitted and willing to stay of their own volition. She was "too far gone" for their 'voluntary' ward and the only solution they could offer was the State Hospital. There was no way I could imagine subjecting my precious daughter to a state mental institution. I had heard too many horror stories.

So back home we went. She began talking a lot about her father who had recently moved to California following our divorce in 1979. She had harbored hard feelings towards him which had never been resolved - so much so that she hadn't even invited him to her wedding. Maybe what she needed, more than anything, was a reconciliation with her father. Possibly just his presence would or could bring her around. It was certainly worth a try.

I contacted him, explained what had been going on, and that I felt she needed him. He agreed, without hesitancy, to come. He could tell by my voice how distraught I was and knew I was at the end of my rope. A tremendous sense of relief came over me just knowing he would soon be on his way - he said he'd catch the first flight he could get. For some odd reason, I felt certain that his presence would provide the magic cure. But I was grasping at straws.

He arrived early the next day enabling all of us to take a much needed reprieve. My older daughter and I went to stay at Wayne's house and my youngest son stayed at the house with Sherri and their father. My oldest son chose not to deal with it at all. Within a few hours, Ken called and said "we've got to get her somewhere - I don't know how you've handled this for three days". In a very short span of time, he also felt frustration and inability to know what to do or how to handle the situation.

A friend had been given me a referral to a chaplain who worked on a crisis hotline. I called. He listened while I talked - and talked - and talked, but he wasn't responding. Finally I said "Look, Ron, this isn't helping. I've been trained for these kinds of calls myself and know you're taught to listen, but right now I'm at the end of my rope and what I need is for someone to give me some clear direction. It was my next question that brought an immediate response. WHAT WOULD YOU DO IF THIS WAS YOUR DAUGHTER?" He said "I'd take her to Havenville Hospital in Lebanon -it's a private psychiatric hospital about two and half hours north of here. I think that's where she'll get the best care. If it were my child, that's what I'd do." At that point in time, that's what I needed - someone to give me direction, because I didn't have a clue nor did anyone else close to the situation.

For the first time since that fateful phone call on Sunday, I felt a small glimmer of hope and encouragement. I then called the hospital and got the ok to bring her in. I called Ken to let him know and, since it was already late in the evening, we decided to leave first thing in the morning. That fateful day was Thanksgiving Day, 1980 -a day our family will never forget. It was the day we stepped into the world of mental illness and were confronted with confusion, frustration, helplessness and pain -all of which were profound and intense. Like adoption, it's a difficult experience to describe unless you've "been there".

The trip to Havenville was a painstaking one. Both Ken and I were experiencing a mixed bag of feelings. Though we had fought most of our married life, we had now been able to come together to seek a solution to this devastating experience. Ken and I were both very tense so I decided to sit in the back with Sherri so he would not be distracted while driving. The ride was one that took us through rolling hills and beautiful farmland, but a beauty we were unable to enjoy or appreciate because our precious daughter was in such distress.

The hospital sits on a hill and doesn't look anything like a hospital - rather it looks like a peaceful chalet. As we wound our way up the road leading to the hospital, I was already beginning to feel a sense of relief. Relief knowing there was someone else to take over, relief knowing she would be getting help, relief knowing that maybe we would get some answers, and relief knowing that I might be able to get my first sound sleep in five days.

As we pulled into the small parking lot in front of the hospital, we noticed that there were hardly any parked cars. The place looked deserted. We stepped out of the car and took in a breath of the brisk fall air. We then got on each side of Sherri, took her arm and led her into the hospital foyer. The silence was awesome in a eerie way; it seemed as though we had entered an empty building. There was no one in sight. Finally we noticed a bell on the wall. Within a few minutes an attendant came out and greeted us. We explained what had been going on for the past four days, that we had called the hospital the day before, and advised to bring her in. He then informed us that they were working with a skeleton crew because of the Thanksgiving holiday. Most of the staff were given four days off. We were led through a set of double doors and down a long stretch of hallway to a locked unit.

There we were introduced to a nurse. By this time, I was in tears. It was the first time since it all started that I broke down sobbing. I kept asking "why" while babbling to this warm, middle-aged, matronly nurse that Sherri had always been a "perfect" child. She didn't drink, smoke, take drugs, nor was she promiscuous. She was just a darn nice kid. In fact, she had been the caretaker for the family - everyone depended upon her. Why was this happening to her. And what had I done to cause it? None of it seemed fair.

I have never forgotten her response. It left a memorable impression on me. She said "Some people cope with alcohol, some with drugs, some with sex- their dependency IS their way of coping; it is the mechanism they use for getting through life; people like Sherri simply shut down. Shutting down is a way of coping too, though the individual has no control over it. Think of it as a circuit breaker that gets overloaded and blows a fuse. Her mind could no longer handle the amount of information coming into it, so it shut off - just like a circuit breaker that blows a fuse. "But there are drugs that can help," she said and then assured me that Sherri would get well and be her old self again. I can't give you a time-frame because it varies with each individual. I thanked her for taking the time to explain a little bit of what was happening to my precious daughter. While it was a small amount of comfort, it was some. We kissed Sherri good-bye and left.

132

On the way home, Ken spoke briefly about what happened after we had left the house, and as he was attempting to bring her back to her senses. She said "Daddy, pick me up and carry me into bed the way you used to when I was little." When she was young, she would sometimes fall asleep on the floor watching TV and he'd pick her up and carry her upstairs. But other than that heavy-duty request, he could make little sense out of anything else she said. Nor could any of us.

Most of the ride home was in silence. It's always hard to express all the mixed emotions going on inside. Though we didn't verbalize it, I know we each blamed ourselves for something we should have/could have done - or certainly something we did that we shouldn't have. It's a natural reaction for parents to blame themselves when their children fall apart. We were both totally drained and anxious to get a good night's sleep.

When we arrived home, the kids and Wayne had Thanksgiving dinner ready for us. We all sat around and chatted for several hours trying to reason through the past few chaotic days. The kids and I decided to visit her on Sunday. We all had a good rest on Friday and Saturday in preparation for the long drive on Sunday. Ken had flown back to CA on Saturday, sorry he had been unable to be of more help. I apologized for placing such high expectations upon his presence. For some reason, I was sure that, whatever conflicts were going on in her mind, would be resolved once she had the opportunity to see and talk with her father again. My solution was obviously too simplistic. This disease was much more complicated.

My older daughter and younger son made the trip with Wayne and I. Linda, who is 14 months older than Sherri, was 20 at the time and Steve, who is 11 months younger, had just turned 18. My 21 year old son could not cope with it at all though he, like the others, was a terrific support system for me. All of us had always been close, but as we look back upon this experience, we all realize that it brought us even closer. Adversity seems to have a way of doing that!

We were nervous as we entered the hospital, uncertain of what to expect. What we faced was worse than we had imagined. We encountered a bewildered, disheveled, zombie-looking young person who did not at all resemble our vivacious, fun-loving, carefree Sherri. Her clothes were wrinkled, her hair stringy and she stared at us through hollow eyes. We didn't recognize this person whose spirit appeared to be absent from her body. It was extremely disconcerting. It didn't take long for us to realize that she was on some heavy-duty medicine. She was barely able to speak though at one point, in a discreet wispy voice, she leaned over toward me and said "Mom, read Matthew 9:18". Thinking that this was just more babble, I didn't pay much attention or think much about it, though I did make a mental note since 9-18 was the month and day of her birth. "Just a mere coincidence", I told myself. It certainly doesn't have any meaning or significance. We only stayed a short time because none of us were handling the visit very well. She seemed totally unaware of our presence. Since it was still the holiday weekend, there was no one to give us any type of progress report. Of course, it was quite obvious that little progress was being made. I had the feeling that the skeleton crew were simply there to baby-sit.

When we got back home, the kids went about their business while I proceeded to get out my Bible and look up Matthew 9:18. As soon as I read it, I began to sob. Wayne held me in his arms as I continued to cry and cry. It had been exactly one week since the fateful phone call telling me that Sherri was in a hospital in WV. Reading the scripture verse catapulted me back to that evening when I first saw her lying flat on the hospital bed and thought she was dead. Matthew 9:18 says "My daughter is even now dead; but come and lay thy hand upon her and she shall live." In her present confused state of mind, how could she possibly have known to quote a scripture that dramatized the event that was played out in the hospital the week before. Chills ran up and down my entire body. Was this a mystical experience? It sure felt like one.

Monday morning I received a call from the hospital. They wanted to discuss finances. There was no hedging - just the facts. The cost of her stay would be $2000 a week! It sounds rather inexpensive by today's standards, but 14 years ago it was one-fourth of my yearly salary. It was overwhelming. Though she was still legally married, they had no insurance. The office informed me that they needed to have a check by Thursday or I would need to come pick her up. Wayne lent me the $2000 which "bought" me the first week. I'd worry about the second week later.

I called the hospital every day to see what her prognosis was. Each day they said there had been no change. On Friday, the doctor told me that he wanted to perform electric shock treatment on Monday if he did not see some significant change over the weekend. But he said he needed my permission to do it. Just the sound of the word, electric shock, horrified me because of the terrible stories I had heard about it. I also thought that it was old method and didn't realize it was still being used.

I got off the phone and began to pray "God, I can't deal with this; please don't let them zap my daughter's brain, but, God, I want her back. What's it going to take?" I felt totally helpless, drained, and confused. Saturday morning around 9:00 the phone rang. I picked it up and was astonished to hear my daughter's voice! What was even more astonishing was the fact that she was talking perfectly NORMAL! It was as though a miracle had occurred overnight. We talked about what

134

she was feeling. She said she could only recall flashes of the past week; bits and pieces stood out in her mind, but for the most part, it was a blur.

Friends of friends who lived close to the hospital had invited me to come stay with them for as long as I wanted so I had already made plans to go up on Monday and spend the week. They were aware of the distance involved and knew how burdensome it was for me to be so far away. I told her I'd be in to see her every day and maybe she'd even be well enough to come home.

Monday was the first opportunity I had to meet the doctor and discuss Sherri's situation. He said that they had diagnosed her schizophrenic and were treating her with Thorazine. It all sounded so horrible and I've always hated labels. But I wasn't at all educated about the various mental diseases or their treatments, so I accepted what I was told. They said it would take some amount of time to work with her, etc. to really get her turned around. They made it quite clear that they discouraged long visits and did not include the family in any of the aftercare. This seemed rather strange to me, but they were the "professionals".

When I finally had a chance to spend a little time with her, her mind seemed clear but her body movements and reactions were extremely slow. She talked a lot about some of the other patients; one particular young man, she said, could not stop talking about the death of John Lennon. I continued to visit her every day that week. The financial office was continuing to press me for a another $2000 payment. I finally borrowed it from a CUB friend, paid it on Thursday which was the day it was due, and knew there was no way I could afford to keep her there another week. So the next day I took her home.

The hospital gave me a prescription to have filled, and she was only home a short time when I noticed how extremely lethargic she was; similar to the first time we visited her in the hospital. She shuffled when she walked, her face was distorted. I knew something was not right so I immediately took her to a local doctor I had been referred to. He took one look at her, scribbled out a prescription and told me to get her to the emergency room of the hospital right away. I later learned that he prescribed a cogenent which would offset the Thorazine. He suggested admitting her to the hospital for a few days so he could get her stabilized on lithium.

By the end of the week, my child was like herself again. The doctor said that she had been misdiagnosed. She was not schizophrenic; she was manic-depressive or what is now more commonly known as bipolar. Sherri said that it was the only time in her life that she felt suicidal. Her mind and her body were totally out of sync. Only a few years before, one of our neighbors had committed suicide. We later learned that she was also being treated with Thorazine which, we believe, may have been the cause.

Personal Experience Leads To Understanding

Life resumed some semblance of normality. We all went about our business. I returned to work; was still involved with CUB, while attempting to get ATM off the ground.

In the late spring of 1981, the AAC National Conference was held in Kansas City, MO. It was the year the bylaws were formulated and put into print. I know, because I typed them! At that time, I was serving as a Director-at-Large, along with Mary Jo Rillera and Betty Jean Lifton. During that conference I met a woman who was being shunned by the general assembly. She acted a little "crazy" and I realized I was drawn to her because of what I had just been through with Sherri. The story of my encounter with Thelma was told in my book *What Kind Of Love Is This?* Suffice to say that I befriended her, kept in touch with her for a few years, fell out of touch for several years and yet, when I arrived home from prison, there was a letter waiting for me from Thelma. I could tell by the tone of her letter that she had not heard the news about me going to prison. But in every letter I ever receive from her, she thanks me for being her friend.

I'm not sharing this to show what a great friend I am - but simply to share the belief that, at some point in each of our lives, we need someone to be a friend. Just someone to reach out and say, "It's ok - I care; I really care". After my recent experience of being indicted, I know this truth more deeply than ever. It's just a reminder for each of us to "reach out and touch someone" - especially someone who is going through a difficult time. It takes such little effort, but can actually have an important or lifesaving impact on someone's life.

On the way home from the Kansas City conference, I was flying high! I probably could have flown home without the airplane! Though I attempted to capture my thoughts on paper, it was impossible. My mind was racing faster than my hand could write; my thoughts were coming quicker than I was able to formulate them. I was giddy, happy, and seeing the world through rose-colored glasses - everything was more beautiful and more wonderful than I had ever known it to be. What I didn't know, of course, was that I was about to experience my first "manic" episode - at age 42!

Seeing the World Through Rose-Colored Glasses

These 'episodes', as they are commonly called today, have never been shared with anyone. I've never felt comfortable talking about them until now. As I attempt to describe the following events, bear in mind that one can only recall glimpses and flashes of what is actually occurring, both mentally and physically, in the middle of a manic phase or episode.

Though I've never used any mind altering drugs, I've been told that the experience has many similarities. This was, I can assure you, a natural high. A more universal analogy that everyone can understand is that it's similar to being in a dream state, but you are wide awake instead of asleep! As we all know, dreams are fragmented, and don't seem to make much sense, but at the time you are dreaming, they seem very real. Likewise, being in a manic state is YOUR reality during the time you are experiencing it. And while the thoughts are usually mixed-up and confusing, some believe there may be a lesson or kernel of truth to be learned from them. Sometimes they seem to have futuristic predictions.

Here is an example of what I can recollect from, what I call, my first 'break' through (rather than 'breakdown'). I remember laying awake all night with my mind flitting from one thing to another. As jumbled as my thoughts must have been, they seemed to make perfect sense and I felt all-knowing. Communicating with others telepathically felt natural.

Earlier in the evening, I had taken my two year old granddaughter for a walk around the block. We walked very slowly and I was acutely aware of colors and sounds as never before. The color of the grass and the leaves on the trees were a vivid shade of green. The sound of the birds singing was melodic. It felt to me like heaven on earth -as though, at that very moment, the Kingdom was being ushered in and this beautiful little blonde child was the fulfillment of the scripture "A little child shall lead them".

Again that evening, I did not sleep. My mind was racing. This time I envisioned lots of airplanes shuttling back and forth across the country, passing one another as they flew from city to city; every plane was filled with people on their way to be reunited with a missing family member. The sky was bright blue and everyone was laughing and chattering. Happiness and excitement filled the air. Once everyone was reunited with each other, there was going to be a giant reunion!

The next day, the kids realized that they needed to get me to the hospital so they took me to the emergency room. The hospital wanted to admit me, but I flatly refused. They took me into a small cubicle, pulled the curtain, and immediately gave me a shot of Haldol. After a brief period of time, a woman, who said she was a social worker, came in to talk to me. The moment she told me she was a social worker, a

137

clear thought came into my mind. The thought was that we are all destined to play certain roles in this lifetime and that there are seven stages. Each of us will have an opportunity to experience each stage, but not necessarily in this lifetime. It was the first time that the concept of eternal life became integrated with reincarnation. For a fundamental Baptist, I can assure you it was a shocking encounter. I also remember requesting a glass of water, not because I was thirsty, but because it seemed to have some special significance for the person fulfilling the request.

Since I had refused to be admitted to the hospital, the kids were instructed to take me home and put me to bed. I was already feeling the effects of the Haldol and was practically asleep by the time we arrived home. I slept for the next 3 days, only waking intermittently. When I finally awoke, I was fine. Life, though hectic, went on as usual.

In January of 1982, Sherri gave birth to her second child. She had natural childbirth since her labor was so short. Danny was born within a half hour of the time she entered the hospital. She was up and about immediately after giving birth. Within a month, she lapsed into a deep depression. We chalked it up to postpartum blues, but it seemed much more severe. We finally had to put her in hospital for three weeks while I took care of the baby.

The national conference that year was held in San Antonio, Texas during the month of June. It was our fourth conference and was memorable for many reasons. Our "adoption family" was becoming closer. Each year we renewed old friendships and created new ones. The prior conference had brought many unresolved feelings to the surface, but this one had awakened them even more. It began a process within me which I could no longer control. A slide show presentation by Triadoption Library was set to the music of "Come Together Now" (the lyrics to this beautiful song are on page 46).

The slides showed a baby being born, a birthmother saying good-by to her baby, and the new parents receiving the child. The stark, harsh reality that I would never, and could never, know my daughter as a child suddenly hit me like a ton of bricks. I began to cry hysterically, and realized that I had never allowed myself to mourn the loss of my child. My feelings had been suppressed for so many years. Even though I had been reunited with my daughter five years before and thought I was "ok", I wasn't. I had never experienced the depth of grief that I was now feeling. These were the first tears to be shed since she left the hospital in 1954 in someone else's arms.

Emotional healing has a different time frame for everyone; just like physical healing, it takes longer for some than for others. Though my healing had begun in 1977 when I first found my daughter, I was now learning that it was a continuing, ongoing, and very painful process.

The same day I came home from the San Antonio conference, I had a compelling feeling to get in touch with my daughter's birthfather whom I had not seen for 28 years. Since our relationship had ended abruptly, I expressed my need to get together in hopes of resolving my ambivalent feelings toward him once and for all. If he refused to meet with me, I was prepared to tell him that I'd be on his doorstep. That wasn't necessary. We made arrangements to meet the following week at a restaurant in Cherry Hill. Our "reunion" was fantastic. All the hurt and anger melted away as he simply said "I'm sorry for not being there for you and for the pain you've suffered all these years."

The next day, I was once again in a manic phase and taken to the emergency room of the hospital. I was placed in a small room with a door and thought it was a tomb. I had no feelings of anxiety since I knew (in my mind) that in three days, I would be released. I also envisioned a birthfather with a great persona who was going to rise up, lead the movement, gain the support of the public and media, and have a tremendous impact upon our adoption reform work. He would be on every talk show in the country. I called my friend, Lee, in the middle of the night to tell her about it.

Other than the images in my mind being different, the scenario was practically the same as the year before. I was once again taken to the emergency room of the hospital, refused to be admitted. , was given a shot of Haldol, sent home to sleep, and within three days I was fine. But this time I decided to seek help. Obviously something was not right.

Sherri had been seeing a therapist whom she really liked so I decided to make an appointment with her. I only spent about six weeks in therapy, but Mary helped me to understand what was happening. She explained that one cannot suppress losses for a number of years and not expect some fallout from them. Primarily, she stressed that I should give myself permission to feel and experience the grief, since obviously I had stuffed it for far too many years. And then she emphasized that, if I were going to remain in a leadership role, I needed to learn how to empathize without taking on everyone else's problem. She referred to me as a "caretaker" who has a strong tendency to want to make everyone's hurt go away - usually at my own expense. She pointed out that I had too much of my own pain and to take on others' pain only compounded my own. It was apparent that it was more than my mind could handle. She said "You need to put up an imaginary clear wall which you are able to see through and still be empathetic, but not allow the other person's pain to get in".

In each session, she reminded me that I could not save the world - only myself. It was not until September of 1988 (over 6 years later) that I would once again experience "mania". Once again, it followed a

139

conference at which I had been invited to give the keynote speech. My husband had attended with me and on the way home on the airplane, I was writing, chattering and laughing. We were having a good ole time. We had only been married for four years and, since he wasn't aware of the disease, he had no way of recognizing the signs.

It was late when we got home, and though it was bedtime, I was unable to sleep. I got up and started making phone calls. I called the kids, my mother, a few friends and my neighbor. It was the middle of the night, but in my mind, it seemed perfectly ok. By morning it was apparent that I needed to get some help. My husband, realizing something was not right but not knowing what to do, called my daughter, Sherri.

She lived 30 miles away, but came immediately. As soon as she came in, she said "Mom, get dressed. We're going for a ride". I did what she asked and never questioned it because I trusted her implicitly. During a manic episode, one seems to have an acute sense of insight as to those who genuinely care about us and those who don't; as if you can almost read what the other person is actually thinking. There is an intense awareness on another level or dimension which is hard to describe. With each of the experiences, that particular feeling was very strong and remains vivid.

This time I was admitted into the hospital at a cost of $1500 for three days. I did the same thing I had done in '81 and '82 - I slept for three days, went home and resumed my life - only this time it was financially costly. I've concluded that it's cheaper to 'sleep it off' at home! I went back to counseling, but only for a short time because I could not afford the $65 per half hour sessions. The doctor diagnosed me as having "unipolar" rather than bipolar, meaning I was only having manic episodes, but not depression. He put me on lithium for a few months and then said I could stop taking it if or when I wanted to.

He advised, however, that I should take it about a week before attending a conference or when I knew I would be in a situation where my adrenaline would be flowing. "Otherwise", he said, "you'll be fine. You appear to have a very mild case." I did stop taking it on my own because I dislike taking medication of any kind and because I didn't think I needed it.

When the indictment hit the paper in March of '93, I contacted him immediately and said I thought I needed to get my prescription filled. He said "Sandy, I think you'll be ok. It's been five years. See how it goes." "OK", I said, "You're the doc!" The prosecution and defense rested my case on Thursday, July 23rd and by Sunday, July 26th I was, once again, taken to the hospital - but this time by my friends.

As I reflect back, I know that the disease was already in progress for at least a week before it was in full bloom It's like the chicken pox; you have the disease before you actually see the marks! It explains my giddiness and flightiness days before the trial began. It explains the numerous phone calls I made. It explains my outburst in Mr. Keith's office. It explains my complete numbness as I sat silent throughout the duration of the trial, in an attempt to be stoic, while my mind was frantically racing and I was falling apart at the seams.

Since I do not wish to remain silent any longer, I have sought a comfortable place to share these personal experiences. This feels like a comfortable place, though I am doing so with a great amount of trepidation. Just as coming out of the closet as a birthparent can be scary, going public with mental illness is no easy task. Being in good company, however, makes the risk an easier one.

When I came home from prison, my daughter gave me an excellent book called **TOUCHED WITH FIRE / Manic-Depressive Illness and the Artistic Temperament** by Kay Redfield Jamison. In it, she lists many writers, poets, artists, and composers with whom I share this strange disease. To name just a few: Robert Burns, Hans Christian Anderson, T.S. Eliot, Charles Dickens, Emily Dickinson, James Boswell, Sylvia Plath, Victor Hugo, Ralph Waldo Emerson, Anne Sexton, Faulkner, Fitzgerald, Hemingway, Robert Louis Stevenson, Tennessee Williams, Walt Whitman, Virginia Wolff, Van Gogh, Michelangelo, Edna St. Vincent Millay, and the list goes on and on; and, of course, Patti Duke has been an outspoken advocate for mental illness based upon her personal experience.

Since making phone calls at all hours of the day and night had been a major symptom of mine, I felt a sense of 'connectedness' to Poet Robert Lowell when I read a quote from a letter written in 1964 to his friend, T. S. Lewis, in which he said:

"I want to apologize for plaguing you with so many telephone calls last November and December. When the "enthusiasm" is coming on me it is accompanied by a feverish reaching to my friends. After it is over, I wince and wither".

And writer John Ruskin wrote of his own experiences with what he called "certain states of brain excitement":

"I saw the stars rushing at each other - and thought the lamps of London were gliding through the night into a World Collision... Nothing was more notable to me through the illness than the general exaltation of the nerves of sight and hearing, and their power of making colour and sound harmonious as well as intense."

141

The depressive side of the illness is expressed in this quote from a note written by Virginia Woolf to her husband before she walked into the river and drowned:

"We do not know our own souls, let alone the souls of others. Human beings do not go hand in hand the whole stretch of the way. There is a virgin forest in each; a snowfield where even the print of birds' feet is unknown. Here we go alone, and like it better so. Always to have sympathy, always to be accompanied, always to be understood would be intolerable. But in health the genial pretense must be kept up, and the effort renewed - to communicate, to civilize, to share, to cultivate the desert, to educate the native, to work together by day and by night to sport. In illness this make-believe ceases."

In the introduction to Ms. Jamison's book, she says: Manic-depressive, or bipolar, illness encompasses a wide range of mood disorders and temperaments. Many are unaware of the milder, temperamental expressions of the disease or do not know that most people who have manic-depressive illness are, in fact, without symptoms most of the time. When many individuals - even those who are generally well versed in psychology and medicine think of manic-depressive illness, they tend to imagine the back wards of insane asylums and unremitting mental illness or madness, and conclude that no meaningful or sustained creative work can occur under such circumstances.

Madness, or psychosis, represents only one end of the manic-depressive continuum, however; most people who have the illness, in fact, never become what is considered "insane". Likewise, work that may be inspired by, or partially executed in, a mild or even psychotically manic state may be significantly shaped or partially edited while its creator is depressed and put into final order when he or she is normal." It has become a fundamental and accepted fact in the medical community that manic-depression is a genetic disease, and is the one psychiatric illness that has been drastically affected by advances in clinical research. Lithium, antidepressants, and anticonvulsants are the standard for the illness and psychotherapy or psychoanalysis alone, without medication, is usually considered taboo.

Ms. Jamison states that many writers and artists stop taking their medication because they miss the highs or the emotional intensity associated with the illness. They feel that the side effects of the drug interfere with the clarity and rapidity of their thoughts or diminish their level of enthusiasm and emotional energy.

In the final analysis, bipolar illness is still very much misunderstood among the general population. While this has been a difficult chapter for me to write, I am hopeful that sharing my personal experience will somehow benefit others. If so, I'd like to hear from you.

The 1993 March on Washington sponsored by the Council for Equal Rights in Adoption. I am on the right, next to Joe Soll and July Taylor.

Here I am giving my speech in front of the Reflecting Pool (reflecting!) in Washington, DC on June 26, 1993. Dave Taylor is on the left; Joe Soll and Judy Taylor on the right.

These are the three oldest of my twelve beautiful grandchildren. L to R - Kristi, Jay and Jill; they were all born the Year of the Child (1979). In this picture, they were six years old. They will soon be 16.

My husband had won a trip to Hawaii in May. In order to attend, I needed the permission of the court since my arraignment was held in April and I had been released on a $10,000 bond, with limited travel.

THE TRIAL AFTERMATH

After I returned home from the trial, my family wanted me to curb my activities. Since I had been hospitalized in the midst of the trial, they felt it would be best for me to slow down and "rest". But I felt it was important to let my friends and supporters know the outcome, so early in August, I mailed out the following letter:

"By now you probably know that I have been found guilty of conspiracy charges in relation to my work of reuniting families. Needless to say, I was shocked, as were those who were present at the trial.

My sentencing is scheduled for October 1st. The federal guidelines mandate one or a combination of the following: 0-6 months in jail; a fine up to $250,000 and probation up to five years. I have been told that I will most likely receive a fine and probation. I have volunteered to serve the six months.

Once again, I want to thank you for all your support over these past several months.

The trial had more of an emotional impact upon me than I thought it would. The prosecution and defense both rested their case on Thursday, July 22nd at noon. The judge then dismissed everyone and said that we would resume on Monday, July 26th for summations and the charge to the jury. By Sunday, July 25th, I was in the hospital. Thursday, July 29th I was well enough to finish the trial. The summations were given as was the charge to the jury which was 95 pages long!

I am still in shock and confused by all this. I was set-up by the New York State Department of Health in Albany. Their investigator created a false scenerio - he claimed to be a birthfather looking for a daughter he had placed for adoption in 1959.

I was told that thousands of dollars and man- hours were spent on this three year investigation.

My attorney said I have ten days from the date of sentencing to file an appeal. I have not yet decided whether to appeal - as I'm not sure I've got enough energy. On the other hand, I believe so strongly in our cause that I feel it's important for us to keep up the fight. Your feelings concerning this matter are important to me. Please let me hear from you or feel free to call me if I can answer any questions."

About 10 days after I came home from the trial, a probation officer came by. Since I was at work, he left his card in the door with a note for me to call him. He explained that it was a routine call to establish that I was physically living there so we set a time for him to come over.

He asked general questions, mostly to do with income; i.e. the value of the house, my husband's salary, etc. At that point I protested. "My husband's income should have nothing to do with this matter. Why should he be penalized for my actions?", I asked. He said it was just to provide some preliminary information for my pre-sentencing report.

I then asked him if he knew what the case was about. He said he knew a little bit, but maybe I'd like to fill him in. I would and did. It had been my understanding that I was probably going to receive a large fine and a long probation since I had not "cooperated" with the government. I told Mr. Davis that I would rather go to prison than pay a fine. "In fact, if I do get a fine, I will probably refuse to pay it", I said in an off-handed manner. It seems apparent that my message was probably passed on to the judge. I took that position for three reasons:

1) Our organization paid federal taxes for the four years we were in operation, and I paid personal taxes, so I didn't feel that I owed the government any money; especially since I didn't believe I was guilty.

2) I did not have the money to pay a fine, and did not want to burden my husband with that responsibility.

3) If I was going to have to "pay" for the 'crime' of reuniting families, then it was my opinion that the government should pay for my keep. By going to prison, the tables were reversed. The cost was $2,000 a month.

60 Minutes Pays Us A Visit

Early in September, the 60 Minutes crew came to the office to interview us. We were all very estatic and eager to meet Lesley Stahl, as well as the two producers we had been communicating with - Cathy Olian in New York and Rebecca Peterson in Washington. From the first phone call we had received back in April to the airing of the program, these two producers were always totally professional people. (This had not been our experience with the talk shows.) We spent the prior week making preparations for this exciting event. Since we knew that 60 Minutes still ranked #1 in Investigative Reporting, we felt inspired, encouraged and exhilarated about finally having our issues discussed and heard by mainstream America. In an early call with Cathy, we also discussed getting to the bottom of why, where, when and by whom the investigation was started. She assured me that was something they would be looking into.

The four-man camera crew arrived early in the morning. These terrific bunch of guys soon turned our office into an obstacle course. None of us had any idea that they would go to such great lengths and do so much taping for such a short clip. Rebecca had come with the camera crew in the morning, and Cathy and Lesley arrived around 2:00 in the afternoon. They had been in Cleveland the day before. There they met with a support group and talked to Bobbie.

The interview began within 15 minutes of their arrival, but lasted for over two hours. Lesley explained that we would stop occasionally in order to give me a chance to say all that I wanted to say. A few times, she would reword a question or I would decide on a better response. Having done many interviews over the years, I found her to be a very easy person to interview with. She has a warm, congenial manner which, I believe, is rare these days in the field of journalism.

We had a great laugh over one part of the interview when Lesley asked "When you get out of jail, are you going to continue doing the same thing?" Since I HAD NOT even been sentenced, I said, "When I get out of jail?? I haven't even been sentenced yet. Do you know something I don't know?!" We all laughed and she apologized. She said she must have misunderstood because she was under the impression I had already been sentenced. Hmm!

The interview ended late in the afternoon.

Sentencing and CERA Conference Coincide

Sentencing was only a few weeks away. In the meantime, the work of the Musser Foundation continued. We tried to wrap up as many cases

145

as we could and kept in touch with individuals whose cases were still pending. Coincidently (?) the CERA conference was held the same weekend as my sentencing which was October 1st. The government had successfully knocked me out of two major conferences within six months. I began to believe that it was no mere coincidence, but rather orchestrated by a clever prosecutor.

I asked Judy Taylor to read a statement for me, which she did. I hoped my statement would explain my position and possibly provide some sort of clear direction:

"By the time this letter is shared with you, I will have already been sentenced for the "crime" of playing a small role in reuniting families. I became part of the adoption reform movement in April of 1976 when I joined the Adoption Forum of Phila., founded and led (for many years) by Penny Partridge, a dear and cherished friend. The same year I joined the Forum, I began a search for the daughter I had surrendered in 1954.

I requested that my name and address simply be placed into the court file in case my daughter was searching also. The judge denied my request. It was that denial by a judge in Media, Pennsylvania that spurred me on to commit myself to this work. Of course, I had no idea at that time that I'd still be here 18 years later trying to open records. And I didn't realize then that there is a MUCH BIGGER PICTURE!

There have been many rumors floating around the movement concerning all that has happened within the last several months. I hope that many of you will consider some of my thoughts.

First and foremost is the fact that we must always keep our eyes on the goal and stretch as far as we are able to understand the underlying financial dynamics of the child welfare system. That's what I mean when I mention "the bigger picture". This indictment was not about Sandy Musser. This indictment is simply a smokescreen brought about by our state and federal agencies, by the NCFA, and by the Congressional Coalition for Adoption.

We are in battle, my friends. The battle is between those of us who believe in family reunification and family preservation; and those who support the current closed sealed secret form of adoption, which first separate a family before creating a new one. The Adoption Subsidy Act was increased from 3 million to 10 million in one year. The goal is to reinstate the Homes for Unwed Mothers. Couldn't that 10 million dollars be better spent helping families remain together?

As long as records remain sealed and we are unable to obtain information that is rightfully ours, our government can continue to perpetuate the billion dollar LEGAL baby-selling business which is one of America's most lucrative industries. It is carried out via adoption attorneys and licensed state and private agencies. Why else hasn't the United States of America ratified the United Nations Treaty on the Right of the Child?

Whether you agree with this or not, or whether your focus is smaller, as group leaders, please keep two things in mind. Though they seem to be in direct contrast, they are both significant for our movement at this particular crossroad:

1) UNITED WE STAND - DIVIDED WE FALL - Difficult as it may be, we must always try to "defend one another's position." Since many of us have been damaged and hurt by this process called adoption, it is not always easy for us to come to one another's defense, but for the sake of unity, it is imperative that we try; so let us commit to caring for one another even though we may not always agree.

2) DIVIDE AND CONQUER - When there are two strong leaders in one large group, then it is time to branch out and create a new group or organization. This is known as the Divide and Conquer concept. Keep in mind that we are barely scratching the surface of the reform work that needs to be done.

One of the primary purposes of The Musser Foundation as stated in our Articles of Incorporation is to 'encourage the formation, utilization and expansion of groups interested in adoption and foster care reform'. We are not sure at this point what direction our organization will take, but we plan to rise up out of the dust like the Phoenix and continue with the work we were doing. If there is anything we can do to assist you in reaching your organizational goals, please let us know."

"You Are Sentenced To...

While Judy was preparing to make the above statement on my behalf, I was preparing to stand before the Judge for my sentencing. My sister had met me in Cleveland to lend her support, as did the same faithful friends. The proceedings began at 3:30 in the afternoon.

Much discussion transpired between the Court, Mr. Getz and Mr. Keith as they made a veiled attempt to reach my "offense" level.

On page 5 of the sentencing report, Mr. Getz states:

"...the defendant was charged as an aider and abetter in the offenses representing nearly all of the 24 counts of which she was convicted. In order for the jury to have found her guilty on those charges, they had to understand that she was aware of the method and means by which the information was being obtained. Clearly the evidence in the case that was brought out at trial, was the manner and means that were used were that Barbara Moskowitz was portraying herself as representing a governmental agency, the Social Security Administration, in obtaining information from other offices, field offices of the Social Security Administration.

As an aider and abetter, the application of the sentencing guidelines are to be applied to this defendant the same as they could be to the principal offender. And in that regard, this particular enhancement would be appropriate because, again, the conduct that was involved was clearly a representation that the activity was being done on behalf of the governmental agency".

The Court: Now Mr. Keith.

Mr. Keith: Thank you, Your Honor. Our argument would be to the contrary. That the evidence does not adduce that Sandy Musser made any of those representations and she shouldn't be given credit for the conduct of Barbara Moskowitz.

The Court: I don't think there is any question about that evidence, she certainly did not.

Mr. Keith: Exuse me?
The Court: Mrs. Musser did not make any representations at all to those folks.

Mr. Keith: That's correct. And I would argue that she would not share in that part of the conduct, your Honor. I think that her activities in that regard are severable from that of Mrs. Moskoowitz.

The Court: There is really no doubt in my mind that she was aware of the general technique of Mrs. Moskowitz in obtaining the information.

148

I'm not sure, Mr. Getz, that she was aware of the particular involvement about it. Are you saying that it is the rule that aiders and abetters are, by virtue of their position, in a position of being penalized by the increase in guideline by reason of their position?

Mr. Getz: Yes, Your Honor. Referring to the guideline, Section 2X2.1 deals, I believe, with the role of aider and abetter, and I think specifically in a very limited way. Basically what it says is that they are to be held in the same standard as the principal of the offense. 2X2.1 on page 236. And I would refer to the background section and application notes under application note 1, where it says "a defendant convicted of aiding a abetting is punishable as a principal."

The bantering continued back and forth. until finally an offense level of 10 was reached.

My attorney then spoke again and said: "This is her first contact with the criminal justice system in any way. I am sure that the court is most troubled by the — I guess the word would be the intensity with which she addressed these matters and went through it. I would suggest to the court that she firmly holds a belief that the fact that these records are sealed and unavailable to individuals in many cases is simply wrong, both from a moral basis that they have a right to know, and also there are some very clear medical reasons that individuals ought to be able to have the information, which in this day and age becomes very important to them for purposes of planning or diagnosis of many of their medical conditions, management of their lives.

I am sure that the government - the government in its opening statement at the trial suggested that this was done for great personal profit. I don't believe there is really any evidence that Mrs. Musser made a great personal profit. I think perhaps there was some money which she paid herself as a salary, the rest of it would have appeared to have gone back into this enterprise and into the advertising of it, into the 1-800 telephone line that was available for people to call and get the information and to disseminating the message that went with it.

The government also spoke in its opening statement and cast some aspersions on the pride with which Mrs. Musser addressed her role in this particular matter and relationship. I certainly can understand the governments feeling about that because there are often two sides to the same coin. I would suggest to the court that Mrs. Mussr could, as well as being accused of sins by her accusers, also in the same text or in the same frame, be treated as someone who took reasonable pride and took a moral stand and pursued something very vigorously.

149

If this was something that was a little closer to being socially acceptable, no one would raise an eyebrow. Her treatment of it is certainly not that of a person who, I think, somehow has no useful justification for it. I'm sure the court may not agree with that justification, but certainly it's something that at least has a reasonable basis both in reality and in her own personal experience. When the court goes to sentence her — I understand that the court will sentence her - - the court must, at the minimum, impose a term of conditions or incarceration, one way or the other, but I would ask the court to take into consideration that this is an individual who for these reasons is perhaps distinguishable from somebody who's simply stealing cars or selling drugs, or doing or committing a fraud.

If the court were to hear the case of the U.S. versus Chichy. The housing — of the Housing and Urban Development folks were being defrauded out of a great deal of money for bogus home loans, and the people benefited through the monies they received. And there was no useful basis in their own experience or personal belief about the issue to suggest a reason for their activity.

I will ask the court to consider those things and to fashion a sentence that would, as opposed to be too punitive, would perhaps put Mrs. Musser in a situation of addressing the issues in her own life. I believe that the court could do that with some sort of community confinement, probation, and perhaps community service in some fashion that would address that as opposed to simply a term of incarceration".

The Judge asked me if there was anything I wanted to say before sentencing.

"Yes, sir. I just have two very brief statements. Number one, I am not guilty of this charge. Number two, somehow we need, as a country, to look at these sealed records. Adoptees all over the country are in need of medical information; people are dying because they don't have the answers that they need. In a country that prides itself on being a free country, something is very wrong with this picture and we should be cooperating and helping instead of punishing and prosecuting."

The Judge then proceeded with sentencing:

"I have read with great interest the presentence investigation, which I will not read from which may well answer many of the questions which lawyers and judges and jurors ask during the course of trial. And I have also read each and every one of the many, many, many letters which have been forwarded to me in your support, and not in your support. And they convey to me a sense, first, of great mission in relation to what you are doing and what you have attempted to do. I have received some letters to the contrary, which I think can be mentioned only because they are to the contrary.

That being so, I think it's probably best that I say to you now, and to those with you, the crime here, and the crime here charged, is not whether you assisted in loved ones finding each other over the course of years. That is a peripheral matter here. It goes to the rationale which began an effort to obtain information.

This court has no view on your efforts along that line. I think that I understand them, I think I understand the feeling of those who have been rewarded and, in instances, not rewarded by your work.

So whatever I say in relation to sentencing is in no manner motivated by any thought concerning the work which you have undertaken. As I've indicated to you, as I read the presentence investigation it became very clear to me why you have embarked on the road that you have in these past few years.

What you have said today is what you said during the trial. It is a sense of saying: I know that the law existed and I feel that it must be changed. And in changing it, if I must violate it to change it, I will violate it.

There is no sense of what we sometimes refer to as remorse for having done so. You have felt apparently yourself justified. So that no matter whether the court accepted the guideline analysis of your attorney or the government's, the court still feels that jail time — a jail sentence of incarceration is well in order in this case.

My body froze as I thought to myself "Did I really hear what I think I just heard?"

And maybe you wish it that way, I really don't know. But I want to make it clear that any sentence in which the court is involved relates and refers to your desire and your activity in intruding into the privacy of the Social Security files. Although your feelings are a very strong one, there is I'm sure an equally strong view that those records should be kept silent, and the United States Congress has agreed with that view. Under that circumstance, therefore, the court will sentence you to the custody of the Bureau of Prisons to be imprisoned for a term of four months. Within 72 hours of your release from the custody of the Bureau of Prisons, you shall report in person to the probation office of the district to which you are released, then to begin a period of supervised release for a term of three years.

The terms of supervised release are as follows:

One, you shall not commit — not commit — any other federal, state, or local crime.

Two, you will comply with the standard conditions that have been adopted by this court which will be given to you in writing.

And thirdly, that you shall be placed on home confinement with electronic monitoring for a period of 60 days, to commence no later than 14 calendar days from your release from custody.

You will be required to remain in your place of residence unless you are given written permission in advance by your probation office or this court to be elsewhere.

You may leave your residence to work, to receive medical treatment, and to participate in any earned leave program of the probation office under the terms set by the probation officer.

During that two month period of time, you shall wear an electronic monitoring device and follow electronic monitoring procedures specified by your probation officer.

You will also participate in any outpatient program for mental health treatment as directed by the Probation Department until such time as you are released from that program by that department.

You shall be restricted from any direct or collateral involvement in obtaining adoption records while you are on supervised relase.

In reviewing the financial aspects of your life, I think probably it would impose an undue burden on you to pay a fine. The court will therefore waive the fine in this case.

The court will require that you pay the cost of the electronic monitoring for the period that I have specified. I'm required by law to order that you pay the United States a special assessment of $1,350, and that amount, of course, is due immediately, as I'm sure you know. That is the special assessment which is mandated by the law.

You will report to the place of incarceration not later than 5:00 p.m. on the lst of November, 1993.

Mr. Keith, I really can make no recommendation in relation to the incarceration, unless you have some knowledge of a place of confinement in the sourtheastern section of the United States. If you do, fine, or if you find one in the next couple of days, you let me know and I'll be glad to include it in the order.

Mr. Keith: Your Honor, I have obtained a copy of the Federal Bureau of Prisons book and I will supply the court with a name of a facility closest to her residence that fits.

Mr. Keith then expressed to the Judge the fact that we were going to appeal the case. The Judge asked me, in light of no funds, if I wanted him to appoint an attorney for me. I said "Yes, sir" and Mr. Keith was appointed. At that point, Mr. Getz rose to say that it was his understanding that I was negotiating with cither book companies or film companies. If so, the government should be reimbursed for any funds that would expended on my behalf for the purpose of pursuing the appeal.

It was over. I was being sentenced to prison for the "crime" of reuniting families. In essence, that's all I was really guilty of. Since my attorney was going to be appealing, at least I would have a reprieve for a few months. He had said that the appeal would probably not be heard until January. At least, I could get through the holidays - or so I thought.

No Stay

It was Saturday, October 30, 1993. My husband was outside mowing the lawn when I heard him call to me. As I glanced out the front window, I noticed the mailman parked by our driveway. As I approached his truck, he handed me a registered letter from the District Court in Ohio, which was postmarked October 22nd. I had no idea what it could be, but opened it immediately. The letter was instructing me to be at Marianna Federal Prison in Marianna, FL by Monday morning, November 1st at 11:00 a.m. Only two days notice! To say I was in shock would be an understatement. It had been my clear understanding that there would be a stay until my appeal was heard.

When I left the courthouse on the day of my sentencing (October 1st), my attorney said he would be filing the appeal within ten days and then be in touch with me. He called the middle of October and said the brief had been filed and he would send me a copy, as well as some papers for me to sign. That was the last communication I had with him. He never remotely intimated that I was headed for prison before my appeal was heard. Now I needed to reach him quickly.

An urgent attempt to get a call through to his office was to no avail. This was such short notice and I was in a panic and confused about what to do. Many questions flooded my mind. Hadn't he filed the proper papers? Why would I receive this letter only two days before I was due to report to prison? Anger, hurt, and fear were all culminating at the same time. I was already upset over the fact that we had lost the case. Though witnesses had been prepared to testify on my behalf, he chose not to use them. Why? He had received his entire payment the month before trial began. Had he lost the motivation to work harder?

My family were all contacted and given the current news. The first thing Monday morning, I called Mr. Keith's office. The secretary didn't seem to know why this had happened, but said she'd have him call me as soon as she heard from him.

Several hours later, he called back. In his laid back, matter-of-fact, nonchalant manner, he said he'd "look into it" and get back to me. Gee, thanks Mr. Keith. I deeply appreciate you taking the time! Considering the fact that I'm supposed to be on my way to prison today, I appreciate your willingness to look into it! Had he dropped the ball? Or was he actually working for the government as I had suspected many times throughout the judicial process. It certainly seemed apparent that something had gone awry.

I called late Tuesday afternoon and again reached the secretary. I asked her if she could explain how something like this could happen. She said she wasn't sure except that "he didn't realize he had to file papers for a stay because most of the people he defends are already in jail!!"

Wednesday afternoon, Mr. Keith called. He apologized and said he "didn't know they were going to send out this notice". The notice had been dated October 18th - the same day he had filed the appeal brief. He said that he talked to the judge and the judge would only give me until Friday at 5:00 to report to prison. There would be no stay! Again, I wondered if he were in cahoots with the prosecution - now I was certain. I was curious as to how long it would take him before he placed a call to me in prison??

RESERVE

They said
you did such awful things -
like broke the law
and pulled some strings.
They said
you disrupted people's lives,
by selling information
but they never thought why.
But I can assure you
none of this is true . . .
For the law
has only yet to see,
ties which were broken
were not meant to be.
They said you must go to prison
to pay for what you have done,
so others won't follow in your footsteps
and your battle won't be won.
But you see - the time given you to serve
is only a time of RESERVE.
RESERVE for the realization
that truth in and of itself
cannot be barred, crushed or buried.
It can only be set free.

Set the truth free - Set free Sandy Musser!

Sherri Lynn

154

THE PRISON EXPERIENCE

Marianna Federal Correctional Institution is located in the panhandle of Florida. It's 35 miles south of Dothan, AL and 60 miles west of Tallahassee. I jotted the following notes as we left for Marianna and throughout the duration of the eight hour ride.

We left the house at 6:45 am. My husband had called the prison on Thursday and was told it was about an 8 hour trip from our home. I kissed my two dogs good-bye and while getting in the car, I noticed a neighbor watering his lawn. The school bus passed and the driver waved. The weather was perfect; a beautiful, pleasant Florida day. Though I am going to prison, the world is still turning. Hasn't anyone noticed; does anyone really give a damn? I am hurting.

I am on my way to prison for a crime I did not commit. Questions flooded my mind - how long will I be held? Will my mail be censored? Will I have access to a typewriter? Will I make new friends? Some say I'm a martyr - I don't feel like a martyr nor do I want to be a martyr. I just want to be true to my principles and beliefs. Others say I'm a scapegoat and that I can agree with. As I understand it, the scapegoat was the one who suffered and died for the sins of the world, while the other goat was set free. I'm not suffering right now, but the "sins" of the movement have fallen on my shoulders, so scapegoat is an apt description. Some say history is in the making - 50 years of sealed records now being challenged by those willing to "pay the price".

As we travel Rt 75N on our way to Marianna, there are moments when I feel as though I am suffocating; my throat is closing up. It's raining heavy. It's 1:50 and we're stopping for gas and lunch. Back on the road again - feeling very sleepy - want very much to get there and have night time come quickly so I can lay down and go to sleep.

I'm wondering how things are going at the office today. My friend, Penny, pops into my mind. She is traveling all the way from Massachusetts to be with me as I walk through the gates. She is indeed a loyal, faithful and true friend and will be recording this historic event.

"It's Cryin' Time Again" is playing on the radio - it makes me smile and cry at the same time - it sure is 'cryin' time'! It's 3:30 p.m. We're now getting off Rt. 10 and heading for Marianna. My stomach is doing flip-flops. Can't let my husband know because he's more nervous than me.

Well, here we are - as we near the prison gates, we see cars parked along the side of the road and recognize familiar faces. We pull over and are greeted by Penny Partridge, Jon Ryan, his son Jeff, and Candy Thorsen. They are carrying signs and hand me a dozen roses from my devoted friend, Lynn Giddens. After taking a few pictures, we decide we still have time to get a cup of coffee. The time in Marianna is an hour earlier so we are in good shape! We find a place to eat and spend the next hour talking about old times in the movement. As it gets close to the time for us to leave the restaurant, my stomach is beginning to churn and do flip-flops - the fear of the unknown is enveloping my entire being. It is 4:30 pm Marianna time. I wave good-by to my friends. I had been told by the court to arrive by 5:00 pm on Friday, November 5th. We arrive at 4:45.

Since it is after 4:00 pm and a weekend, I am immediately informed that there is no one who can "process" me; therefore I will be placed in a "holding" cell which they referred to as "Administrative Detention". In actuality, it was "solitary confinement" or today more commonly called "isolation" or "segregation" (isn't that an interesting word to use?!)

To Hell and Back in 3 Days

The following writing was done within a few hours of being placed in the isolation cell where I spent my first three days. When I was finally able to mail letters out, I sent it to the office to be permanently recorded. It's being copied as originally written.

I arrived at Marianna at 4:45 p.m. As we pulled into the parking lot and started walking towards the door, we were met by an officer who looked to be in his early to mid 20's - a rookie? He informed my husband that he was not allowed in the building. (I learned later that this was not true, but this young rookie wanted us to know who was in charge). We said our quick good-byes and I was ushered into a large room and told to sit down. He asked my name and "ID number". "Sandy Musser 51963-060". He called someone to tell them there was a "self-surrender" waiting to be processed.

About 20 minutes later, a male and female lieutenant showed up. I was handcuffed, put in the back of a police car and taken to maximum security. The female officer told me I would be placed in a "segregation cell" until Monday. The reason was because there was no one at the camp who could process me. In order to be processed, I would have had to arrive before 4:00. Then why did my letter of "commitment" say 5:00? We pulled up in front of a large building. I was taken inside, went through security and led into a room with nothing in it but a counter and photography equipment. I was fingerprinted and photographed; three sets of fingerprints and eight photographs. It had been raining which added to the eeriness of it all. By now it was 5:45.

The next stop was a small shower stall with bars. I was placed inside and told to strip. The female officer remained outside the bars and proceeded to check the inside of my mouth, behind my ears, under my arms, between my toes, shook my hair; "turn around, bend over, and pull the cheeks of your backside apart and cough"! It was only then that I began to cry and wondered how I could possibly be paying this big a price simply because of my commitment to the goal of reuniting families. I feel as though fate has dealt me a very cruel blow and I search my mind for an answer that makes sense - but there doesn't seem to be one. The guard hands me an orange jumpsuit and tells me to put in on. It fits snug. I am given no underwear. She unlocks the shower bars and takes me to my cell which is only a few doors away.

It is now 6:00 pm and I have just been placed in my cell. My mind is beginning to race. Is this all a game? The feds against the little people?! They said it was a conspiracy to defraud the government. Wasn't it really a conspiracy by the government to defraud adoptees of their real identity? Isn't everything topsy-turvy? Shouldn't the attorneys and agency workers and judges who falsify documents in the name of "adoption" be in here instead of me?? I keep trying and trying to make sense of it all, but keep coming up blank. My mind just can't fathom the insanity of it.

I had brought a purse with a note pad, thank you notes, a few paperbacks, some makeup and $120 cash. It was all "held" to be checked in - more importantly, my jewelry consisting of my wedding band, necklace and watch. So far no receipt for any of it. When I asked why I couldn't keep my wedding band, the officer said it was because it had a few diamond chips in it!

As you enter the 6 x 10 cell, a metal bunk bed is on the right; across from the bunk bed in the left corner is a metal desk with a swing-out stool attached; to the immediate left as you come into the cell is a lidless steel toilet attached to a metal sink. Everything is bolted to the wall.

There is a long, narrow window with safety glass, probably 12" wide by 48" long, at the end of my bunk which looks out onto a small courtyard. The courtyard is completely wired across the top. The door of my cell is solid steel about two feet wide; on the left side of the door is a long narrow window, similar to the one at the end of bunk, but smaller. About three-quarters of the way down the door is a 4" x 12" slot (like the old mail slots) which allows for the passing of towels, toilet paper, food trays, etc. A small plastic mirror above the sink gives a distorted view, like the view most people have of adoption - strangely distorted.

It is approximately 9:00. A guard comes by. He unlocks the little slot door, and places 2 sheets, a pillow case and a wash cloth on it so that I can retrieve them. I told him I needed my medication and saline solution. He has disappeared and not yet returned. I didn't get my medicine or saline.

Before going to sleep and through a mist of tears, I write the following poem which is in its original form, but later expanded:

THEY TOOK YOU (AND ME) AWAY

1954 I screamed with pain, then you were born (though no documents we can see). They snatched you from my womb to sever our bond that they said could never be. They forbid me to lay eyes upon you, but they could never remove the memory of you from my heart, no matter how hard they tried - for years and years I silently cried! Because of the day - that terrible day
THEY TOOK YOU AWAY!

1976 I spoke of you today for the first time in 22 years. I announced to a group of 8 adoptees that "I gave her away, but I never forgot her". My heart began to scream with the pain that had been suppressed all these years. And now my journey to find you begins. It would be a journey to end the awful pain, to put to rest the longing inside and to finally find peace. Because of the day
THEY TOOK YOU AWAY!

1988 For the past 12 years I've devoted my life, my heart, my soul to helping others find the peace I found when I found you. I built a national organization. Loved ones around the country were being reunited. I was pegged an adoption reform activist as I spoke out against the government's practice of sealed records. I was devoted, committed, dedicated. Because of the day
THEY TOOK YOU AWAY!

1993 And now I am in a locked cell 6 x 10 - 325 concrete cinder blocks - no sunshine - no contact with anyone - something like the hospital room where it started 39 years ago. They punished me then for giving birth to you - I hadn't obeyed the rules - there was no ring on my finger - Punishment required - to sacrifice my first born!

And now they are punishing me again in my work of reuniting families - again they said I broke the rules. Adoption records are sealed - shall not be broken. Punishment required - Jail!
AND SO TODAY, THEY TOOK ME AWAY!

I decide to make a mental list of my closest supporters and 'donate' one hour of my time to each one. Kind of a dedication to them for their steadfastness and willingness to stand by me.

I finally fell asleep and slept fairly sound. I awoke about 6:00 am - no way of knowing time. I do some minor exercises. I feel completely isolated and alone. I am. Still wondering what I did wrong. Someone made a comment that my fate was in the hands of 12 people who didn't have enough sense to get out of jury duty. (An attempt to humor myself). Though I'm sure they were all intelligent people, I know they didn't have the whole picture; few people do when it comes to understanding the atrocities done in the name of adoption.

I just discover that my tooth brush can double for a hair brush. What a discovery! I've been stripped of everything -- my wedding band, my watch, the necklace my son gave me last Christmas which said "I love you MOM", and other personal items I had brought, were all confiscated.

First AM breakfast to pass through the 4"x8" opening is grapefruit and fruitloops cereal - no utensils! So prisoners in solitary are expected to eat like animals? I cannot even see as I write since I've never been given my saline solution. It must be around 9:30 am. I don't eat - I fall back to sleep and wake up to the noise of my lunch tray. By now I'm hungry. Lunch consists of a biscuit, two eggs, grits and a banana.

I see a guard passing by my door and again ask for my saline solution and medication. He brought my saline solution. I ask about utensils and he brings me a plastic spoon - he said that's all we're allowed to have! Lunch was good, especially the coffee. I had been given a handbook when they placed me in the cell which I took time to read. I do more mental gymnastics, but in vain - still no concrete solution. The only concrete is on the floor and in the cinder blocks - I start counting them - there are 325 - they are grey, a dull light grey. I decide to go back to sleep but not before realizing that I've now missed two of my pills. I write a note and leave it under the door.

159

Someone calls my name and I awake. A young man was kneeling on the floor outside the steel door by the little slot opening. Are they afraid if they open the door, I'll attack them? I sit on the floor and peek through the little mail slot in order to talk to him. He introduces himself as Jeff and says he will be my case manager when I get to camp on Monday. He has a pleasant manner and is the friendliest person I've met so far; he actually talks to me like a real human being. He reiterates what I had been told - had I arrived by 4:00 on Friday, I could have been processed and gone right into camp, but since it was 4:45 when I arrived, everyone had gone home for the weekend. He explained that I was being held in "Administrative Detention". Oh really? (The fact that these are the same cells used for punishment and disciplinary problems is just a coincidence??)

I asked Jeff the time. It is 4:00 pm Saturday so I've almost got 24 hours under my belt. Only 117 more days to go. Jeff told me that camp will be a piece of cake - this was just an unfortunate timing problem - no punishment intended!! You sure could have fooled me!! He had seen the note I slid under the door, concerning my medicine, and said he'd let the medicine man know about my missed medication.

Soon after he leaves, dinner arrives. The portions are generous, but bland. Trying to eat a large piece of roast beef with a spoon is a difficult task. Guess that's why God gave us fingers (for times like these!). An odd thought comes into my head - 'Treat someone like an animal long enough, they will become animal-like' - or maybe it's not such an odd thought. The meal consists of string beans, kidney beans, and overdone potatoes. Also included is a salad, a very hard roll and a tasteless brownie. Two drinks are provided - soda and iced tea. I eat the meat and salad.

The time is dragging. There is no radio, no time, nothing to read, and no one to speak to. The only thing you've got to keep you going is your mind. The past two evenings, I've tried recalling favorite songs - the old-time hymns I learned as a child help to lift my spirit. As the tears stream down my face, I begin to sing quietly - "On a hill far away stood an old rugged cross -the emblem of suffering and shame, and I love that old cross where the dearest and best, for a world of lost sinners was slain; so I'll cherish that old rugged cross, til my trophies at last I lay down. I will cling to the old rugged cross and exchange it someday for a crown". I fall asleep.

Meal times are welcome - something to look forward to and a chance to catch a glimpse of another human being (the guards) as they pass by my door and deposit the meal at the small tray-like trap door. But they do not speak. Still no medication ... Doors clang constantly just like they do on television. I always thought that awful sound was intensified for

160

effect, but it's real. It's so loud that it wakes me in the middle of the night. The temperature has been comfortable.

As a member of the Hemlock Society, I'm thinking of Dr. Kevorkian and wondering what he's doing? We were both giving people choices and both landed in prison the same day. Both freeing people from their pain, bringing them peace. On the radio, while coming to Marianna, they mentioned his plan to fast during the term of his incarceration. I wish I had the stamina and determination to fast, but I'm much too weak - both mentally and physically and would it make my cause any more deserving or prove the point any stronger?

And what about Heidi - she, too, was giving people choices. Apparently it's "OK" as long as you're not public and flaunting it. Dr. Kevorkian, you can keep doing what you're doing - after all, doctors have been helping their patients die for years, but they just don't talk about it. How dare you bring it out into the open! Heidi, you were much too flamboyant. Though we all know your services are needed, we can only deal with such things if they are done "in secret" -

And YOU, MS. SANDY MUSSER - just who do you think you are? How dare you initiate reunions on shows like Maury Povich and advertise your services! Don't you know it's against the law to do these things!! I guess we showed you who's boss! You were a bad girl and now you must pay the price.

Dinner - Sunday - large portions - fried shrimp, but very dry; rice, bean mixture, peas, salad, roll, strawberry shortcake. The day passes slowly. I inquire again about reading material. I get lucky - two newspapers! One from early September and the other in Spanish! 48 hours have now passed - hopefully only another 12 to 14 and I should be out of this lockup hole in the wall. I'm ready for conversation. I miss my family, my friends, my dogs. All this because I arrived too late for "processing", even though I was actually on time according to my court order. But I should have known - how stupid of me!! The Bureau of Prisons (hereafter called BOP), like other government agencies, stops functioning at 4:00 sharp and apparently no one else "on campus" is capable of doing the "processing!" "It's not my job, man!"

It's Monday a.m. - I don't know the time. I told the guard who brought breakfast that I had not received my medication since Friday, and that I'm supposed to be "processed" this morning. He said he'd check on my medicine. He came back about a half hour later and asked why I hadn't said something sooner!! I shout a silent, but very loud, primal scream and then inform him that I HAD mentioned it several times over the weekend to various guards; he said they are "looking into it"! Ah, those infamous words! As usual, a bit too late, but who really gives a damn!

161

I'm now beginning to lose my composure. I feel myself falling apart. My hands are shaking as I drop a note outside the door asking to see a counselor. I am sitting on the floor in the corner next to the locked solid steel door with my knees pulled up to my chin. The walls are closing in and I feel as though I am suffocating. My claustrophobia is in full bloom. Panic has me in its tight grip. I start crying and then sobbing hysterically. A female officer comes and kneels down by the door so she can talk to me through "the slot". Where did I come from, how did I get here, and when? Was I a self-surrender? Was this my first offense or am I a repeat offender? She then, like the others, assures me that I was only placed here because I arrived after 4:00 pm on Friday. No one on duty who could screen me - so I had to be placed in Administrative Detention. You'd surely think I'd be convinced by now. I'm not. She asks about my medication, name of doctor, etc., then promises to be back shortly. She keeps her promise.

In about five minutes she returns with another officer; they open the solid steel door which had been locked shut for three solid days and as I step over the threshold into the hallway, I felt an instantaneous and overwhelming sense of relief. My entire body relaxes to the point of collapse; the guards steady me, handcuff me, and take me to a front office where I am given a blood level test. I am then escorted back to my cell, given a dose of medication, and assured that they will be transporting me to the camp very soon. I feel as though I've spent the last three days of my life waging a battle - a battle to simply survive.

About 15 minutes later, a thin male officer in his early 30's comes to take me to Camp. Before leaving maximum security, I am taken back to the same room where I had originally been fingerprinted. I'm told to change from the orange jumpsuit back to the clothes I wore when I came in on Friday. The officer goes thru the rest of my belongings which had been literally thrown into a paper bag. He tosses it all into a box as though it's junk. He tells me it will be shipped home. My jewelry, consisting of my wedding ring, watch, and necklace had been haphazardly thrown into a white business-size envelope. As he gets ready to put it in the box, I ask why I can't keep my wedding ring. He dumps my jewelry out on the counter, looks at it, and says "Because of the diamond chips - it's policy."

I tell him that it's my understanding I could keep a religious medallion. "True", he says, "but you don't have one." I show him the necklace my son had given me the previous Christmas which says "I love you, Mom" and tell him that I wear it 'religiously'. To my surprise, he gives me permission to keep it, as well as my watch. I denote a soft spot and think he's probably a fairly decent guy. But then he makes a phone call to the camp and his comment makes me believe he's a real jerk. He said "I've got **one** here I'm bringing over". Not - I'm bringing Sandy Musser over or I'm bringing a new inmate over - but I've got **ONE** here...! Like a piece of steer that had just been roped! Why didn't he just say the word convict! Ah, man's inhumanity to man!

Just as we get ready to get into the van to go to the camp, he realizes he doesn't have any of my paperwork with my fingerprints and photographs. We return to the building to look for them, but they are no where to be found! Can you believe this - we have to go through the whole process of fingerprinting and photographing again! So what? The taxpayers are generous people! Finally, I get into the van and we drive the half mile to the camp. It's 11:30 am.

I follow him into the processing office called R & D which usually stands for Research and Development, but in prison it stands for Receiving and Discharging. I am turned over to a female officer who leads me to a back room. She's not at all friendly or pleasant. By now I'm totally convinced that being miserable goes with the territory and is probably one of the qualifications on the Bureau of Prisons application form. (I begin some mental bantering with myself. "Do you think you're in a country club, MS. MUSSER? This is prison, you know! Nice and prison don't go together. Why not? Maybe if we turned out nicer prisoners, we would have less crime. But think of the jobs that would be lost!") Again, I am strip searched! Why?? I can't believe this - I have just left an isolation unit! (Ours is not to question why, ours is but to do or die! - was it history class where I first heard that axiom?) Is this simply for the sake of humiliation or do they think maybe one of the guards put drugs on my food tray and I inserted them into my vagina so I could have a coke or pot party with my newfound friends when I got into camp??? Sorry family. This is what I learned in prison.

I am issued my uniforms. Brown pants, brown t-shirts, beige shirt-blouses, a brown jacket, and brown shoes. Like a puppy, I follow behind my newest captor and am led to the front counter where I am about to experience "processing". Now I figure that this part must really be a big deal because I just spent three solid days in solitary confinement staring at a cold concrete floor and 325 cinder blocks, for lack of someone to do this "process" thing. 10 minutes later when my "processing" is complete, I'm madder than a nest full of hornets that just had their home torn apart! Processing consisted of the need for me to sign my John Hancock to several pieces of paper. "Just sign on the line where the X's are." I still didn't understand why one of the guards or officers couldn't have slapped these papers in front of me and had me sign them on Friday? They kept telling me that no one was "qualified". Now this was definitely a tough job for someone to handle! Making sure someone signs their name on the dotted line takes a great deal of skill!

163

By signing each one of the papers, I was promising not to hold my government responsible for anything that might happen to me while I am in their care (including death). I've just been convicted of a "crime". How much validity does my signature have? Of what value are these silly papers? They are in total control so my signature means absolutely nothing! Who's kidding who? What a silly game. One more time my picture is taken! They now have many, many mugshots on file. This particular one is placed on my commissary card. Since I had been crying, my eyes were puffy and swollen so my picture looked like it should be added to the Top 10 of America's Most Wanted list.

I'm excused and at the same time am greeted by a "Big Sister" who has been assigned to show me around. We walk out the front door, down a short strip of pavement to the Laundry where I am "issued" (note the military jargon) bed linens, pillow, and nightgown. The appearance of the building(s) is that of a small mini-mall. Is that what the architect intended? Does it make it more palatable? Might some of us decide we like it enough to want to stay?

As we step out of the Laundry and round the corner of the building, I am awestruck by the beautiful landscaping and meticulous grounds. I see some middle-aged and elderly women raking leaves; they smile and say hello as I pass by. The trees are glistening as they display their beautiful colors and project serenity - almost an eerie serenity. It looks like a college campus. Yea, I can handle this! A piece of cake! Before the month is out, I will be eating my words.

My Mini Experience with Prison Life

As I continue this chapter, I want to make it clear that I do not consider myself an authority or expert on prison life. Especially since I served time in, what is sometimes referred to as, Club Fed or the Kiddie Camp. In addition, and without question, four months is not enough time for anyone to make that kind of claim. This is simply my own personal experience as seen through my eyes as I lived out my term of 118 days in a federal prison camp. If you are a birthmother, you may feel as though you're back in a home for unwed mothers. The similarities were uncanny.

Straight ahead are two buildings that look like dorms. Maria, my big sister leads me to the building on the right called Seminole. It's divided into A and B. I've been assigned to B. This will be my home for the next four months. As we enter the building, I can't help but notice the spic and span floor - it shines like glass. My "room" is on the second floor so we climb the 16 steps and pass one cubicle before getting to the one that is mine. The cubicles are small - approximately 6 x 8.

164

Maria introduces me to my roommate whose name is Lorrie. Lorrie, who is a large woman, greets me pleasantly. She could tell I had been crying and mentioned how hard it is when you first come in. She said it takes longer for some to adjust than for others. "How long do you have?" "Four months", I reply. "Oh, that'll go by fast! It takes a couple weeks to get acclimated, but after that, it's not too bad. I have ten months, so you'll be out before me!".

She then shows me which locker is mine. We all have a four foot metal locker in which to keep our clothes and other personal items like toothpaste, shampoo, etc. The lock, she says, will have to be purchased from the commissary. Since I didn't have anything with me of value (except the necklace I was now wearing), I didn't see the need to buy one. Though I had just been victimized by the government, I still had a certain amount of faith in my "fellow-women". I never did buy a lock - does that mean I'm still naive and idealistic? I proceed to put my "new" clothes away.

I've been assigned the top bunk. I look for a ladder, but don't see one. Lorrie then points out that there is a 12"-15" wide one soldered onto the end of the bed, inside of the metal horizontal bars. Because the cubicles are so small, it is up against the end of the wall and the locker is at the foot of the bed. In other words, it is not practical or useable.

Lorrie had a "medical" for a lower bunk because she was so heavy. It would have been impossible for her to get up on the a top bunk - especially in light of the manner in which one had to accomplish this feat. She proceeded to explain the procedure. First, it was necessary to get in a standing position on a folding chair, then climb onto a small wooden desk and from there you are able to pull yourself up onto the bunk. Does OSHA know about this? And why isn't the Bureau of Prisons, a government agency, held accountable to the same standards as private industry?

Lorrie fills me in on some of the rules. "Rule #1 and most important of all is DON'T MISS COUNT." "What's a count?", I ask. "Counts are held five times a day. The purpose is to be sure everyone is 'accounted' for. The most important count of the day is the one at 4:00 pm. It's the only count where every inmate must be in a standing position directly by their cubicle. The other count times are 10:00 pm, 2:00 am, 5:30 am, and 10:00 am. The other important matter is Inspection Day which is every Tuesday. That's the day the big wheels come around with their white gloves and check out our units. Though we're each responsible for our own cubicles, we all have to be out of our units all day while the inmate orderlies clean every nook and cranny."

"Well, I can't think about those things right now. I've been locked up in a small room for three days, but it seemed like forever. My main concern right now is to call home. No one has heard from me since Norm

165

dropped me off at the Administration Building on Friday. I know my family is worried. How do I make a phone call, Lor?" "

"You can't until you go to commissary; when you fill out your commissary sheet, you'll fill in how much credit you want applied toward phone calls each week, but first the counselor has to assign you a pin number. What day do you go to commissary?"

"I think I go on Wednesdays."

"Well you're allowed to make two phone calls when you first come in, so just go to Mr. Rush's office and let him know you want to call home".

"OK - well, I'm going to go do that now because I know my family is concerned that they haven't heard from me".

The counselor's office is on the first floor. Usually there is a line waiting to see him, but right now, the coast is clear. I knock on the door, wait for his nod (an absolute must) before opening the door, introduce myself and ask him if I may call home. He asks how I'm doing and what crime I committed. He seems fascinated as I briefly tell him the story. I learn he is Muslim. (Maybe he has a good handle on this family thing). He asks for the number I want to call, dials it and hands me the phone. He stays put as I have my conversation.

Mom answered and I filled her in on what had transpired after Norm left. She was, of course, shocked. She said she had called the prison over the weekend and was assured I "was doing fine". You mean they lie?? I then explained that I wouldn't be able to call again until I received my pin # and my money credited, which wouldn't be til the end of the week. I asked her to call Norm later and explain the situation. Since he is on the road most of the time, I knew I wouldn't be able to reach him. We said our good-byes and I returned upstairs.

Lorrie takes me on a tour of our floor while explaining that each floor is designed the same way. The three shower stalls, three toilets and three sinks are enclosed in the center of the floor, surrounded by 8 cubicles on two sides and 2 at each end for a total of 20 cubicles; 40 women per floor. i.e. 80 women a side (Seminole A/Seminole B) or 160 per building. There is another building called Cherokee A & B. Capacity is 320. When I got to camp, there were approximately 295-300. Before I was discharged, there were 350. Some of the 2-women cubes were transformed to 3-women cubes.

Items available from the stockroom at all times are writing tablets, sanitary pads, razors, (how about that!) soap, toothpaste and toothbrushes. The phone is located at the end of the hall and there is a sign-up sheet that hangs next to it. Each person can sign up for a 15 minute block of time. A note posted above the phone has a warning: Attention: All inmate telephone calls are monitored and tape recorded.

As we walk around, Lorrie introduces me. I notice that many of the women are working on crafts; mostly knitting and crocheting, but also cloth covered photo albums and frames, jewelry, painting t- shirts, homemade cards, and many other miscellaneous items. As time goes by, I am impressed by the number of women in one small camp who exhibit such tremendous talent.

Like a new kid on the block, I feel kind of strange, but it doesn't last long. The women are all friendly and make me feel accepted. It's almost 4:00 and everyone is migrating toward their cubicles. It's not until someone downstairs yells "THEY'RE COMING" that everyone scrambles to their feet, stand at attention outside their cubicle and become quiet - in fact, silent. Two guards come up the stairs; one goes to the left and one to the right. As they pass, they are counting to themselves. By the time they meet, they each have a 'count' of heads - which they hope match.

Now we wait for count to 'clear' and then we can go eat. It usually takes about 15 minutes for count to clear. If the numbers don't jive, the process has to be done all over. Today it clears. "Now it's time for chow", Lorrie says, "but we have to wait our turn." Important notices are all posted on the bulletin board right inside the front door which includes which unit goes to the food line first, the schedule for the use of washers and dryers (there are only two per unit), and the "call-out" sheet. The 'call out' means that you are being called to go to a specific place at a specific time i.e. for a medical exam, to see one of the education teachers, an appointment with the psychologist, etc. It was imperative to check the call-out sheet each morning.

The food in solitary confinement was not good at all so I wasn't expecting camp food to be any better. In fact, I was hopeful that I was going to be able to lose weight. The opposite occurred. The food, though certainly not low cal, was both filling and tasty. We had a good variety, large portions, and a salad bar and dessert at every meal. There were two serving times for each meal except for breakfast. Breakfast was served from 6:00 - 7:00 since work details began at 7:30. Lunch was at 10:00 and 11:30, dinner at 3:00 and 4:30. The lines were long, but who's in a hurry?

After dinner the first evening, I decided to take a tour of the grounds. As you stand outside and face the cafeteria, the doors for entering are on the right side of the building, and the exiting doors are on the left. As you exit the cafeteria and walk straight ahead, you pass the library, a few classrooms, a few offices, an aerobic room with a large screen TV called the large multipurpose room, another room with a pool table and a smaller TV called the small multipurpose room, and then you come to the track.

Within the circumference of the track is a basketball court, a softball field, racketball and handball. So this is why they call it Club Fed! I return to my 'room' and Lorrie is there reading one of her many romantic paperbacks. She had stacks of them. We were talking about our "crimes" when a call came over the loud speaker that mail call would be held at 6:00 in the visiting room for Seminole unit. Though I didn't expect to have any mail, I went along to see how mail call was handled and for something to do.

As you walk in the front door of the Administration Building (we called it the "ad-min" bldg.) from camp side, the visiting room is to the left and the "admin" offices are to the right. Mail call was usually held in the visiting room except when it was raining; on rainy days, it was held in front of our units. The visiting room could be more appropriately named an "all-purpose" room. It's about half the size of a basketball court with movable or portable seats which convert the room, in a moments notice, to a playhouse, a chapel, an athletic meeting, a Christmas skit, Black History programs, etc.

But what makes it so special are the two most important purposes it is used for - visitation on weekends and mail call every week night. Every evening at 6:00, it becomes the place where friends and family make their connections. There is no doubt at all that mail (besides visitation on week- ends) is the number one morale booster in prison, so few people ever miss mail call.

I always felt as though my mail was a "mini-visit" from the individual who was writing to me. The guards are instructed not to give mail to anyone other than the person to whom it is addressed, but a few of the more lenient ones do. So if someone couldn't make mail call for one reason or another, a friend could sometimes pick it up for them. The guard who distributes the mail sits at a desk in the front of the room. The mail bag is emptied onto the desk. He then proceeds to call out the names and as your name is called, you go and retrieve your mail from the officer. We had some good laughs over the mispronunciation of names. I often felt guilty about getting so much mail when there were many who didn't get any. Some of the women joked about the amount I received and asked if they could help open it.

It was quite a surprise when I received eight pieces of mail the first evening. Before leaving for Marianna, I had contacted my friends, Lynn Giddens and Penny Partridge, and gave them the address which Norm had been given when he called the prison for directions. Lynn and Penny had obviously spread the word quite quickly and the mail began to pour in.

At the end of the second week, I was called to Mr. Savid's office. He was the Unit Manager in charge of the day to day operation of the camp.

Mr. Savid was a very handsome light-skinned black man with beautiful green eyes. Though very attractive, he was also very arrogant (which seemed to go with the territory). He wanted to make me aware that my mail was being 'returned to sender' because of the large volume being sent to the incorrect address. "Then how come I've been getting it delivered to me for the past two weeks," I inquired.

He proceeded to explain that even though the camp was on the same property, the street address was only to be used for the maximum and medium security part of FCI (Federal Correctional Institute). The camp had a P.O. Box # and that was the address people were supposed to be using. So my mail was being stamped with "Addressee Unknown" and returned to the sender! Why hadn't I been given the new address sooner? How was I to know if I wasn't told? "Since all the mail gets sorted at the main building, including the mail picked up from the PO Box, why is it such a problem," I asked. "Well, you know, Sandy. Rules are rules."

After returning from mail call the first evening, another call came over the loud speaker. "All A & O's report to the Administration Building now!" "That's you," Lorrie said. "Every time you hear A & O", you have to go to the Administration building and an officer there will assign you a duty. A & O stands for Admitting and Orientation so new recruits are dubbed A & O's. There were only two others who came in the same day I did. New recruits were called upon to do odd jobs throughout the day, including trash duty every evening, until they were assigned a "full-time" job. Job assignments were usually within ten days to two weeks.

Orientation for new "recruits" was held every Wednesday from 9:00 to 4:00. It provided an overview of prison life - the rules, the punishment for breaking them; various programs available and eligibility for same; introduction of key staff members and their specific programs; etc. There are no fences at camp - only signs that say "OUT OF BOUNDS". We were informed that we could leave at any time, but the punishment for doing so was a minimum of five years in the "big house". The camp at Marianna was built in 1988 and had not had an escapee yet. I remember thinking that if I had been given 5 - 10 years, like many of the women, I may have been the first. Fence or no fence, it was still confinement.

About a week after I arrived, the mother of one of the women in Cherokee Unit passed away. It was a Friday evening when she received the call. Since it was a weekend, she was not able to get "authorization" for a pass until Monday! I recall being aghast, shocked and angry and thinking, "if that were my mother, I'd want to be on a plane within a few hours!". When she FINALLY did receive permission on Monday, she was required to pay the expenses of a guard to go along with her! If she couldn't afford to pay his way, too bad - then she couldn't attend her mother's funeral! The officer would remain by her side the entire time. Keep in mind, my friends, everyone in camp is a **NON-VIOLENT FIRST-TIME** offender. Is there any reason why an officer, in the city she would be traveling to, could not meet her at the plane and attend the funeral with her? Wouldn't that be more logical and make more sense?

This was just one of the many things that didn't make sense. We joked about the fact that if it was BOP policy, it wasn't supposed to make sense. One quickly came to understand that rules were made to show who was boss, not out of any sense of fairness.

60 Minutes Film Crew Visits Prison

I had been in prison about 12 days when 60 Minutes sent their film crew to get pictures of me in my new environment. Since the interview had been done in September, they were there to film the fact that I had been sentenced to prison and was now serving my time. The Public Relations prison personnel officer stayed with the crew and myself throughout the entire filming. At one point, one of the film crew asked if he could speak with me briefly and was told "No". He was informed that it was not part of the agreement. They were there to film - not to interview.

They filmed my cubicle every which way they could and were running out of angles. How many ways can you film a 6x9 room? I suggested they shoot the pictures of my grandchildren that were in frames on top of my locker. The prison PR man nixed the idea by saying "Do you really think that's a good idea? What if their friends in school see their pictures and start teasing them about their grandmother being in prison!" Ah, secrets again! I assured him that my grandchildren were aware of why their grandmother was in prison and that most of them had written reports about the subject of adoption reform. They could handle it.

Naturally, everyone was curious about what was going on and within a short period of time, word had spread about "one of their own" being featured on a major investigative show. Several of the women wanted to know how to get the 'ear' of 60 Minutes and though I didn't have any special connections, I did pass along the producer's name, address and phone number.

One day while I was in line at the cafeteria, Mr. Savid approached me and asked if I was wearing contacts. I said "yes". He then wanted to know the color of my eyes. I told him they are hazel, but my lenses are aqua. He then told me, "You'll have to send your color contacts home and get clear ones because you're not allowed to wear color contacts in here". I told him I didn't have any clear contacts, nor did I have glasses, and that I would be unable to see without them. Then I inquired as to what the problem was. He said the problem was that they could accidentally release the wrong person based upon eye color! I reminded him that "Numerous photographs have been taken with my aqua contacts so if I get clear ones, my eye color WILL be different!"

The discussion ended, but the battle raged on. I had very little saline solution left and saline wasn't carried on commissary. About six weeks before I was due to get out, I filled out the necessary forms in order to have it sent in. Mr. Savid said he would not approve it until I had clear contacts. Since there was no reasoning with him, I decided it was necessary to go over his head and filed a complaint with the camp administrator. It was approved.

All in all, it should have taken no more than a week for the saline to come in. R & D assured me they would notify me soon as it arrived. After the second week, I spoke with Mother to be sure she had sent it and she said she had. I checked with the office two more times.

Finally, the week before I left, I spoke to someone different and was told "Oh, yeah, it's been here for awhile, but the slip you need to sign hasn't come over from the main office!" I explained that I had been using old saline solution for the past month and a half and could someone get me special dispensation. She had me sign a piece of paper stating that I was accepting it. There is no way to know how long the solution was sitting in R & D, but I suspect about a month.

During the second week of camp, I was called to my counselor's office and informed that they didn't have a copy of my high school diploma in the file. My word, of course, was not sufficient. I would be given 30 days to have it sent in; otherwise I would be required to attend GED classes (at a cost of $2500 to my government). My diploma was surely stored somewhere at home, but I wasn't sure where and didn't want to have to ask my husband to search for it.

My small high school in Yeadon, Pennsylvania had since merged and became part of a regional district. I wondered how difficult it was going to be to get a copy sent in time. Since my sister was still living in the general area, I asked if she'd take care of it for me. One of her close friends, Rita, went to the school and made a personal request. The verification letter arrived the day of the deadline and stated, "This verifies that Sandra Kay Musser, date of birth, January 3, 1939, graduated from Yeadon High School June 14, 1956." I was spared the GED classes.

On Tuesday, November 23rd, two days before Thanksgiving, I fell getting down from my top bunk. It was about 6:15 in the morning so it was still dark. As I went to place my foot on the desk, it slipped and I fell straight to the floor. My back caught the corner of the desk and my right ring finger somehow got twisted. The noise, of course, woke Lorrie who yelled for someone to go to medical and obtain help. The lights went on and everyone had assembled to see what was happening. By now, I was lying on Lorrie's bunk moaning from the pain. My back hurt and my finger was throbbing.

In about 10 minutes, a Filipino nurse, who spoke little English, appeared. She asked where I was hurting, and I told her I had hit the small of my back on the desk as I fell, but that my finger seemed to be hurting the most. She then said "you walk to medical in 15 minutes and I examine you there". So 20 minutes later I shuffled up to the medical office, was examined and told I was fine! "If I'm fine, how come I hurt so much?" "You be ok - little bruising, that's all". "But why is my finger so swollen?" "Old injury", she replied. I did have a deformed nail on this particular finger, but I had never injured it per se. Since my finger was still throbbing so much I said, "Well I'd like to have an x-ray because my finger doesn't feel ok." "OK.", she said, "I make arrangements for you to have x-ray".

At 11:30 the same morning, I was called to Administration and told that the bus was there to take me to FCI for the x-ray. A woman from the Cherokee Unit was also going. She and another woman were moving a desk in preparation for our Tuesday inspection. The desk had slipped and fell on her foot and since she had slippers on, the weight of the desk smashed her toes. We were bussed over to the FCI building for x-rays. Since we were entering the "Big House", we had to go through a security check just to get to the x-ray room. It only took a few minutes for each of us to be x-rayed and we were told to check in with medical when we got back to camp. Medical said they'd let us know when our x-rays were back. I never heard anything though I checked with them periodically.

Because of the incident, I was given a seven day "reprieve" from work which I had just been assigned to a few days before. I was "the window washer" of the cafeteria and I had a partner; we washed the inside and outside of 72 window panes. The panes were quite large, so it wasn't a difficult task. Our compensation was .12 cents a hour.

The day after my fall, I attended a pre-scheduled meeting with the "Team". It's called a Team Meeting because you meet with the Unit Manager, the Counselor and the Educational Director. The purpose of the Team Meeting is to discuss your individual educational goals, whether you will be assigned to a halfway house or home confinement upon release, your release date, etc. At the end of the meeting, I was asked if I had any questions or any particular problems. Since my finger was now purple, I showed it to them and explained what had happened. My question was in the form of a request - could I have a lower bunk as

I found it difficult getting on a chair and then onto a desk in order to get into the bunk. The Unit Manager asked me how old I was. I responded that I would be 55 within six weeks. He said "Well, we don't have any lower bunks available right now, but if one becomes available, I'll let you know." There were, in fact, two lower bunks available on our floor. Was I going to challenge him or call his bluff?? Not wanting to end up back in isolation, I didn't.

The following day was Thanksgiving. My husband had driven up to Marianna on Wednesday evening, so he could be at the prison when the visiting doors opened. Visiting hours were Saturday, Sunday and holidays from 8:15 to am to 3:15 pm. He visited on Thanksgiving Day and then came back Saturday and Sunday to visit. He had to spend Friday alone since it was not a visiting day! After seeing my swollen finger on Thursday, and hearing what occurred at Team, he returned on Friday to talk to one of the staff members about a lower bunk.

He had no sooner left the building when I was called to Administration and told I was moving to a lower bunk on the first floor. I asked if I could "check it out" (only because I couldn't understand why they weren't keeping me on the same floor). The female officer shouted "CHECK IT OUT? WHAT DO YOU MEAN - CHECK IT OUT? WHERE DO YOU THINK YOU ARE - HOTEL HILTON? YOUR HUSBAND WANTS YOU IN A LOWER BUNK AND YOU'VE BEEN ASSIGNED A LOWER BUNK. NOW GET YOUR THINGS AND MOVE THEM!" "Yes Ma'am. Thank you, Ma'am!"

I gathered up my belongings and moved to the first floor. I was now in a 3-women room - the quarters were quite a bit more cramped, but at least I didn't have to perform gymnastics to get into bed. My new roommates were both young black women. Cassie was terrific. Knowing I was "new" to prison life, she went out of her way to make me feel comfortable.

Catie and I didn't have much of an opportunity to get to know each other. She worked the midnight shift at the Power House and the first evening I was in her room, she received a "shot" at work. A "shot" meant she got herself in trouble and was being punished for it. Apparently one of the furnaces was filled with soot and needed cleaning. She was told to get inside and clean it out, but she protested by explaining that she had asthma and the soot would get into her lungs and cause her to have an attack. The officer in charge didn't want to hear any excuses and gave her 30 days in segregation!

Since I had been unable to handle 3 days in "segregation" (a new term being used instead of solitary confinement), I was horrified to hear what happened. How could anyone survive 30 days? When she returned to camp, she was assigned a new room.

173

Her bed wasn't empty very long; within two days it was filled. Mr. Russ, the kindest officer in the camp, called me to the Admin Building and said he was assigning a new "recruit" to my room - would I be her "big sister" and show her around?

Ann was six years younger than me, married, with two sons. She, too, had four months to serve. We spent a lot of time walking the track together and talking about our future plans. Ann was more faithful than I when it came to walking. In fact, she was walking 7-10 miles a day in any kind of weather. I was doing 3-4 until the temperature began to drop! I was in awe of her determination and steadfastness. She was a terrific roommate and had a wonderful gift for crocheting which she passed onto me. She also became one of the cooks in the kitchen, so I always had an inside track as to what we were having for lunch and dinner.

Though we had become very close, we have not been in touch since we've been out of prison. One of the first rules discussed in orientation is that you may not associate in any way with an "ex-felon" until your probation is complete. If you do, you are "breaking probation" and could be in jeopardy of being sent back to prison. I think it's called the "fear tactic" and that's what a police state is all about.

The women in the cubicles on both sides of us were terrific On one side was Ellie and Shelly. Every night a few others joined them and they played cards til 10:30, which was lights-out time. The wild conversations kept Ann and I laughing. They were great fun to be around.

After two weeks following my fall, I still had not heard anything about my the x- rays. In the meantime, my finger was still swollen and throbbing. I checked with medical every few days, but they always said they were still waiting for them. Again my husband intervened after I had complained to him on the phone about the lack of medical treatment. The next day, I was called to medical and a young, snippy medical clerk said to me "Who do you think you are to have a legislator call here and claim that you've had no treatment on your finger. Just look at this chart!" There before my very eyes was a nicely filled out chart of all the times I had supposedly been seen! II was shocked, but I quickly realized that this was a game I could not win. He who has the power has the control. I said "You know and I know that I'm in a no-win situation. May I go now?" End of story.

Though the prison discouraged phone calls to the media, Cathy Olian, Producer of 60 Minutes, had given me her home phone number. Since I was allowed to list 20 family and friends, I included hers. I had only been in prison less than a month when I made the now infamous call to Cathy in which I told her, in no uncertain terms, that I would

174

probably be getting out of the adoption reform movement; that if being in prison was to teach me a lesson, I had learned mine! At the time of my call, I was feeling completely drained and emotionally depressed. I couldn't seem to shake the solitary confinement experience and there were nights when I would awake in a cold sweat from nightmares of suffocation. The problem of my contacts, my fall from the bunk bed, the 'trumped-up' medical report, the hassle of getting my diploma in on time, etc. had all converged at once and really had me down.

In retrospect, those problems now seem minor, but they loomed heavy as I lived them day to day. I was also feeling empathetic toward the women I had met. So many of them were there for ridiculous charges and I was angry at the bill of goods that was being sold to the American people concerning "criminals" - especially now that I was considered one of them! I had been blind, until now, to what is really happening in my own country and feeling totally helpless to do anything about it.

I remember thinking that I never, ever wanted to hear the word adoption mentioned again. I emphasized it over and over to Pat, Mom and Norm each time I spoke to them on the phone. Norm would try to tell me about an adoption show, and I'd cut him off and tell him I wasn't interested. At one point, he ignored what I said and I raised by voice and said "I AM NOT INTERESTED IN HEARING ANYTHING ABOUT ADOPTION. DO YOU UNDERSTAND? I DON'T REALLY GIVE A DAMN!" That feeling remained for the entire term of my imprisonment and for a brief period after coming home.

The weekend following Thanksgiving, my Mother and sister came to visit. Since it was such a long drive, they would leave home early Friday evening, rent a motel and stay until 1:00 or 2:00 Sunday afternoon. Since there was a TV in the visiting room, and mom is such an avid football fan, she was able to keep up with the games - especially the Super Bowl. There were also snack and soda machines, but we were dependent upon our family for change. Though we were allowed to "buy" change on commissary, we were not allowed to take it into the visiting room. You figure it out - I've tried and can't!

Before entering the visiting room, we (the inmates) had to enter a small room to be 'frisked'. My daughter-in-law had just sent me pictures of my grandchildren (her son was only 14 months when the twins were born). Excited about showing them to my family, I took them with me. I had them in my hand as I entered the little "frisking" room. What a shock to learn that I was not allowed to take two little pictures of my grandchildren into the visiting room with me! We could take nothing in and we could take nothing out! Security, you know.

In spite of all the restrictions, looking forward to each weekend made the time go by more quickly and getting to see my family helped to maintain my resolve. The family all took turns coming to see me which meant that I had visitors every weekend, except one. That particular weekend, the end of January, my appeal was being heard and I wanted Norm to be at the hearing that was being held in Cincinnati.

The second weekend in December, my two daughters came to visit. Linda lives on the west coast of Florida and Sherri on the east so Linda drove three hours across the state from West Palm to Pt. Charlotte. Because they were both working and raising families, they seldom had time to get together. This afforded them the opportunity and they always came in with lots of funny stories about their trips. The first time they drove up, they were so busy talking that they drove 100 miles out of their way! They fell in love with the town of Marianna. It's a small, quaint town with older homes - similar to the one where they grew up. And because it's in the northern part of our state, there are "real" trees as opposed to Palm trees.

Pat and Jerry stopped for a visit the week before Christmas, as they traveled north to see their family over the holiday. Pat had continued to keep the office operating while I was "away". Other visitors included my friend, Carol, from Michigan, and her husband. Also an active birthmother from Illinois stopped to visit as she was passing through the state.

The visiting room, though generally not crowded, always had children running around. It was great to see them romping and playing as they climbed on their moms, their aunts, their grandmas, or their sisters. There was also a small playroom provided for them with reading books and coloring books. Many women never had any visitors at all and I felt very sad for them. It made me realize how fortunate I was.

Christmas day was, of course, packed with visitors and Santa Clause came to visit. Big girls and little girls alike had their picture taken with Santa. Our Christmas meal was Roast Duck and, turned out to be one of the two worst meals I had. The other one was "Desert Storm" meatballs.

A couple weeks before Christmas, everyone got involved in the holiday spirit and we began to decorate our units. There were a lot of trees on the property so we painted leaves and put holly branches and pine cones across dividing walls on top of our cubicles. The artistic women (and there were several) drew Santa and his sleigh with all his reindeer, painted them, cut them out and taped them to the cinder block walls. We taped Christmas cards to the wall in the shape of a Christmas tree. It looked great. There was a warm and cozy feeling as we worked together to make our quarters look as good as possible under the circumstances.

Inspection Day arrived and it all came tumbling down! The bosses would not allow the decorations to remain. They should arrest and hang the big mahoffs for murdering the Christmas spirit! Such a shame with no real rhyme nor reason - just because they said so! Naturally we were disgruntled and morale was way down. Ladies and gentlemen, I submit to you that this kind of inane decision-making on the part of the "decision-makers" is about one thing - and that is control!

My sister, Betty Ann and her husband, came to visit the first weekend in January which was my 55th birthday. I had already spent Norm's birthday, Thanksgiving, and Christmas in prison; before I was released, two of my grandchildren had birthdays and my mother celebrated her 81st birthday one month before my release.

The 60 Minutes Show finally aired on January 2, 1994, the day before my birthday. We had been waiting for it so long that the excitement had lost its lustre, but I was still quite nervous. The TV rooms in both buildings were packed as never before. One of my friends put my name on a folding chair and plopped it right in the middle of the first row. Air time arrived - more waiting, since ours was the second segment! The women were so supportive. They could see how nervous I was and had only nice things to say. When they played the tape of me and Mr. Investigator, they moaned and groaned.

I felt very disappointed and letdown over the 'final product'. I'm not even sure why except I had hoped it would be positive. There were two specific parts that made me very angry; the first was the connotation of the phrase "she hired an accomplice" and the other was the way they cut off my sentence on the "setup" tape. Mr. Flavin had asked the question "Is this legal?" and my complete response was "I don't know if it's legal, **but sealed records aren't legal!**" All the audience got to hear was "I don't know if it's legal." That seems to me to be unfair reporting.

Lesley made a comment at the end of the show. She said I had contacted their station a month before the show aired and informed them that I was feeling depressed. "She said she may withdraw from the adoption reform movement altogether" Lesley said. The comment brought shock waves to many in the adoption reform movement. Pat said our office was flooded with calls as people questioned whether I had actually made the remark and, if so, I should reconsider. They told Pat they could not believe I could walk away since we had come so far. I DID make the comment. One adoptee apparently saw the picture clearly as she wrote:

"If you discontinue your search methods, my hopes are dead. How can I be supportive of you to continue your successful searches, when I don't have the guts to do what you have done? I feel like I am saying, 'Go for it Sandy. Break the law and risk more jail time so all of us adopted people can find our families.' How incredibly selfish is that?!"

177

The next month was Black History Month and the committee had various programs and plays going on throughout the entire month. I considered it a great learning experience and attended each one of them. The talent and initiative that went into the programs was astounding.

A 'Typical' Day in Camp

Most of the people who wrote to me wanted to know what a typical day in prison was like. It can best be described as a "city within a city". By its very nature, it is self-contained and operates like any small municipality (i.e. with the inmates as the employees of the city). It has its own power plant, construction, electrical and plumbing departments, maintenance and landscaping crews, educational and recreational departments, a medical staff, a library and a store known as the "commissary". Military jargon is commonplace.

The jobs are performed by the inmates who work for these various departments, while prison superintendents and staff oversee the work of the inmates. Right before I arrived at camp, the inmates on the construction crew had just finished building a $3 million Training Center for the BOP staff, officers and their families. Since some of the departments operate three shifts, a large prison staff is necessary to keep everything functioning. In addition, there is a psychologist and chaplain who can be seen by appointment and who sponsor diverse support groups on an ongoing basis. Drug classes are provided and mandatory for drug offenders. If there is something you didn't know about drugs when you came in, this class provides you with the knowledge.

Everything must be purchased from the commissary which provides the BOP with millions of dollars of revenue each year. Since everything I had brought with me was sent home, I was forced to purchase the necessary items from the commissary. It's the same reason that we were not allowed to receive anything in the mail, except paperback books. Paperback books are not 'yet' a commissary item (though I 'spect they'll soon be). Even Christmas presents may not be sent - though you can send money which can then be spent at the "company" store.

Non-denominational church services were, of course, optional and were held on Sunday evenings. The choir was primarily black and the music was always outstanding. The recreation department handles crafts, movies, scheduling of sports, etc.

Every morning, we were awakened at 6:00 am by a loud speaker. "Time to rise and shine ladies!" They called us ladies - maybe hoping we would act like one? Breakfast was served between 6:00 and 7:00 and work began at 7:30. There were many different types of jobs, and while you could put in a request for a certain job, you had to take what you were assigned.

UNICOR - The Federal Prison Industry

UNICOR is the federal prison industry (or the "company") which operates in every prison. Each UNICOR has 'specialty contracts'. In Pete Earley's book entitled *The Hot House,* he states that the inmates in Leavenworth prison ALONE produced $27 million worth of goods in 1986 netting the BOP $5 million. That's just ONE prison and that was 8 years ago! It is common knowledge that the BOP plans to double the number of prisons. The United States puts more people in prison than any other country. It has been said that the day is not far off that America will have as many people inside prison as outside of prison. For many reasons, I believe America is creating slave labor camps; the following may help to explain how they're going about accomplishing it.

The women in our camp typed U.S. Patents all day long for UNICOR. Because the pay scale started at .29 cents an hour (as opposed to .12 cents for other jobs), it was considered to be one of the more "prestigious" jobs. You could work your way up to $1.15 an hour after five years of "service"! In order to keep this illustrious job, you must maintain a certain number of keystrokes per day!

Most of the men's contracts are primarily building furniture, welding, etc. for government offices and military installations. i.e. one government bureaucracy (Bureau of Prisons) working for another government bureaucracy (U.S. Military) at slave labor costs. The other jobs were of a more menial nature, but since monotony in prison is a major problem, it does help pass the time.

As part of our orientation, we were given a tour of the huge two-story UNICOR building. When you first walk into the building, you see rows and rows of computers with women sitting at the keyboards busily performing their data entry jobs. An eerie chill ran up and down my spine. The book *The Handmaiden's Tale* popped into my mind. The women who choose to work for UNICOR usually do so because of the higher pay-scale and the need to send money home to help support their families.

If you're a "short-timer", like I was, you cannot get a job working at UNICOR. They don't want to take the time to train you, only to have you leave in a few months. Since money has never been very important to me and since I did not have a family to support, I would not have chosen to sit in front of a computer all day and work for the government for .29 cents an hour.

I spoke with several women in camp who shared a theory with me and asked me to pass it on. The theory is basically this: Under our

179

capitalistic system, punishment under our law is inherently unjust and is not really designed to control crime for the good of society, but rather to keep the population in subjugation. They perceive imprisonment less as a punishment for convicted offenders and more as a way to control surplus labor. Imprisonment rates apparently climb during times of recession and high unemployment. By imprisoning people for minor infractions, they can reduce the unemployment pay and put them to work for UNICOR (prison industry) at slave labor wages. The primary purpose for obtaining **frivolous** arrests is repression while the long-term propensity of the legal system is to reflect and protect the interest of the capitalist class and oppress the working class. This is simply one theory. Having "been there", it makes sense.

The women I met in Marianna Camp were all nice, average people. I never once experienced any fear from other inmates. I encountered a general caring attitude for one another and a unique bond exists among the women. The majority are middle and lower class who are constantly struggling to make ends meet. None of them, of course, were well-to-do. As we all know, people who are well-to-do seldom go to prison. Only on rare occasions do the elite serve any time.

While society generally believes there is a lot of homosexuality in prison, it was practically nonexistent in our small camp. By the same token, deep bonds of friendship do occur when you are living in such close quarters. I became good friends with two women, in particular, who were serving long sentences for drug conspiracy. One had been setup by a federal agent and has served four years of a 10 year sentence. I think about these women on a daily basis.

Because of the close living quarters, I acquired a special caring for women of color and nationality. Of the camp population during my confinement, there were approximately 50% black, 25% Hispanic and 25% white. The age range was 19 to 80. The longest sentence was 15 years; the shortest, a month; the average was 7 years and that was for low-level drug offenders. Of the 50,000 women in prison today, 80% of them are mothers

A very important fact that I had not understood before is that when you are committed to a federal prison, you are required to serve 85% of your time (unless your sentence is under a year). In state prisons, only 15% is actually required and, due to overcrowding in **state** prisons, rapists and murderers can serve less time than a woman selling marijuana or embezzling to feed her kids! For the sake of emphasis, let me repeat it. **Someone who commits rape and murder will serve less time than someone who distributes pot or embezzles.** This insane imbalance has been created out of fear - the government sold us a bill of goods when they convinced society (through the media) that drugs are the primary problem. The "War on Drugs" takes precedence over violent acts of murder and rape. This is insanity and has GOT to be turned around.

Of the people in prison today, 62% are casualties of this war on drugs. I was astonished to learn that most of them are serving time for conspiracy to distribute marijuana! Imagine! In our small camp alone, there were young women with small children serving 5 to 10 years for "conspiracy" because their husbands or boyfriends were selling pot. The theory is that as long as they are living in the same household - they must have known what they were doing, and if they know, they should turn them in.

Personally, I don't smoke marijuana , but I know that 25 to 30 years ago there was quite a bit of discussion about legalizing it. Millions of lives have been lost and millions of others adversely affected by society's 'acceptable' drug known as alcohol; the weed called marijuana holds no such claim. But it's more profitable to keep it illegal. If it were legalized, the minimum security prisons and practically all of the camps would have to shut down. When you consider that two-thirds of the prison budgets go for salaries, then you begin to understand the need to keep them filled.

U.S. Surgeon General Joycelyn Elders knows whereof she speaks, but her proposal that we decriminalize drugs will never fly because, like adoption, it's much too profitable for those in power - did you ever wonder what they do with all the drugs they confiscate? Though many do not choose to believe it, it is the government who keeps the flow of illegal drugs going, just as it does with the trafficking of babies and children.

A perfect example is a former aide to President Reagen. He was 'caught' smuggling drugs into the country in a big time way. He turned in 22 people in "his organization" and walked, having never served one single day in prison. In fact, he is still living the life-style of the rich and famous. Possibly his real job was/is confidential informant, assisting in making arrests in order to keep the justice system functioning. Likewise, a 72 year old farmer, featured on Inside Edition, is spending time in prison on a ludicrous charge. The bank foreclosed on his farm and he sold some hogs to get some money to feed his family. The bank said he had no right to do that (since they owned them as part of the foreclosure) and prosecuted him! We are really living in a sick society when you consider just these two cases alone. What has happened to our Justice System? It has gone mad! Not only is it blind, but it is also deaf and dumb! Of course, those who are drawing large salaries from the "Justice System", at taxpayers expense, will probably not agree.

181

Something has to change, but I fear the ongoing struggle between our government and its people will continue to exist; primarily because we are in the process of creating a 'police' state environment. A quote from a prison guard may help to explain what I mean. He said "In our world, there are only two sides: them and us, and there are a bunch more of them than us." My question is 'who is them and who is us'? If you work for the government as he does, then you are 'us', but if you think that many people who work for the government are some of the biggest thieves and lawbreakers, (and many think so), then 'us' becomes 'them'.

To expound upon this theory further - our police agencies within the justice system, which include the FBI, DEA, AFT, and CIA, have confidential informants all over the country who get paid just to "whistle-blow" on others. The scary part is that Big Brother is all around and the sad part is that it's causing the breakup of many families. Family members are going to prison simply because they refuse to testify against their own family members. The "conspiracy" charge is like a net that drags in anyone within reach.

To try to explain it in simple terms, what the government is saying is this:

1) If you know your brother has his hand in the cookie jar and you don't tell me, and I find out and think you knew, then you're going to be punished.

2) By the same token, if you get your hand caught in the cookie jar, but can convince me that your brother talked you into it - it was really his idea - then I'll reward you. I'll punish your brother and you can go out and play.

3) If I catch you in the act, but you are willing to tattle on your brother and say he did the same thing you did, even if he didn't, I'll still punish him and let you go out to play because you "cooperated."

To illustrate further using my own case - my co-defendent admitted to doing what she was accused of doing, but in order to escape punishment, the government needed her to "cooperate" by testifying against me. She also had to supply them with names of other "perpetrators". I did not commit the crime I was accused of which was conspiracy (knowing what she was doing and how she was doing it). But on the stand, when specifically asked if I knew what she was doing, she replied "A lot of times I would call Sandy after a search that just wasn't working out and I would say, 'Sandy, I've run it upside down, inside out, sideways'. And she would know exactly what I was talking about." That was it! By inferring that I must have known, she was then free to go out and 'play' and go about her business as usual. I went to prison and served time and am no longer permitted to continue my work.

If none of this makes sense to you, you've just joined thousands of others who are confused by the actions of our Justice System who have created, then used and abused the plea agreement and plea bargaining system to further their own agendas. i.e. Why arrest one major kingpin when you can arrest 50 people who work for him. Imagine how many arrests a major **government** kingpin can supply to keep the system functioning.

The government even establishes their own investigative companies as part of their 'sting' operations in order to entrap organizations like ours, or other investigative companies, by offering to be of "assistance". When you fall into their trap, you are well ensnared. It's like having your best friend turn on you. You just don't expect your own government to "play head games", but that's what the game of espionage is all about. It's being played out every day in our good ole U.S.A. against our own citizens. The police branches of the Justice System have been given carte blanche to do as they please with little or no accountability. And then we wonder why we've got problems in this country.

As an article written in Issue #29 of **Full Disclosure** states

"The government arrested and convicted twenty-three private investigators and information brokers around the country for obtaining confidential information from the government. Its records are actually millions and millions of files compiled on each and every one of us in America. Stored in their facilities, the government protects these records judiciously. But wait a minute...isn't the government" of the people and by the people" made to serve our needs? This may be a very superficial statement in today's society but the founders of the Constitution really believed in this statement.

Now with the cold war over, numerous FBI agents are sitting around with nothing to do. The government, attempting to be efficient, has apparently turned these unproductive agents loose on U.S. citizens. In the latest governmental escapade to protect "their" records, the government has arrested a nonprofessional citizen. On March 27, 1993, Sandy Musser, 54, an adoption--reunion specialist from Cape Coral, FL was enjoying a cup of coffee and reading her local newspapers when she read about her own indictment. It was one of the FBI's formatted news releases that they are infamous for. ... One can only wonder who Big Brother will attack next? Have you ever wondered what those excess FBI agents are doing? Will we be attacked in our own homes for using computers next?"

The second most common crime for women is embezzlement or a

form of it. To share a little humorous story - right before I left prison, a 58 year old woman with a strong southern accent came into camp. She had us all in stitches as she told her story. When asked what she had done, she replied in her slow southern drawl, "Weelll, I was just cashing checks. They was Momma's checks. Me and Momma lived together for many years and we had a checking account together. Social Security kept sending Momma's checks and I just kept depositing them for her! Problem was - Momma's been dead for 12 years!" "Well, was it worth it?", someone asked. "I have to serve 10 months, but I collected checks for 12 years!" We all wondered why the social security employee who was sending her the checks wasn't arrested!

A young woman, who became a good friend, had embezzled thousands of dollars from the bank where she was employed. Because of my inquisitive mind, I always asked a lot of questions. "What were you thinking?", I asked. "To tell you the truth, I was just trying to keep up with the Joneses. My husband didn't make much money and all my friends were buying new homes and new cars; I just wanted to keep up. It was really stupid." And now her 8 year old son is without his mother.

There were some pretty ridiculous charges. One was a young 23 year old who had a job as a telephone solicitor selling water purifiers. She said they came into her place of employment like gangbusters and told her they were all being arrested. She said "I thought it was a joke. I had boots on that day and I said 'Oh, I'm shaking in my boots'". They were accused of operating a scam. The owner claimed his employees knew what was going on and they all went down!? The employees got a year and, of course, the owner got off with a lighter sentence.

Again and again, I wonder - how many of these companies are established by our own police agencies in order to keep the flow of arrests going. I suspect quite a few!

The other most absurd charge was a young girl who was attempting to get a car loan. She exaggerated her income on the bank application; the bank then called her place of employment, found out she did not make the income she stated, and they prosecuted her.

While it is possible to get a college education in prison, you are responsible to pay for your classes (or credits) and you must be serving at least a year to warrant it. I was excited to learn that a computer class offering Word Perfect was available. It was a program I wasn't familiar with, but one which the business community seemed to be requiring. The class turned out to be a complete farce. I signed up for the class within a week of arriving in prison, but was told the classes were full. What I couldn't understand was that every time I passed the computer room, it was either empty or only a few computers were in use. I inquired a few more times (believing that the squeaky wheel gets the oil), but was told my name hadn't yet come up.

Finally, a month before I was due to be released, I got assigned to the computer class. An inmate, who was the "teacher's assistant" was available to offer help, but she quit only a few days after I was assigned. She said that, aside from having total responsibility while the teacher was chitchatting with friends, she was also treated poorly and not appreciated for the amount of work she was doing. She came to the conclusion that .12 cents an hour wasn't worth it while the teacher was drawing $25,000!

It didn't take me long to understand exactly what she meant. The teacher was seldom available to offer assistance and the few times she was, she seemed annoyed at being interrupted. It explained why most of the computers remained empty day in and day out. Though people had signed up for the class, they were not able to get the help they needed. Other women complained of the same problem and brought it up at the monthly "town meeting". We were reminded that it is setup to be a 'self-taught' class. Then why have a teacher on the payroll for teaching a computer class she's not teaching?? The complaints only fell on deaf ears. On several occasions, "visitors" came by to visit the facilities. Of course, when they are shown a roomful of computers, it looks very impressive but, in actuality, is a farce.

The "town meeting" is held once a month and is directed by the Unit Manager. It was my understanding that its' purpose was to provide interaction between the BOP staff and inmates, as well as to keep the inmates informed of updated policy changes and/or corrective measures that need to be made. In reality, only the latter is applicable and no real interaction takes place.

The following article, written in satire, emphasizes succinctly how the government has taken the CONSPIRACY charge and made a mockery of it. Many arrests can be made based simply upon this new catch-all "conspiracy" charge. Every single day, innocent people in our country are being convicted for who they know, what they know or **are supposed to know if they don't know**! If you happen to be at the wrong place at the wrong time, you are considered just as guilty as the person "caught in the act" and you will serve time for something you did not do.

This article written by James Johnson of Sandstone, MN is entitled:

The Latest American Phenomenon

"Yes friends and neighbors, step right up and get your very own Grand Jury Indictment today. For this you could receive an extended prison term

185

in a Federal Prison at taxpayers expense. Yes you, too, can participate in America's Fastest Growing Taxpayer Mugging.

It's easy. If you're a first time, non-violent, victimless offender, you could be eligible for a fun-filled term of at least five years. If you're interested in an extended term, try a conspiracy indictment and conviction. Under the guise of conspiracy, you don't even have to commit a crime. All you have to do is talk about it, and if you're real smart and make sure that you talk about it on tape, you could be the lucky recipient of 10 or more taxpayer supported years in one of our approximately 67 beautiful Federal Facilities in an area of our choosing, with more Facilities coming soon!

Even though you've worked all your life to support your family, pay your taxes, and have a meaningful life, you will not be excluded from this chance of a lifetime. Think about it - you can leave your worries behind. The taxpayers love picking up the tab for your family responsibilities.

Your new conviction will set you up for the good life. Within two weeks after your arrival at one of our ultra modern facilities you will be placed in one of the many myopic job positions available, and if you do 15 minutes of productive work a day, you had a busy day. Yes folks, this system is designed to put stability in your life, and teach you how not to function in society.

Along with your new job, you will receive taxpayer paid benefits. First, you'll have 3 hot's and a cot, medical attention usually within 3 days after an injury, censored mail, disrespectful and degrading treatment daily and plenty of mental anguish to ensure that you'll probably never be yourself again.

Finally, as an added extra bonus, you'll escape from the violence and violent people on the street. Yes, that's right. You'll be able to enjoy a safe and secure existence around the non-violent people that are here.

And just think, all of this is prepaid by our hard working taxpayers. Only in America could this kind of logic be so successful.

Yes folks, I highly recommend the new overcrowded Federal Prison System - it's a nightmare come true. After careful consideration and the undying help of DEA agents, the conspiracy plan was chosen by them for me. My conspiracy was created by the DEA. They're a great bunch of guys who are more than *willing* to help you commit your crime in any way they can. Why without their help I never would have made it here. But thanks to them, and a cruel Federal Prosecutor, who fortunately for me rejected the facts of my case, I qualified.

Yes folks, under the conspiracy plan chosen for me, I became a first time, non-violent, non-drug, moneyless, victimless offender. With this, I became one of the lucky ones that received an excessive and unwarranted 14 year taxpayer supported Federal Sentence, and was placed a mere 1600 miles away from my wife and 7 children. Just think, my unnecessary stay in a Federal Institution will only cost the taxpayers a paltry One Million *dollars after including the costs of investigation, prosecution, incarceration and welfare for my family. A deal at twice the price.*

So don't hesitate, get that indictment today and join the 80,000 plus inmates whose life and families have been destroyed in The Latest American Phenomenon and try a Mandatory Minimum Sentence in a Federal Prison. You owe it to yourself, but you'll have to hurry, bed space is very limited.

For detailed information call your local DEA office. There's one near you."

The following poem was written by the son of my good friends, Judy and Dave Taylor. It speaks to the corruption of power that seems to exist in our country.

That Which Makes All Around Me Evil

...To have the power.
And not only to have
But to want it, and need it,
To crave and desire it,
To roll in it like a dog
In dirt and stick to it.
And to be proud of the foulness
That emanates.

And to use it,
Like a tool,
And not only use...
But abuse, misuse, and distort it,
Twist it, turn it,
Shape it and smith it
And wield it like a weapon,
Not against equals carrying
A similar arsenal,
But upon the weak,
And defenseless.
The powerless...
The People...

By Derek Taylor

These were taken 11/5/93, the day I entered prison. Friends Penny Partridge, Founder of Adoption Forum; Jon Ryan, Founder of National Org. of Birthfathers, his son, Jeffrey, and Candy Thorsen, Founder of Mother/Child Reunion, met me at the prison gate.

This is a picture of the Federal Prison Camp in Marianna, FL, that I called 'home' for four months.

MINI-VISITS BY MAIL

I know I've said this many times throughout the book, but I can't emphasize it enough. The cards and letters I received while in prison were the basis of my survival and ongoing recovery. I considered them "mini-visits." I've saved them all and still read them from time to time.

In the beginning, there was some confusion about the correct address. My husband had called the prison to get directions and the address he was given was the same address I had passed on to a few close friends; they, in turn, spread the address around to others.

After the second week, I was called into the administration office and told that many of my letters were being returned to sender because of an "incorrect" address. Though I had received the mail addressed to the street address for the first 10 days or so, the rest were being returned to the sender marked "addressee unknown - not at this address!" In spite of the address problem, I still received an average of 20 to 30 letters a day.

Many people responded to the 60 Minutes program and especially to Lesley Stahl's comment at the end of the show. I came to think of these letters as "mini-visits" because it usually took me an entire evening to read them. The depth of concern, caring and frustration expressed by my family, friends, and acquaintances was overwhelming, astounding, and deeply appreciated. Sue, Jane and Carol, adoptive parents from Adoptive Parents for Open Records in NJ wrote me regularly and sent lots of reading material. And it was an adoptive mother (of an adoptee whose search we had done) who made the largest contribution to the defense fund.

Mindy, an adoptee from IN and my good friend, Sandi, from NJ, as well as my brother, sent me a card every single week. Many others wrote on a regular basis. A most touching note came from an adoptee in New

England who said she fasted on Thanksgiving Day because of my imprisonment. One of my daughters did likewise. Another adoptee, who we completed a search for, and is now a good friend, sent notes to her family and friends and asked them to drop me a post card. They did! All of sudden, I received a batch of postcards wishing me well.

Several people tried to send gifts, but since gifts were not permitted, they were returned to the sender. I then received a form showing that a necklace (for instance) had come in, was being returned, and who it was being returned to. Many people tried to send stamps knowing that I responded to all my mail, but they were not permitted either. One person wrote a four or five page letter and stuck the tip of six stamps to the top of the last page, so occasionally they would slip through. They either got through unnoticed or maybe an officer, with a heart ,decided to let them through. Self-addressed stamped envelopes are OK, so when writing to someone in prison, be sure to enclose one.

Funds that were sent in went directly into your individual account and you never saw it. In order to let you know that monies had been received and deposited, the back of the mailing envelope got stamped with the amount and date it was received. Though all the mail is opened and 'censored', the volume is such that most of the mail is not read word for word. Their main concern is making sure there is no "contraband" coming in. i.e. smuggled goods!

These are just a few excerpts, chosen completely at random, from the hundreds of letters I received. Though I wish I could include all the letters, that would take another book. These few excerpts will provide you with a glimpse of the outpouring of love, kindness, and dynamic thoughts I received day in and day out from around the country. They were my primary source of strength. For the sake of protection, only initials are being used.

●●●●●●●●●●●

"I felt sad and disappointed when 60 Minutes ended the segment on you by saying you had called them and were depressed and rethinking your cause. Selfishly I was sad because I've always had in the back of my mind that if I decide to spend money, your foundation would be successful in finding my mother. If you discontinue your search methods, my hopes are dead. How can I be supportive of you to continue your successful searches, when I don't have the guts to do what you have done? I feel like I am saying, 'Go for it Sandy. Break the law and risk more jail time so all of us adopted people can find our families.' How incredibly selfish is that?!" J.P./FL

●●●●●●●●●●●

"I viewed 60 Minutes this evening. I was both saddened, depressed and angry to learn what has happened to you. I know you are not guilty.

Our country's laws are archaic when it comes to adoption. I want you to know that I applaud and respect the work you have done in reuniting families throughout the years. The only thing that hurts me is that your dedication to the cause must be wavering. Hopefully, in time, you will throw the depression aside and continue on with your work. You're a wonderful, compassionate, knowledgeable, giving woman! It would be a travesty if you remove yourself from something that brings so much fulfillment, peace, love to many. R.S./NY

• • • • • • • • • • •

"I hope this letter finds you well and in good spirits. I have wanted to write you so many times, but never had the right words to say. I wish there was something I could do to make the time pass quickly, but be brave and hang in there. When you look back at this experience someday, you'll wonder how you did it. I have faith in you and I know with God's help and all our prayers, you'll do fine. There's an old saying someone told me - "And this too will pass". L.K./FL

• • • • • • • • • • •

"I just learned of the witch-hunt against you at an AIM meeting. I am a birthmother who reconnected with my daughter 3 years ago. What I want to say to you is thanks for being who you are ... a courageous, clear thinking, honorable woman. You can gauge the importance of your impact on the strength of the backlash from the patriarchal system - which I understand was beyond reason - against you. In other words... you're doing a great job.

Keep up the good work and be proud, Sandy. P.C./MI

• • • • • • • • • • •

"The purpose of life is not to be happy, but to matter: to be productive, to be useful, to have it make a difference that you lived at all. Sandy, you have made a difference and I hope you will continue to make a difference. You have contributed a lot to peoples lives! Thank God for people like you." W.H./NC

• • • • • • • • • • •

"I am saddened to think that you may drop out of the adoption movement. I hope that you will reconsider. You are a pillar of strength to many of us and a pioneer in the adoption reform movement. Please try and be strong. I can't even imagine how difficult this part of your life must be. I wish there were some way that I could help you directly. Without the work you've done, many of us would have never been able to search and find, for you have paved the way." D.W./VA

• • • • • • • • • • •

"I've really had a hard time sitting down to write this. I keep procrastinating because I'm feeling like you're paying with your freedom, enduring so much discomfort, to change a system that has

191

taken away MY basic human rights to know my heritage, and I'm not. Things are so unfair when ethnic and sexual rights come before human rights. And it's not fair that you're stuck there. I'm so heartbroken for you. I pray for you constantly. What can I do to help you. I wish I could let you see inside my heart so you'd know how much I wish I could do something!" L.W./SC

●●●●●●●●●●●●

This letter was sent to the court of appeals on my behalf by an adoptive parent. "Ms. Musser is a woman of high moral character, and the cause for which she has jeopardized herself - that of the full emancipation of the last of this nation's truly second-class citizens, adult adoptees, those individuals among us who are the only ones to still be denied their full legal rights under the law, that of access to their own histories - is a just and righteous cause.

Adult adoptees are the only remaining of this nation's citizens - since slavery - who are not legally allowed access to their own histories, including but not limited to, their birth records and/or the adoption contracts that were entered into on their behalf by others without their knowledge, consent, or control, and to gain access to which, they have no legal redress. No other United States citizens are as legally disenfranchised, or treated so shamefully under the law, as the adult adoptees in our midst.

The fact that our current laws disallow this moral civil right of the adult adoptee, a taken-for-granted right fully enjoyed by all the other adult citizens of this nation, including you and me, no doubt, is deplorable. That Ms. Musser, and others like her, have hazarded their own lives and fortunes to remedy this injustice on behalf of our adopted fellow-citizens, is highly commendable, and certainly not worthy of the censure of the court." N.L./CA (adoptive mother)

●●●●●●●●●●●●

"Today, November 24th has been designated your day. You are not forgotten even though you are on a four month holiday compliments of the United States. Thanksgiving is tomorrow and a lot of people out there have you to thank and will have you in their thoughts and prayers when they give thanks. We who believe in what we do will continue to do so." C.W./NY

●●●●●●●●●●●●

These two letters were sent to 60 Minutes with a copies to me:
"I have been on my own since my adoptive parents abandoned me at age 17, after a messy divorce. At age 18 I began my search for my birthmother. I hired several other organizations and private investigators, all of whom were not able to help me. In fact, one ripped me off and one gave me a wrong name. In June of 1993, I was told to contact Sandy

Musser. I paid Sandy a total of $150 and within one month Sandy knew where my birth family was. Unfortunately both my parents died in 1991. I found aunts, uncles and cousins. If it weren't for Sandy, I would still be looking for the wrong person." J.A./CA

• • • • • • • • • • •

"After watching the 60 Minutes broadcast of 'Who Am I', January 2, 1994 on Sandy Musser and the work she has done to help so many people looking for a loved one given up for adoption or looking for a birthparent, I've felt the need to stand with Sandy and try to do what I can to overturn the adoption laws the way they are today. I have always thought it is the right of all people to know from where they come. We are human and we wander this world looking into the eyes of passerby's thinking 'are you a family member I'll never know,' looking for that one face in the crowd that looks like you. Always searching, screaming Who Am I! Who do I look like. The list of who's, what's, when's and where's is endless.

This is a civil rights movement. Sandy Musser is the Rosa Parks for the adoption movement. She is being charged for trying to unravel the lies and deception that these courts deemed legal. The law states that it's a CRIME to find your blood relatives, but who committed the first crime - the government was the first one to break the law by sealing adoptees' records! Adoption is for puppies, kittens, and bunnies. Stop Closed / Sealed Adoptions now!" J.M./WA

• • • • • • • • • • •

"I am writing to let you know that you are in my thoughts and prayers. I believe in what you do and have done to find the information that is so important to the lives of so many. I am a friend of Ruth's and was with her as she struggled to search for ANY information she could find on her birth family. We spent hours and hours together in libraries finding nothing. I remember her talking about the possibilities of hiring an agency/person to help her with her search to find her birthmother. I remember her finally making the decision to 'hand-over' the information she currently had to 'this agency'

The weeks that followed were stressful, anxiety-filled, full of emotion, sad, angry, and joyful. We celebrated and mourned the information that would come to us as you would call with new information. When the packet of information came in the mail for Ruth with HER information, from your agency, we celebrated. Finally, she had confirmed information on her birth family.

Thank you Sandy for creating THE MUSSER FOUNDATION and the ADOPTION AND FAMILY REUNION CENTER. In closing, I thank you for all you have done and continue to do to help reunite families, especially for Ruth." H.P./MI

●●●●●●●●●●●

"I saw the 60 Minutes interview last night and thought it was a great story. I want to let you know that what you stand for is wonderful. Please don't let this reflective time away from your friends and family dissuade you from your civil disobedience and the rights of adopted children and birthparents." D.M./FL

●●●●●●●●●●●

"Last night we all sat and watched you wanting to give you a big hug; hoping to take away some of the loneliness that we could see. My thoughts have been with you and I remind everyone at the group meeting to say a prayer to keep you going. Remember that what you ask for you will receive, and I'm sure that "strength and endurance" has been a much requested prayer for you. You know that we are all with you, yet it is easy for us to say, but until we have walked the walk you have been on for two months; there is no way we can say 'I know how it is'.

In thinking about the two things we all never have enough of, money and time, I am sure that in your present situation, that time is more of an enemy right now. It won't be long before there will be more time behind you than in front of you. What you have stood up for shows tremendous generosity and your reward will be abundant. When a person believes in something they put their all into it and your actions are loudly heard by all of us. The important thing is to believe in yourself and I pray that you will do that; you will not become disillusioned by the hand of men. Sandy I believe that you will be strong and that we will see your smiling face again; looking back on this as a mile point gained in the issue you stand for." B.L./VA

●●●●●●●●●●●

"I've been meaning to write for so long but every time I sat down with pen and paper, I could not find the words to express my outrage at your verdict, my sadness at your incarceration and my frustration at the state of the adoption reform movement. I saw the 60 Minutes segment. Considering how unfriendly the media can be, I thought they did an ok job at presenting our side, but I thought you presented our side wonderfully! At the end of the segment they said you had recently called them to say that if the purpose of your sentence is to make you think twice about it, is working with you and that you may drop out of the movement altogether. How it broke my heart to see how they have broken your spirit." L.R./NY

●●●●●●●●●●●

"I know in some ways what it is like for you there in lockup because when I was young (14), I was sent away to a "Home" for girls. I kept running away from there because it was so terrible and always ran back

194

home. Then my parents' social worker convinced them to send me to a very expensive mental hospital. Since it was so expensive, I eventually ended up in the State Hospital. I was only 15 and in that snakepit for over six months for "exhibiting antisocial tendencies". How I survived that period of time is a mystery. I still have flashbacks and never seem to get too far from the experience which is indelibly imprinted on me. I repressed the memories for years and even now have trouble telling people about it.

When I joined the sorority of birthmothers two years later, it was just icing on the trauma cake. I always believed that losing my firstborn was further punishment for being so bad. It's taken me over three years of therapy to put things in better perspective. I'll never fully understand why I had to endure those experiences. But, I'm a survivor and you are too.

I'm not trying to be a 'Pollyanna', Sandy, but I'm certain that what you are going through now has some greater meaning for you and those who care about you. After you are home, and the house arrest is over, you'll be free to explore options in your life. Just follow your bliss. Try to do whatever it is that makes you happy and comfortable. After all you've been through, God knows you deserve an extra measure of happiness for the rest of your life." A.W./NJ

• • • • • • • • • • • •

"I am one of the many people you were trying to help locate their families. I know that things look bad for you now, but try to smile. Your foundation was the first organization to offer hope of me ever finding my family. I don't know if you can possibly imagine the horror of never knowing your family. For one, it nearly killed me. I was put in the hospital because the people that adopted me didn't look at my medical records. This is nothing next to the psychological abuse, trauma and frustration of the situation. Words cannot express the joy you have brought me and millions of other people. Those who have friends are never alone. Thank you for your support." S.R./NJ

• • • • • • • • • • • •

"I send you a message, my dear friend. Picture yourself years from now with your own cherished family around you - your friends beside you, and your name emblazoned into a monument to sacrifice, dedication and courage, the only one of such distinction in what was meant to be a movement of purpose. Also know that you will surely know who deserves your friendship in the future. Keep strong, keep your faith, the steady course, and perhaps it will be likened to the torch of liberty some day - that you showed the way despite the bushel that was put over your light." R.R./FL

• • • • • • • • • • • •

195

"Though you and I have never met in person, we have spoken a few times on the phone. I have a great deal of respect for you and the work you have done. The system is really a little messed up to say the least, when people like you are persecuted, while murderers and rapists and the armpit of our world are actually protected by our system. I pray that you are well and that your days have not been too terrible. You are a good caring person and I hope you know just how unfair we all feel, the system has been to you. I hope you will continue to always know in your heart that you are supported and loved by a lot of people. By the way, I learned at the ripe age of 45 I was adopted! G.D./NJ

• • • • • • • • • • • •

"I am so very sorry you are there in prison. I admire you for standing up for what you believe in. As far as I'm concerned you can hold your head up very far indeed. I, too, had to hire a searcher to help me find my precious son. No price can be made on what it is worth to both he and I. I was just so glad that somehow, someone could help me!! We know that God is a just God and that we are fighting for what we know God is about. He is about TRUTH, LOVE, HONESTY and the institution of family! None of which our society and, particularly adoption is about. I'll keep you in my prayers that God will let you know what you shall do next in your place in adoption reform and reunions. Remember you are not alone in this! It looks like a conspiracy against you, but the rest of us are with you in heart and spirit." E.A./NM

• • • • • • • • • • • •

"I watched 60 Minutes cause I saw in the paper where Lesley Stahl had interviewed you. I think she does a good job but yet I was concerned because CBS was holding the camera and had the power to cut and snip at will. Sometime I suspect that in an effort to be sensational (and make the facts fit into a seven minute segment) the editors will allow statements to come across as they were not actually intended. Since I am familiar with your opinions on the subject, I listened with a critical ear and was glad to observe that the entire discussion seemed to appear to come across in a straightforward way.

For me there were no surprises - until the end - when I heard that you were considering giving up your searching permanently. For you to come to that conclusion, I know, can only be the result of severe depression. Certainly understandable in the face of what has to be a most dehumanizing experience - disappointing, but understandable. I don't want to believe it. Wouldn't it be possible to continue family research by conventional methods? Or have you thought of another way to champion the cause of open adoption records without effecting reunions?" G.G./FL

• • • • • • • • • • • •

"I was shocked to read in the News-Press that you were already at FCI. I'm with you in spirit and always have been; you gave me the courage and direction to start looking for my son - you have made history, Sandy - and now with a declaration of 'Sandy Musser Day' during National Adoption Week - wow! I just hope and pray someone with clout is watching and listening. You're a brave woman and have always stood by your convictions (wrong choice of word there)! You have made your mark on society and will be known and remembered for a long time! I love you." M.Q./FL

• • • • • • • • • • •

"When Pat called me to tell me what happened I could hardly believe my ears! It was bad enough to hear you are in prison, but putting you in solitary confinement for 3 days was ridiculous! I simply don't understand why you are being treated so harshly - especially when you haven't done anything. (Is having a big heart against the law?) I hope you know how special you are to so very many people. Without you, Sandy, there are many of us that would still be longing to know what happened to our babies. Wondering if they are alive or dead! Wondering what kind of families they were raised in - we would still be in that world of limbo! You don't know what it has meant to me to know you." V.B./MI

• • • • • • • • • • •

"I am a 52 year old birthmother. Early this month I saw the 60 Minutes coverage of you and your efforts on behalf of family reunion and adoption reform, and I am writing to thank you from the bottom of my heart and soul. What you have done and (I hope) will continue to do is an inspiration to all of us who are in big or small ways waging war on the terrible system of adoption in this country. You have certainly paid a price, but I hope that the postscript on 60 Minutes was just a smokescreen and that you will continue your efforts against a morally unjust system, and on behalf of those of us who have been harmed irreparably by it." G.G./MD

• • • • • • • • • • •

"I recently saw the 60 Minutes segment, and wanted to tell you how sorry I am that you ended up where you are just for trying to help people. It's no consolation, I'm sure, to know that Rose Furman went to jail for helping the poor get legal services and, after paying this terrible price, did see changes in the laws of many states regarding the services of paralegals.

I'm not an adoptee or a biological mother, but I am a sister who not only cannot find the sister given up for adoption when I was two and a half, but also endure my family's denial of her existence. I remembered her existence over fifty years after we were split up and have since located proof that she did, and may still exist. The pain of our separation has greatly diminished the quality of my life and, indirectly the quality of my children's lives.

Even today, I experience the same sort of thinking. 'Why do you want to drag all this up now? Why do you want to hurt your parents this way?' The answer is simple. Annie is my family. Her absence is like having part of my identity missing. Not knowing what happened to her and who she is, is just as horribly painful as losing a child and not knowing where that child went to. If there is anything I can do for you, let me know." A.P./AZ

• • • • • • • • • • •

"Just saw the 60 Minutes show - excellent job. It is indeed as important as Rosa Parks and the Civil Rights Movement. Perhaps God has appointed you as the Rosa Parks of the Adoption Movement. I'm sure prison is no fun, but any of us would go for the same reason. I would go to prison for the cause, and I thank you for being willing to go for this cause. Your heart beats, lives and breathes what is truth. These are archaic laws and must change. I thank you again from the bottom of my exuberant heart. You are loved by all of us. You did what's right. Take care of yourself." R.M./WA

• • • • • • • • • • •

"I asked you to help find the 58 year old daughter of Babie Hoover, a blind wheelchair- bound 77 year old woman who gave birth in Winfield, Kansas. I saw 60 Minutes last night and I am so impressed with what you do to get people their rights. Please accept the enclosed donation to help with your cause." M.S./KS

• • • • • • • • • • •

"I've wanted to write you for a while now, since the article about you was printed in the News-Press. I also saw the segment on 60 Minutes. What a difficult position to be in. Some people think you are very wrong, others can't applaud you enough. You have made some people very, very happy, and some people very uncomfortable because they have never faced the issue and dealt with it. I believe that the adoption process should be changed.

My real reason for writing is to tell you that you don't need to feel bad. You have been through a lot of things and you should just take this quiet time you have to take care of you. Realize your strengths. Take time to nurse some real hurts. I'm sorry you have had to go through so much. Realize a lot of people care about you. Use this time to strengthen your mind and body." J.E./FL

• • • • • • • • • • •

"I am shocked that AAC is silent about your conviction. I guess that's a statement of how serious they really are about open records. It is characteristic of many of the people I encountered upon my comparatively recent entry into and peripheral activity in the movement. There are times when I feel there is some activity toward open records, but that is more individual than universal. You mentioned an army needed to fight city hall- I think part of the problem is that there may be too many city halls which deludes what should be a very strong and dedicated focus. Certainly lots more people should be joining the risk taking. It's OK to not want to continue - be true to you." E.W./WI

• • • • • • • • • • •

"Love is the strongest force there is and I hope you can visualize the amount of love from all of us that you have helped coming to you to ease your pain and fill your heart with warmth and love. Each and everyone of us knows how it feels to have a helping hand reach out after many years of pain, shame, questions, guilt and sorrow and lead us to the answers that begin to heal. You, Sandy, were the helping hand. You will always have a special place in my heart. As I watched 60 Minutes the other night, I thought of being 17 and lying on a delivery table tied and blindfolded, pleading and begging for my child. Where was the legal system then? The legal system did not ask if this was my decision, if I had been mentally abused, if I was informed of my rights; no, instead they allowed the kidnapping of my child! I was the one sentenced to be a prisoner. Every day women are manipulated into surrendering their children. This must stop and I feel sure that your efforts are an important step in changing the laws. God Bless You! C.A./FL

• • • • • • • • • • •

"Thank you! Thank you for having the guts to do what so many of us will not - to stand up, to speak up, for what you believe in. Yours is truly a case of the "victimless crime." I have wanted to write to you since I heard about your indictment ... but the words clog in my throat as I try to sort through where I can possibly start. I am sickened by what has happened to you.

Sandy, I hope that somehow you are finding strength and solace in your heart; that you are receiving all the love, support, and comfort you deserve from your friends, family and supporters. You have made your mark on history! That much is true. Even if your work before the indictment didn't do that (which it did), you can surely look back now and say, "Yes, I did it. My life meant something." Your life and efforts have meant, and will continue to mean so much more than you will probably every realize.

Frankly, if I never heard the word "adoption" again, it would be too soon. Does this feel familiar? Somehow I suspect it does. Sometimes I wish I could just forget I was adopted. But I can't. So I go to conferences, give workshops, write books and articles and talk, talk, talk to groups,

199

people on the streetcar, radio hosts, and tell them that CLOSED ADOPTION IS INHUMANE!

Enclosed is a copy of my book *Adoption Reunions*. I sure hope the book gets to your hands. (Gee, do I sound distrustful? Do I sound like an adoptee who was placed in the hands of the "authorities" to decide my fate? Do I sound like maybe I have a problem with the system? Do I sound a tad bitter...? Damn right!)

Sandy, you are thought of, respected, and loved. Thanks again for your work, your strength, your life. Hang in there." M.M..Ontario
• • • • • • • • • • •

"I am writing to you to express my support and admiration of your strength. I cannot imagine what you are currently enduring, but what you did was right and what the system is doing is wrong.

Society and the court system puts adoptees through so many unjust, painful and degrading situations. As Nancy Verrier states in the *Primal Wound*, "society validates and attempts to help victims of sexual or emotional abuse heal, while adoptees are asked to bury their pain and simply be grateful". This must change.

We are all in this together, and things will only improve when adoptees refuse to "be silent and grateful" any longer." R.L./OR
• • • • • • • • • • •

"How appropriate that I'm writing you on Valentine's Day. I think you are a sure example of what Valentine's day symbolizes - love. You have brought people together and reunited them bringing much love and job into their lives and we are all - adoptees and birthmothers - very grateful for the work you have done and the sacrifices you have endured.

My birthmom and I are still in touch and are very close - as are my siblings. I can't tell you how grateful I am to you for bringing about our reunion. She is so accepting of everything about me and my life - and she is a great joy to my heart.

I saw you on 60 Minutes - you were *wonderful*! Very strong and convincing. I didn't like the way they portrayed you as a hard convict. If anybody is committing the felony - it's the government! I'm hoping you don't lose your determination because there's a lot of people out there that need you to open their eyes to the truth - that need to know something more than the lies typed on paper. Keep smiling - better days are just around the bend." K.W./FL
• • • • • • • • • • •

"I just learned that you were in PRISON and were finally going to be on 60 Minutes. It was surreal watching it and listening to you defend what you did and realize that, according to law, you were viewed by

200

many as a CRIMINAL. I wish I could serve some of your time for you. I have long admired your strength and determination to help so many people whose grief weighs heavily upon them each day of their lives — people who must live each day without much hope of ever seeing their own flesh — many of these people turned to you as a last hope.

Sandy, it doesn't seem real that you could be locked up in a prison uniform - locked up as if to protect society from certain threats. And maybe it's that simple. You pose a threat to those who are devoted to keeping records closed - a threat to insecure individuals who would sacrifice another's human rights to insure their own continued fearfully controlled lives. I know your inner life is rich ... it is what gets us through - beyond survival - that nourishes our spirits to seek and to thrive. I hope you are well and thriving. I send you love and hope - never give in - just keep on going - as an old wise black lady from the south once said to me "Don't step in it, step over it!" M.C./OH

● ● ● ● ● ● ● ● ● ● ●

"I just watched 60 Minutes along with the member of my support group. I felt compelled to write you and offer support. I, too, feel the adoption laws, as they are, are immoral, unlawful and inhumane. They must (and will) be changed through the efforts of dedicated and outstanding people like you.

I applaud your work over the years. You are a Godsend for all of us who have been deeply (and perhaps permanently) hurt by the closed adoption system. You are a strong and clear voice for people who are brainwashed into thinking there is nothing wrong with the system. I am horrified at what you are being subjected to. To be treated like a criminal when, in fact, you are a miracle-worker is a gross injustice. I cannot imagine what you must be going through. I only hope you can find the strength to endure. You are in my thoughts, and prayers. As you've said, "Praise the Lord and pass the ammo!" We cannot be silenced! May God be with you." K.G./MI

● ● ● ● ● ● ● ● ● ● ●

"Just a note to let you know that you have my support and gratitude for all the work and commitment which you have shown towards helping to reunite adoptees with their birthparents - I spoke with you in the fall of '93. I hope when all of this is resolved, you will not forget those of us who are still searching. I am forwarding a request to the Court of Appeals to overturn your conviction. Again my thoughts are with you." J.M./CO

● ● ● ● ● ● ● ● ● ● ●

"I want you to know that our group is thinking of you and we are angered, frustrated and saddened by this latest development in your case. It is a sad commentary on a country that professes to be the land of the free. It is unfortunate that there are enough distorted, self-serving personalities with power within our "democratic" form of government, bent on maintaining that power no matter what the cost is to those that pay their salary. But I will not be intimidated by government power, even though I am well aware of the extent to which that power can invade and destroy. It has probably left you feeling used and unappreciated. Most leaders must face feelings of loneliness and frustration and take the risk of losing all. There are very few people with the strength and wisdom to sustain the blows you have endured. C.G./MI

• • • • • • • • • • • •

"I FOUND MY SON!!! If it wasn't for you -I never would have started the search 7 years ago and filled out the ISRR form - he's been looking for me for 3 years!! No thanks to Catholic Charities! He registered in October '93. They called me for a match! We met 9 days ago - he graduates May 3rd from USF and gets commissioned as an officer in the Army in Military Intelligence the same night! I'm so happy - I'm ecstatic! I'll write longer later, but I had to share the greatest news in my life! What a feeling! He tells me he loves me and those are the most precious words I've ever heard. My mom is thrilled also. I had always prayed they'd meet before she passed on - she's 70 years old. Thank you, Sandy, for your drive and fortitude." M.Q./FL

• • • • • • • • • • • •

"I think of you often, and hope you are well. I can not comprehend what the last weeks have been for you, so in some ways, I feel at a loss as to what to say. Anything I could say will seem trivial compared to the journey you are on. I guess mostly I want you to know that a lot of people care about you. My opinion and regard for you have not and will not change in the slightest. The trial you face is meant to dehumanize you, to tear you down. You must not let this happen. I know you are a good soul. A good human being. You are also a gentle person. And gentle people sometimes care too much about what other people think. If they didn't, they wouldn't be empathetic. Take care of yourself and stand tall. Godspeed Sandy. My prayers are with you for the holidays and the days beyond." J.S./MA

You can understand why these letters brought me so much encouragement and comfort. Each one was so uplifting. They were a constant and present reminder as to why I had always been willing to "pay the price". Just a few days ago, there was a message on my answering machine from a young man for whom we completed a search soon after we began doing search work. The excitement and enthusiasm in Paul's voice reminded me once again why I was so committed to family reunification. He said:

"This call is for Sandy. My name is Paul A. from Southern California. Several years ago you helped me find my birthmother in Yuma, AZ. I went down to meet her and wrote you a letter about it. It was a fabulous thing. Since then I've been to Wyoming to visit with them several times - they moved from Yuma to Wyoming - and I just finalized everything for this next weekend. It's kind of like the final chapter in the book for me. My birthmother and my mother have been wanting to meet forever, so many parts of the family on my birthmother's side are going to meet in Loughlin, NV. My mother (adoptive) and a couple of her friends and everybody are all going to come up and we're all going to meet in Loughlin and it's going to be a really, really neat thing for my brothers and my sister to meet my mom and for my mom to meet my birthmom and everybody to talk. We're going to spend two or three days together.

I'm really, really, really, really sorry that you had to go through what you went through and I wish there was something I could do to repay you for what you've done for me. The first person I thought of calling was you and your organization. I live in Los Angeles and I don't what I can possibly do for you after what you've done for me, but let me know. I know you like pictures so I'm going to take lots of pictures and I'll send some out your way so you can see what you've been a major part of. You've got my address cause you just mailed me your little bookmark after you got out of your incarceration. You take care and as I said, if there's anything I can do for you -anyway I can repay you for what you've done for me, please don't hesitate to write or call. Thanks again and I'll keep you up to date. I'll let you know what happens after this weekend." P.A./CA

Reform Voices

"From the data being reported, there is good reason to believe that when they surrendered their children, few mothers understood the full meaning of the confidentiality agencies now say they implicitly promised them. Are agencies forcing on these mothers the 'right' to a confidentiality they never intended to have and may not wish to maintain with respect to their children?"

Doris H. Bertucci,
Social Worker

The following letter was sent to President Clinton by the Rev. Keith C. Griffith, MBE Methodist Minister, Wellington, New Zealand.

"*I understand that Sandy Musser, an adoption search worker in Florida has been sentenced to four months jail at a federal prison on the indictment for "conspiracy to defraud the government" for providing adult adoptees with the truth of their origins and identity.*

No doubt the due process of law will take its course and I do not seek to influence or interfere with that process. However, I do wish to raise the issue and need for adoption law reform concerning access to adoption information...

*We in New Zealand have been very grateful for the lead given by USA in the area of Democracy, Human Rights, and research on adoption issues. These principles and research from your country were a very important factor in instituting adoption law reform in New Zealand. They were thoroughly studied by your Government and adoption workers, and in 1985 the Government instituted adoption law reform allowing Adult Adoptees to know the truth of their origins as a **democratic fundamental right**.*

Since then about 50% of the adult adoptees have asked for and received the truth of their own origins, with very few complaints or complications. Australia has now implemented similar legislation and England granted adult adoptees that right back in 1975.

I hope that the USA may take steps now to address the issue of adoption law reform regarding adult adoptees' access to the truth of their own origins. While I realize that the matter is finally up to State Legislatures, some comment and encouragement from the President could play an important role in facilitating the process."

*P.S. I have been privileged to visit your country three times to speak at Conferences on adoption issues and have recently published a comprehensive book in Canada **The Right To Know Who You Are**.*

Almost A Birthmother

I have been touched by adoption in numerous ways. I, myself, am an adoptee, who was almost a birthmother. At age 18, a senior in high school, I was pregnant with my son, Jason, now age 10. I was thrown out of my adoptive home and into St. Agnes Maternity Home run by Catholic Family Services in Hartford. This was the same agency thru which I had been adopted. I experienced all the coercion and manipulative ploys of the adoption social workers there.

Fortunately, I left the home and stayed with various pro-choice homes in my community until my son was born. As an adoptee, I knew that my baby would be the only person in my life who would be genetically related to me. The thought of giving him up was unthinkable.

204

It was very difficult to do this, but I was very lucky to have felt I had the choice. So many others before me and after me have not had that choice."
Margaret Jones

"If you are a legislator ... please beware of special interest lobbyists offering only conjecture instead of real statistical evidence supporting the need for adoption secrecy. Ask why, when so many social work professionals are seeing the need to end adoption secrecy, certain special interest groups are willing to devote so much time, money and effort to preserving adoption secrecy for its own sake.

Attend a meeting of any of the 350 adoption search/support groups throughout the country. Ask what its members have uncovered regarding unethical and deceptive adoption practices perpetrated on them by adoption brokers, both agency and independent, whose actions have been effectively shielded by decades of "confidentiality."

Ask about birthmothers who have been coerced, browbeaten or emotionally blackmailed into signing surrender papers; ask adoptive parents who were given falsified background information about their children, preventing their seeking proper treatment; ask adoptees who have suffered disabilities because agencies refused to pass along vital medical information which had been added to their files by birthmothers after adoption. As one articulate male adoptee put it, 'Secrecy and ethics cannot coexist, because ethics, by definition, asks for honesty.' So when you see an agency obsessed with secrecy, ask why!

In light of today's propensity for malpractice and liability litigation, explore the possibility that those enjoying the greatest protection through continued adoption secrecy may be the adoption brokers themselves, agency and independent, who have been totally immune to accountability / responsibility / liability, both to those whose lives have been affected by it and to the greater human community."

Joanne Swanson
Birco Publications

Rene H. is a social worker from Holland. At the CERA conference in NY in 1993, he suggests that America needs a new policy that starts at the beginning - not at the end when the adoption has already taken place. He explains:

"In European countries we have a clear sex education course

205

that starts in elementary school and goes on to secondary education; secondly, an agressive birth control system in our countries - you see it everywhere -you can buy the things you need when you need them; and thirdly, to give up a child, to surrender a child, to relinquish a child - whatever words you use, **is not done - it's just not done!**

Grandparents care for the child in our culture. The social workers educate young girls who are unexpectedly pregnant - not to surrender the child - instead they influence the girl and her parents to rearrange their economic situation and the situation at home. So **surrendering is just not done.**"

"Imagine going through life wondering who your birth parents are, your heritage, whether you have brothers or sisters and worst of all having no medical history. Unless you are an adoptee or birthmother in search, Dad says you have no idea of what the process is like, especially in the state of Indiana. Adoptees aren't criminals but are sometimes treated as such by insensitive people from the state, court system and welfare department who play "God" with lives of adoptees and birthmothers. Living with my dad while he was so obsessed with finding his birthmother wasn't easy."

Michael Rigg,
Son of Adoptee

Michael's father, Randy, wrote to me in prison in late November to tell me he had located his mother, but he had not yet had contact. Ironically she lived in my area. Then this message from Randy came soon after - "This message went out on the FIDONET Adoptees Echo. I found my birthmother November 24, 1993 and talked with her the first time on December 8th. My mother's first letter to me was received prior to Christmas, 1993."

"Today was like any other... just another day ... until I stopped at the Post Office to get our mail. The last envelope I pulled out was from my mother and I just completely lost it. How I drove to work, well I don't know, I must have been on automatic pilot. Inside the envelope were pictures and a letter. I cried some more. I couldn't even read the letter. My wife had to tell me what it said. I cried even harder and she didn't help matters because she was crying too! I'm sure if people saw me they must have wondered if I escaped from the State Hospital. If I looked at those pictures today once, I must have looked at them a thousand time, maybe more."

Randy Rigg,
Reunited Adoptee

"I have sat behind the desk facing adoptees scores of times during the past years, and I honestly admit that I cringe now as I recall my attitude and my behavior with them. That they remained polite and controlled is an indication of how pitifully eager they were for even the little I told them. I know now because of the many adoptees I have spoken with during my research. They have described their intense anger at that woman, me, who had the power to keep their records from them. The stranger, me, sitting there deciding what facts of their lives would I permit them to know."

An Adoption
Counselor

The following letter, written by a birthmother to the child she found, is one which could have been written by any birthmother. It says exactly what has been expressed by birthmothers all over the country.

They Told Me I'd Forget

We are meeting again after many years of being apart. You are an adult now and I am no longer a teenager. We probably both have had our share of pain in our lives over the years. You, because you felt rejected and abandoned by your original mother and I, because I was convinced that I could not raise you on my own.

The person you are meeting now is much older and wiser than the scared teenager who sat in a social worker's office so many years ago. You are meeting someone who has asked herself over and over how she could have done that? I wasn't even allowed to see you, hold you or even say good-bye to you. I was told I was going to "forget". Then I was told to "get on with my life". It must be hard for you to understand how alone and afraid I was. I am no longer afraid of the authority figures or the system. I was influenced by them, as well as by the birth father who was not willing to help me raise you, and by a society who looked down on single mothers.

When I was pregnant with you, I always hoped that someone would come to me and say, "It's OK. I'll help you and you can keep your baby". But no one came. The only encouragement I got was to place you for adoption, not to keep you. They told me I'd "forget". They told me to keep it a secret and not to talk about it and it would all go away. They told me everything was over and done with ... now get on with living, the past is the past.

They never told me about the pain of not knowing where you were or if you were all right. They never told me how I would feel on Mother's Day without my child (when someone else would celebrate it with you). They never told me about the emptiness that overcame me every single Christmas while I watched other mothers take their child to see Santa.

I never forgot your birthday. The month before and the weeks leading up to your actual birthday were always the hardest for me. I never got to hold you, see you, or touch your face ... instead, you were taken away. I can't even remember signing the papers. I was numb, I cried a lot and went into a deep depression.

Now we have connected once again. It is so wonderful to see you and to know that you are ok. The blanks are beginning to fill in the years that have gone by. Sometimes it's painful for me to realize that I have already missed many important parts of your life. I have finally completed my circle. It is a beginning ... it will be only what we choose to make it.

●●●●●●●●●●●●

"As when slaves who got their freedom had to take it over or under or through the unjust forms of the law, precisely now must women take it to get their right to a voice in this government . . . and I shall earnestly and persistently continue to urge all women to the practical recognition of the old Revolutionary maxim, "Resistance to tyranny is obedience to God."

Susan B. Anthony

...And so my friends, we too, as adoptees, birthparents, adoptive parents, and extended families, must take it over or under or through the unjust forms of the law if we are to reform our archaic system and become free from the chains of adoption that keep us enslaved.

THE LEADERSHIP SPEAKS OUT!

The Board of Directors of the American Adoption Congress refused to take a position or stand concerning this historic case, for reasons still unknown. However, there were many other leaders who did. This chapter shares the thoughts and views of those who stood by my side, spoke out on my behalf and came to my defense whenever it was deemed necessary. All of them, in their own way, are calling for drastic changes of an adoption system which is no longer working.

Though I've known them all as peers, many are also special friends. Within adoption reform, they are considered the "cream of the crop". After reading their writings, I'm sure you'll agree.

A few, myself included, have been labeled "radical". If calling for honesty, openness, guardianship and family preservation is considered radical, then the label probably fits. But for those of us who carry that label, the shoes of other "radicals" like Lincoln, Ghandi, King, and other civil rights leaders feel quite comfortable.

Jim Gritter is the Director of CFCS, a Catholic Charities agency for the Diocese of Gaylord in Traverse City, MI, and is in the forefront of Open Adoption. We first met when he invited me to speak at the Second Annual Conference for Open Adoption in the early 80's.

Jim is the Editor of Adoption Without Fear and is currently writing a book entitled Adoption Without Shame. He is one of the most unique professionals I have ever met; he is warm, caring, sensitive and understanding, and he is having a tremendous impact upon adoption practice all over the country. Here are a few of Jim's thoughts concerning the indictment.

MISREPRESENTATION BY WHOM?

There is a great unrecognized irony in the jailing of Sandy Musser. She is accused of misrepresentation, a specter which appalls the establishment and leaves them aghast. "Open and shut situation," they say, no ifs, and or buts about it —misrepresentation is always terribly wrong." There is actually something encouraging about the government's intolerance of misrepresentation, if only they would apply that standard to the root issues as well as the symptoms.

Completely overlooked in this pique of bureaucratic indignation is the enduring misrepresentation. The establishment came painfully close to addressing the most critical issue in all of adoption - identity - without even realizing it. Just like the government, Sandy Musser is deeply concerned about the issue of misrepresentation, but her concern goes to a much deeper level. She is grieved with the fact that countless adoptees struggle forlornly on a daily basis with the question "Who am I?" She is moved to action because so many adoptees feel like they are misrepresentations. Many of them wonder if they are imposters or frauds. They have an ascribed script to live out, but they feel the unsettling tug of another set of possibilities. Often they are unsure as to what is real and what is representation.

Webster defines a fraud as "one that is not what it seems or is represented to be."

The system is fickle in its treatment of misrepresentation. When the system encounters a sly response, a clever effort to counter its own original charade, it cries foul. It doesn't like a dose of its own medicine.

There is another irony to it all, and that is the question of who is the prisoner? Obviously, the episode proves that the keepers of secrets have the power to incarcerate those who seek the facts, but one wonders whose heart is more imprisoned? As the keepers of secrets surround themselves with fear, as they growl with threats and punishments so people will keep a distance, as they put their creative energies into the building of formidable boundaries so no one can get to them, the prospect grows that someday it will occur to them that they reside in self-imposed solitary confinement.

The system has once again opted for secrecy. In reaffirming that position, it is suggesting that the game must go on. As long as secrets are held, it is axiomatic that sleuths will emerge to secretly counter them. Now the game escalates. The establishment has launched an effort to counter those who counter the keeping. No doubt the search community is sufficiently determined and resourceful to figure ways to counter the counter-counter activity.

210

In some ways I suspect both sides enjoy the detective work — the hunt, the intrigue, the creativity. It is all very interesting and somehow a weird tribute to human nature and the human spirit.

We must never allow it, though to distract us from the heart of the matter. We must always return to the core question:

Are all Americans entitled to fundamental information about themselves, or just those who are born into a context of propriety?

Tragic as this entire episode has been for Sandy Musser — an ironic hero in the effort to address misrepresentation - - to the extent it highlights this over-arching question, it will serve a useful purpose.

Annette Baran and I first met when she spoke at an Adoption Forum conference in the late 70's. The last evening of the conference, I had a gathering in my home for anyone who wanted to attend. This afforded me the opportunity to chat with this wonderful warm human being and we have remained friends ever since. I am pleased to count her among my strongest supporters. She presented the following speech at the 1993 CERA conference in New York City - an extremely timely speech in light of what is happening in the field of Open Adoption.

HOISTED BY OUR OWN PETARD

What does hoisted by our own petard mean? It means we provided our own noose, hung it in the right place, ignored its slow descent down toward our necks and were surprised and undone when the noose was tightened and the blood supply was cut off.

Other metaphors like that could be planting a rose garden and being surprised at the blood poisoning the thorns give you. In adoption terms, we experimented with the idea of Open Adoption placement selectively, carefully and almost apologetically at the beginning. When we first started thinking about it, the idea was for older toddlers who had been kept by birthparents for a few years. When it looked hopeful, we extended its use and created the definition of Open Adoption. Finally, we came out saying that all adoptive placements of all children should be open. For older children, it was a must because older children had history and identity that could not be amputated without extreme harm to the child. We finally came to believe that all newborns had the same need and the same right to Open Adoption placement.

Since we believed it was so good for the child and their adoptive parents, we propagandized about it, took a lot of flack originally, but kept on because of our ideals. It was the one chapter in our book, *The*

Adoption Triangle, that we thought was most important from a long range point of view. It took a long time for it to be even partially accepted. We were blessed and rewarded when people began to practice more open placements, but were we naive - were we blind to what was also going on out there in the real world of marketing and business in adoption.

We had no idea that the entrepreneurs and vendors shrewdly understood what we didn't - that the idea of Open Adoption had great potential for increasing their business for getting more newborn babies for infertile couples. We were and we remain naive. They are not. They recognize that to offer pregnant women contact after relinquishment and placement is a convincing ploy to get them to give up newborn babies more readily. Who was to say that the offer was really a lifetime offer - that open meant staying open? Suddenly there was a whole Open Adoption market of newborn babies operating out there and we didn't have a clue as to how it all came to be in place. We were still talking a lot of theory - everybody else was using the phrase Open Adoption, only it sounded different somehow. It sounded skewed, a bit sleazy, a bit coercive.

We can't blame it on anybody but ourselves, and I include not only Reuben and me, but a lot of you - my fellow naive colleagues in this group. When we said open - we meant open forever. When they said open - they meant open until legal adoption and then WHAMO, it could close and close as tight as they wanted so that's what is meant by "being hoisted by one's own petard". We gave them the ammunition and the weapons to shoot us with because we were too dense to recognize the potential danger. Where does that leave us today? What can we learn? Is there anything positive to be gained from this whole experience. We think so.

Adoption is not one phenomenon. Adoption wears many hats. There is relative adoption where grandparents, aunts, uncles, etc. adopt a child whose birthparents cannot assume care. There is stepparent adoption which is self-explanatory. I have a favorite stepparent story. My good friend had a baby in her first marriage. Her first husband was a tightwad and he offered to permit her second husband to adopt the child so he wouldn't have to pay child support. He knew he could have continued contact with his daughter after the adoption - which he did; the second marriage ended in divorce also, but with the child having continued contact with both fathers. Her mother finally settled down in the next marriage and it was the third husband who really was the father for most of her childhood and teen years.

When she graduated high school, she invited all three fathers to her graduation and they all came. She's now an adult - almost 40. She has cared for and buried her adoptive father, is caring for her aging ill birth father and is preparing to help her mother care for her stepfather when the time comes. That's one kind of very open step-parent adoption.

Another type of adoption is what I call the Dale Evans type of adoption where families take into their homes all kinds of handicaps and races, etc. and operate a kind of group home giving children a safe place to grow up. It's not a nuclear family setup in any sense of the word, but it works.

There are also those families who adopt particular problems - downs syndrome, hearing impairments, spinal bifida, fetal alcohol syndrome, crack addiction, HIV positive, etc. They usually specialize in a particular problem and raise numbers of children with the same problem.

There are foster parent adoptions where foster children become permanent members of the family through legal adoption or guardianship. There are international and/or transracial adoptions where children are removed from their homeland and transplanted into this country. Then there are subsidized adoptions which may fit into any one of those categories. The ones I have just listed are adoption cutting edge - that is they are most of the time adoption for the children.

And THEN there is adoption of newborn infants for infertile couples. Let me stress that adoption for newborn children, most of the time, is not for the children - it's for the adults. There is a big difference! In very rare incidences is it necessarily in the best interest of the child.

This is the kind of adoption that gets the most publicity, causes the most grief, and results in CERA conferences, CUB conferences, AAC conferences and, of course, the NCFA opposition lobby in Washington headed by Bill Pierce. In reality, the numbers of newborn infant adoptions are smaller than the other groups, yet it is the group that generates the salaries of attorneys, adoption services, middlemen, etc. It is the romanticized role of ordinary couples who often, because they can't conceive a child, are elevated to sainthood and made into virtuous beings as opposed to the birthparents who are usually seen as lacking in virtue, status and value. Conversely, these couples are also the folks whose unmet needs lead to desperation and makes them great targets for the dealers who charge whatever the market will bear, and who somehow convince the couples that more and more money buys better babies. That is the world where so-called open adoption is the new recruitment technique and tactic.

I would like to offer the thesis that it is also the world where adoption of a child into a nuclear family is still an attempt to make it the same "as if" it was born to them; that complete ownership is the only conceivable way of thinking for most of the couples involved. Then ergo the notion of open adoption is really an oxymoron - two opposites in conflict with

213

each other that don't have much chance of succeeding.

Over the years I have received scores of cards from couples after court-action finalizing the adoption. The cards read "Legal at last!" - "Ours finally!" - "No more jitters!" - "We've been to court; now we have the pink slip and we can stop worrying". Need I go on? If adoption is legal ownership, then how can it be open and allow free mingling of birthparents. If adoption means getting rid of legal authority of the birthparents and taking it on themselves, then it really means getting rid of them altogether in the minds of the adopters.

Adoption of newborn, healthy, normal Caucasian babies as it is perceived in the United States is, by its very nature, by its very fabric, really closed, not really open. For us to believe that we can take this institution, leave it as it is and tack on open, really doesn't make a lot of sense. We have to change adoption of newborn babies before we can add open to it.

Perhaps this is a good time to bring up the Baby Jessica case. The media consumed us with information - but more important misinformation, about this case. What can we learn from it? All of the old myths, prejudices, class distinctions, moralistic notions and stereotypes came back with a vengeance. I felt that I was catapulted back to 1950 or maybe earlier.

I have my own scenario. When the DeBoers met Cara, they liked her and were delighted at the prospect of adopting her baby. They treated her like a friend, and were respectful of her feelings and needs - until Jessica was given into their care at 40 hours, and suddenly the friendship and caring evaporated and Cara became their adversary, their enemy to be feared and denied. When Cara came back pleading for her child and indicating her feelings that she could not continue with the adoption, the DeBoers figuratively, and maybe literally, slammed the door in her face. Here, in my scenario, were two mothers facing each other and no where is there an indication that Mrs. Deboer tried to understand Cara's pain and need to have her child returned to her arms. Continuing my scenario, Mrs. DeBoer tightened the hold on Jessica and said in essence, "no go away, you signed a paper and this is now our child, too bad for you " and then began the delays and evasions and unlawful behavior.

I read somewhere that Mrs. DeBoer said that the only reason she hung onto Jessica and did not return her to the birthmother was because she truly believed they were better parents and it was all for Jessica's sake. What an elitist notion! And that elitism and prejudicial stereotyping grew and grew with the DeBoer's being perceived as the loving good guys and the Schmidts as the unfit parents who didn't deserve to raise their own child. A lot of this type thinking has always been there - just below the surface. This case brought it out into the open and maybe that has its positive aspects. Maybe now we know more clearly what we have to battle in this institution of adoption as it is currently practiced. Maybe this case is the best one that can shed light on the adoption experience.

We need to return to the original purpose of adoption which was to place a child who needed a family, not to create a family by placing a child who already has one. Friends, it's time for us to come of age and stop pulling our own nooses so tight that we cut off the flow of sanity and oxygen.

*Reuben Pannor and I met at the Second Annual Open Adoption Conference held in Traverse City, MI in 1983. He is the coauthor of **The Adoption Triangle** which has become a cornerstone for adoption reform. Reuben, a social worker of the "old regime", now works feverishly to undue the 'sins of the past'. Following are excerpts of a speech Reuben presented at the 1993 CERA conference.*

In our conferences over the years, we have spent a great deal of time with workshops that are, in a sense, trying to patch up a wounded system. Much has happened in the past year that brings us face to face with the need to reexamine what adoption is really all about and, most important, to face the fact that it's time to stop the 1950 soundbites and concepts and begin to think 1993 - on the cusp of a new century and accepting new sensibilities. Other groups in our society built on the fulminate and the ferment of the 1960's and 70's, and expanded their concepts to freedom and individual rights. This has not been so in the world of adoption.

Adoption not only stayed put, but energy has been poured into rationalizing and defending and perpetuating a system that is outmoded. That, I think, needs to stop. Freedom of information, for example, is now accepted by almost every group within society; every group except adoption. We are still begging and pleading for open records.

Why? It is time to recognize that every part of the triad has the constitutional right to enjoy the same freedoms and rights guaranteed to everyone in our society. We represent a segment of the population denied basic rights that the rest of the population takes for granted. There is nothing ambiguous about this issue. We are entitled to these rights and we should demand them now. People who are denied their basic rights are often driven to desperate acts.

I recently attended a play in Hyde Park depicting the life of Eleanor Roosevelt. An interesting part of her life caught my interest. She was invited to a conference in one of our southern states and when she arrived

215

at the conference, she sat down in the section that was designated for blacks. A friend pulled a chair up next to her and began talking with her when a policeman came over and said "Mrs. Roosevelt, you'll have to leave - you'll have to sit in the white section." And she said "The constitution guarantees us all - all Americans equal rights and I'm going to sit here" and she did. A few moments later the Chief of Police came over and said to her "You'll have to move. Our State laws (which were the Jim Crow laws) forbid whites and blacks to sit together" and she said "those laws are inhuman" and she just sat there.

We need to keep in mind that sealed adoption records are also unconstitutional and inhuman, and if Eleanor Roosevelt could sit and defy the laws of that state, then I think we can understand how Sandy Musser could decide that sealed records are inhumane and she deserves every bit of our support.

Our efforts to unseal records is an issue that must be settled and must be settled now. Constitutional challenges must be remounted in the climate of 1993 and it's time for the adoption reform movement to demand that this issue be resolved. In the early days, the founders and supporters of organizations like Orphan Voyage, CUB, ALMA, American Adoption Congress, were brave risk-takers for all of us who did not have the courage to speak out openly. Those days are long past. It is time for everyone - adoptees, birthparents, adoptive parents, professionals, relatives, concerned people, to come out of the closet and to clearly and openly identify themselves, their feelings, and concerns.

The silent ones are still reflecting on the dignities and shame of an earlier time in history. Too much energy has been consumed in maintaining the silence, pain and secrecy. Those who remain silent are carrying a heavy burden for which they are paying a terrible emotional and psychological price; a burden that spills over into every aspect of their life. Speaking out gives emotional relief and dignity to all of us and it makes us strong and it gives us an opportunity to educate others. Let's make a vow here and now that the self-imposed, self-destructive silence will come to an end for all of us.

In 1976 I read an article in the Philadelphia Inquirer *about a reunion story. It mentioned the name of P. Partridge. I called her and she invited me to a support group meeting of The Adoption Forum which she Co-Founded. In 1979, Penny was elected the first President of the American Adoption Congress. Following is a speech she gave at the Adoption Forum conference in Philadelphia on March 26, 1994 shortly after my release from prison.*

216

WATCHING SANDY MUSSER GO TO JAIL
What We Can Make It Mean

I want to talk about something that has happened to us in the last year. It has to do with Sandy Musser going to jail, but it is something that happened to us as well as to Sandy. The way I see it is that - people against the reuniting of relatives, separated by adoption, exerted influence and got one individual woman PUNISHED TO DISCOURAGE OTHERS from trying to facilitate reunions.

I think this is a big deal, and I have felt compelled to be as good a witness as I can - not to The Truth - but to my own perceptions and my own experience of what has happened. I am going to tell you a very personal side of this story, which may make sense for you of why I see it the way I do.

Sandy and I go back to 1976, a very important year for both of us. In 1976, I found my birthmother. In hopes of getting a little publicity for the Adoption Forum, I wrote to my neighborhood weekly, *"The Germantown Courier"*, and they did a story about my reunion. Someone at the *Philadelphia Inquirer* saw it and did one too. Sandy, mother of four in Merchantville, New Jersey, saw the Inquirer article, called information for my number, called me, and wanted to know the time and place of our next meeting.

This fall, when she was in lockup isolation unit - without seeing another human face and without her prescribed medication for three days, Sandy wrote a poem, which includes the following segment:

> "1976 - I spoke of you today for the first time in 22 years. I announced to a group of 8 adoptees that 'I gave you away but I never forgot you.' My heart began to scream with the pain that had been suppressed all these years. And now my journey to find you begins. It would be a journey to end the awful pain, to put to rest the longing inside and to finally find peace".

So that's how Sandy and I came to be part of this web in which we are all of us in this room somehow connected. Some of you are connected to each other in exactly the same way. I think the people you connect with when you are just waking up to this stuff, or searching, or find, remain very important to you - maybe for the rest of your life.

Sandy and I both stayed pretty involved in this web of connections among people affected by adoption. But we went our separate ways. We had different parts we played, different styles, and different beliefs. I remember reviewing one of Sandy's book for the Adoption Forum

217

newsletter. One of my sentences was something like, "I don't happen to believe such and such, as Sandy does, BUT..." and Sandy liked that. We didn't talk much over the years, especially after Sandy moved to Florida. But I think we always respected each other and really appreciated that the other cared and stayed involved.

I have to say that I was very uncomfortable when I learned a year ago that Sandy was being indicted for a federal offense; conspiracy to defraud the government. There was nothing I was THINKING about it, in particular. I didn't WANT to think about it. At the AAC conference in Cleveland last year at this time, I didn't go to a special meeting about Sandy's situation. I didn't sign a petition supporting her.

But eventually, I couldn't STOP thinking about Sandy in connection with the underground railroad; people breaking laws to help other people escape from slavery. And I realized that for me, helping people find lost relatives was worth breaking the law for. I have a close friend, Pam Hasegawa, who had thought for fifteen years that she had found her birthmother, even though this woman didn't acknowledge Pam as her daughter. She turned out to be the wrong person. Pam is now fifty-two. I would gladly break a law if it would turn up Pam's birthmother for her. And I like to think I would gladly go to jail for it, with apologies only to my family.

I still hadn't reached out to Sandy. I didn't do that until last August when I was with Pam, who knew someone in touch with Sandy and had heard more than I had.

Together, Pam and I wrote a note to Sandy, basically, "We're sorry. We're thinking about you." Then Sandy called me. She was going to be sentenced on October 1st, when I was planning to be at the CERA conference in New York. So I said, "Well, if you want to let me know about your sentencing, I'll announce it at the conference." That is how I got more involved.

The morning I woke up in New York City, at the conference, I knew I was going to make a little speech about Sandy. It was coming up out of me. This was a couple days before we heard what Sandy's sentence was. What I needed to say was that if Sandy went to jail, I was going to be there and hoped others would join me. What I was feeling was that if I were going to jail, I would want my friends to be there to give me a hug at the gates before I went in. I also felt that this was an important enough event in the history of the struggle against closed records that it deserved eye-witnesses. I also hoped we could use this event to publicize the idea that until we have open records, people will do whatever they have to find each other.

I knew I hadn't made a complete fool of myself when Sophie Janney came up to me after my little speech. I don't want to embarrass Sophie, but I do want to thank her for letting me know I had said something that had some meaning to someone else. Sophie said she hadn't cried when she went to see "The Joy Luck Club," but that what I had said had made her cry. That gave me courage. And Sophie, and several others asked me to keep them informed so that they might at least try to be there, if Sandy did go to prison.

The fax came in at the Roosevelt Hotel. Sandy had "gotten":

- four months in a federal prison to start November 1st;

- after her release, two months house arrest wearing an electronic device around her ankle (for which she has to pay a monthly fee, which is like having to rent your own shackles)

- after that, three years probation, during which time she cannot do any searching for anybody, which includes referring for search help elsewhere.

WHAT HAD SANDY DONE? This is how I understand it. She had a quite visible business for helping searchers. She had to make a living, and this was how she chose to do it. A man had called for help finding his daughter, only he was really a New York State Department of Health investigator. Sandy farmed out the detective work, so to speak, and the person to whom she often farmed out such work got caught obtaining information illegally. Why didn't THAT person go to jail? Because, in order to avoid going to jail herself, she turned state's evidence against Sandy. She testified in court that Sandy HAD to have known that laws were being broken. If she had not been willing to testify against Sandy, it's unlikely that Sandy would have been convicted.

I am making no judgments about anybody here. Sandy herself has said that the other woman was understandably very scared about going to jail. Sandy did no testifying at all, even on her own behalf, because she did not want to risk getting any more people into trouble. I don't think there's any doubt that Sandy has been made an example of. People get into records they don't have legal access to all the time. The U.S. Attorney involved in prosecuting Sandy was quoted in a newspaper as saying, "I hope this will have a chilling effect on people who do these things." I think he meant adoption searches.

Not long after the conviction, a New York adoption agency told a California couple who were trying to help the woman's mother get her birthmother's name, "Why don't you just stop this? You know, people are now going to jail for this. What some people hated most about the 60 Minutes segment on Sandy was that it might leave people thinking that any adoption search involved breaking the law. They thought it might scare some people away from even contemplating a search. The best part of 60 Minutes - I thought was that it showed three different people clearly saying, "This is worth breaking the law for." This is desperately important.

Sandy thought she probably wouldn't have to go in until January because her lawyer was appealing her conviction. But he had failed to file for a postponement of the serving of the sentence, which is the usual thing when there is an appeal. So practically at the last minute, Sandy found out that she was supposed to report to the Federal Prison in the panhandle of Florida.

She got a brief extension and then she left me a message that I got Wednesday night that she had to report by 5:00 PM on Friday. I called and let everybody know who had asked me to and got myself on a plane the next day, thanks to a frequent flyer certificate of my husband's and to his help in other ways. And Friday afternoon, I drove into Marianna, Florida. There were four of us waiting, when Sandy & Norm arrived after a ten hour drive from their home in Cape Coral. In your folders are some pictures we took that afternoon.

Sandy is now home wearing the electronic device. The four months went by! The worst thing that happened to her was at the very beginning. Sandy had been told to report by 5:00 pm, and we watched her get to the right building by 4:45. No one had told her that after 4:00, the person wasn't there to process her in. So she was put into solitary confinement until sometime on Monday. Sandy is extremely claustrophobic, and she was on an anti-depression medication that she asked for repeatedly for three days but never got.

A couple weeks later, she fell while she was getting down from her bunk bed, which was about six feet off the floor. The ladder for the bunk bed was on the wall side of the bed, so she had to climb to the desk, and then a folding chair and then the floor. But she slipped on the desk and broke her finger. She knew there was an empty bunk across the hall and requested it. A male prison official said to her that he supposed a fifty-five year old woman should have a lower bunk but they didn't have any available. At that point, Sandy held her tongue. She did eventually get a lower bunk.

She liked the prison food and she liked her fellow prisoners. One thing about a women's minimum security prison - and Sandy told me this, but I had also read it - is that for some of the women there, it's a better environment than where they've come from, so it's a relatively good time in their lives. It's a time that women aren't isolated from each other, that they have each other.

The best thing that happened to Sandy in prison was your cards and letters. She usually got between twenty and thirty a day. Now here's the interesting thing. These were generally not from old timers like me. Most of them were from people who are relatively new to all this and haven't gotten entrenched in stands about how things ought to be done.

You see, some people didn't like it that Sandy got a lot of publicity. She wasn't discreet about what she was doing. Some people didn't like it that she charged money or that she charged as much money as she did. Some people didn't like it that there was any illegality involved. Some people said they wouldn't want anyone getting into their Social Security records. Some people didn't like it that Sandy could make a living this way and also talk about civil rights. They said acts of civil disobedience have never been performed by those who are paid. These are some of the ways that people said "This is not about US".

I wouldn't be surprised if there has also been a class thing. I think some people have been uncomfortable with or about Sandy because she doesn't look or sound like they do. She doesn't have a fancy education or fancy credentials. I feel like I'm breaking a code in bringing up these things, but they are things WE have to get BEYOND.

Now I want to read you excerpts of two letters I received by people whom Sandy had helped. The first is by one of our own Ruth Almen a former President of the Adoption Forum, who now lives in the Upper Peninsula of Michigan. Ruth sent out a "mass mailing" to her friends, asking them to write Sandy a friendly note on a stamped addressed post card that Ruth provided. This is the beginning of Ruth's letter.

"Through your involvement in my adoption search, you helped me realize a lifelong dream, by loving and supporting me through the hard moments and days to my first joyful reunion with my brother. Another person who played a significant part in making this happen is my friend Sandy Musser. Sandy is the head of the Musser Foundation, which found Sarah for me in 1989, in two and a half months, AFTER I HAD SEARCHED FOR 7 YEARS..."

This is from a woman in Illinois.

"I spent several years searching for my son on my own and made no headway. I was put in touch with Sandy's organization by a Florida State Representative. In less than 30 days she found my son. I would not have the "peace of mind" afforded me by knowing the simple facts: his name, what he looks like and he's alive and healthy."

I had written a letter about Sandy that was reprinted, among other places, in the CERA newsletter ACCESS, which goes out to over a thousand people. Because of that, I got a letter from a Methodist minister in New Zealand who was also sending me a copy of his letter to President Clinton that he had written after reading my letter. Here is a paragraph out of that letter:

> *"No doubt the process of law will take its course and I do not seek to influence or interfere with that process. However, I do wish to raise the issue of need for adoption law reform concerning access to adoption information. I FIND IT REPUGNANT THAT IN ANY DEMOCRACY A PERSON MAY HAVE TO BREAK THE LAW TO DISCOVER THE TRUTH ABOUT THEMSELVES."*

Let me just add to that a tiny item from the press release sent out by the Musser Foundation after Sandy went to jail:

> *"We must sign the UN Treaty on Children's Rights. Our own United States has still not signed this treaty which emphasizes that every child shall have knowledge of and access to their birth family!"*

Here's what we can learn from watching Sandy Musser go to jail. A little step in the right direction can go a long way, when you realize how it fits together with other people's little steps. We're all in this together. The divisions among us are not as important as our connectedness. We don't have to approach differences AS divisions so that we don't talk to the people who don't sound exactly the same as we do on a given subject. We can disagree about many things and at the same time agree on SOMETHING. What I think we all should have been able to agree on, in this case, is that until we have open records, some people are going to have to break laws - and will - in order to learn something that is essential to them. Even people who could agree only with this could have done more to support Sandy personally, by acknowledging the price she was paying for doing things her way.

What I WANT all this to mean is that we can learn to STAND BY each other against the backlash against the open records movement - even if we disagree about means, even when we come from various walks of life. Sandy wrote something fairly recently that is kind of a prayer that her imprisonment did some good. It ends:

> **IF MY BEING IN PRISON** starts a fire burning within the hearts and souls and minds of those who are committed to this cause; or **IF MY BEING IN PRISON** simply gives courage to you, my friend —

THEN MY INCARCERATION WILL NOT HAVE BEEN IN VAIN!

I know that Sandy Musser's going to jail reinvolved me with the adoption community and with the struggle for open records. And Sandy WAS a model of courage for me. I pray that her going to jail reminds us how much we want people to have legal access to the identities of their parents and legal access to the identities of their children.

In August 1989, I presented this speech at the 1st March on Washington. In 1993 I would see my own words come to pass.

THIS TIME MUST COME

I stand here before you today as a civil rights activist for the adoption reform movement. But I want to talk about three well-know activists of other eras who loudly and clearly proclaimed the need of freedom for their people.

If a man named Moses were standing here before us today, I believe he would be speaking on our behalf and saying to our present government - Let My People Go! Because Moses was not only the leader of the Jewish nation - he was also the most famous adoptee - one who had been adopted outside of his Jewish heritage and Jewish faith. But when he became aware of the bondage his people were in, he fought and persisted to see that they were set free. The Bible says that God heard the heartcries of His people. Our heartcries are now beginning to be heard around this country. We fight against the plagues of the adoption and child welfare system - the plague of the SEALED RECORD, the plague of CLOSED ADOPTIONS, the plague of CONFIDENTIALITY which always equals COVER-UP, and the greatest plague of all - a corrupt system that has become a billion dollar business!

But I believe that we're well on our way to the Promised Land, and that most intelligent, caring individuals really want TRUTH AND OPENNESS - NOT SECRECY AND LIES.

This will be a land that will not see the need to sever birth roots nor eradicate the family name; a time when guardianship is a more cherished role than ownership. It will be a land that will not require the control of the social work profession, nor legislated rules and regulations; a land where no money need exchange hands (known as "fees") in order to adopt a child. Our Promised Land will be a land where adoptees, birthparents, and adoptive parents can come together and form a circle of love that will be immersed with openness, honesty, and heartfelt caring.

If Susan B. Anthony were standing before us today - she, too, would be speaking out on our behalf. She, too, would be saying - let these people go. She knew what it meant to be denied rights - rights that her male counterparts enjoyed. She fought and led the women of American through the streets and halls of justice so that they, too, could have a voice at the ballot box. In 1873, she and 16 other women marched to the voting booth and exercised their God-given right to vote - and for this, she stood trial. She was prosecuted and fined - a fine she refused to pay. How many of us are going to have to stand trial, pay fines, and be prosecuted for demanding or exercising our God-given right to our original birth certificate or other records concerning our own lives?

If Martin Luther King could be here today, he would most likely be at the forefront of our March. He would be raising his hands, his head, and his voice, heavenward and shouting to the world - Let these people go! In one of his famous speeches, Martin Luther King said, "I have a dream that someday our people will not be judged by the color of their skin.." We share a similar dream - that the day will soon come when we will not be judged or branded because we bear the name of 'adoptee', 'birthparent' or 'adoptive parent'.

We pray for the day that we will not have to bargain, plead beg, petition or pay for what is rightfully ours. We anticipate the day when legal documents called birth certificates will no longer be falsified - when birthmothers are no longer signed into the hospital under an assumed name, given them by an agency or attorney - we look toward the day when a simple request for information will be granted - and when Big Brother no longer stands over us with folded arms guarding our most prized possession - our BIRTHRIGHT!

Finally, I want to share the words of a poem written by Mary Anne Cohen, a birthmother with great insight and foresight. Mary Anne has written hundreds of poems over the past several years; this is one of the early ones. I consider it her best.

THIS TIME MUST COME

TIME WILL COME when our tragedy will not be replayed,
When no child will be torn out of the arms of love into the arms of money.
When all births will be blessed, all equal,
And there will be no word remembered to brand a child born outside society's ties, no recording of legal lies...
When love is more lasting than papers, and no child is deprived of either heritage or nurturing, even when they come from separate places.

224

And it is finally seen that blood and home are not the same,
And neither replaces the other, and there is no quota for love...

TIME WILL COME when social workers are to serve, not to sever;
When they know it is better to unite than separate,
To be true than to lie, to be seen than to hide,
To accept than renounce, that the giving and the nurturing of life are
both sacred and deserving of respect;
That all parents are real parents, not rivals,
That love is stronger than fear of laws or time, and cannot be
terminated, cannot be legislated, cannot be denied...

TIME WILL COME when all children can grow, become real, cast
off shadows, renew or sever ties by their own choice, be responsible,
BE FREE!
When our bondage ends, and we answer to our children;
Answer with the gift of sight, gift of words, gift of sorrow...
When every person has the right to trace their roots in their mother's
face, father's eyes...
When nobody is condemned to eternal childhood, and no mother
cries forever...

THIS TIME MUST COME

*The following article is a reprint from the **American Journal of Adoption Reform**. It is written by Jon Ryan, President of NOBAR (**National Organization of Birthfathers & Adoption Reform**).*

The Federal Government
Conspires To Suppress Adoption Search

What is this case really about? Does in involve a conspiracy to obtain highly classified, confidential information from the federal government - or is it about one person (Barbara) getting some current address information from Social Security and then having the feds and others capitalize on that mistake to launch a nationwide effort to suppress search?

Who is behind this effort? Is it just the federal government or are the national pro-closed adoption (anti-search) organizations involved? From the circumstances of the case, it appears most likely that the pro-closed adoption organizations have finally found a way to enlist the feds in their efforts to suppress search activities.

The only real mistake in this whole scenario is that Barbara used the Social Security system to obtain information that she could have obtained elsewhere.

Having previously obtained the name of the person for whom she was searching, Barbara needed only a current address. It was more efficient for Barbara to make one simple phone call to Social Security for the current address information than to search many other public records for the same information.

By trying to obtain a current address from Social Security, Barbara violated the U.S. Code. The evidence was indisputable that Barbara had obtained information illegally from Social Security. The feds then used that crime to simply heap on more charges and build a much larger case.

The feds took a molehill and made a mountain out of it. A close examination of the indictment indicates that the only real crime was Barbara calling Social Security.

One phone call would have been enough to charge her with a violation of the U.S. Code. However, an impressive, 39-count indictment against both Barbara and Sandy Musser was created when several phone calls were made by Barbara (several search cases, one phone call per case) and then everything else was tacked on against both women for good measure: conspiracy, wire fraud, and mail fraud. Getting a current address was considered to be theft, retention, and sale of government property.

Repetition and embellishment of the charges made the only real "crime" look much bigger than it actually was. From a purely tactical perspective, a jury is more likely to convict on a huge, multifaceted indictment rather than one dinky, technical violation. In this case, it worked for the feds.

For the record, it should also be noted that some of the search cases in the indictment against both women were cases that Barbara was working on for other people. These were cases that had absolutely no connection whatsoever to Sandy. Apparently the government just piled on whatever they could find and hoped that something would stick.

The real opportunity for the pro-closed adoption organizations to suppress search activities came when Sandy used Barbara to help with obtaining search information.

In the normal course of business, a client would call The Musser Foundation to do an adoption search. The case would, in turn, be farmed out all or in part to researchers around the country. These researchers would try to get relevant information. If the search was a success, the researcher was paid a set fee, Sandy's organization kept the remainder of the client's fee, and the client would get his or her information -thus enabling her or him to be reunited with other family members. Sandy used Barbara for many searches and that was the connection that the feds needed to close the circle and charge them both with conspiracy.

All by herself, Barbara was not important to the government. Many people get into Social Security records every day all over the country to obtain the same kind of current address information that Barbara obtained. It would be a waste of time and money for the feds to bring federal charges against Barbara for such a harmless, relatively insignificant, and commonplace violation.

Sandy, however, was someone who had a national, highly visible, long-term, pro-family, search and reunification business.

There wasn't much that could be done to Sandy because she had a legitimate search organization. Sandy's business was much like many businesses that offer search services to find people who don't pay their bills or deadbeat moms and deadbeat dads who don't pay child support. Searching to reunite family members separated by adoption is much different, however, than searching for people who owe money: reuniting family members separated by adoption interferes with those who profit, and profit well, by doing closed adoptions.

When the feds found some way to link Barbara and Sandy, a golden opportunity for a federal indictment was created. This case reeks of conspiracy, but it is on the part of the pro-closed adoption organizations and the feds, not Sandy Musser or Barbara Moskowitz.

In an article on 7/30/93 in the New York Times, the Asst. U.S. Attorney Thomas Getz, who prosecuted the case, stated, "From the beginning, this case was not about adoption records or adoption reunions, but about people breaching the security and confidentiality of government records."

If this case was really about "breaching Social Security" and did not involve adoption records or adoption reunions, then why did Thomas Getz bring in a birthmother from Florida and an adoptive mother from New York to testify against Sandy at the trial about adoption issues? These two women did not work for Social Security. Sandy's attorney told the judge that if the prosecution wanted to open up the case to witnesses involved with adoption issues, then he would bring forth hundreds of birthparents, adoptees, adoptive parents, and adoption professionals to testify on Sandy's behalf. The birthmother and adoptive mother were quickly taken off the stand. The damage, however, had been done by the brief adoption-directed testimony of these pro-government witnesses: whatever instructions from the judge to the contrary, the idea had firmly been implanted in the minds of that jury that this case was definitely about adoption.

Another interesting facet of this case is the timing. After such a long investigation - from August 1989 to January 1992 - and then a wait of 14 months, the indictments were made public in Ohio just the week before the 1993 National Conference of the American Adoption Congress (AAC) in Cleveland, Ohio. Apparently it was expected that Sandy Musser, who lives in Florida, would be attending the AAC conference and she could be served with the indictment when she was at the conference.

How did Mr. Getz know about the AAC Conference in Ohio if his only interest was the violation of getting into Social Security records? How did Mr. Getz know that Sandy Musser would be attending the AAC Conference and why did he wait 14 months to go public with the indictment? If this was such a heinous crime that threatened the security of government records and was such an imminent danger to our government and citizens, why was the Musser Foundation allowed to conduct business as usual and continue their search efforts for an extended period of time between the end of the investigation and the indictment?

Did Mr. Getz, as a representative of the federal government, intend to use this indictment as a political opportunity on behalf of the pro-closed adoption organizations - a chance to disrupt the AAC Conference and gain additional national exposure? Was the AAC information supplied to Mr. Getz by the pro-closed adoption organizations and was there a joint decision to go public at that time?

When the prosecution finished its case, Sandy's attorney did not have any witnesses testify on Sandy's behalf because he thought, based on his experience as defense attorney, that the government had simply failed to prove its case of conspiracy and the other charges. (For example, when Sandy sent printed literature about her services to people who inquired - the feds alleged that this was "mail fraud"). There was no direct evidence that Sandy knew how Barbara was obtaining current address information in her searches through Social Security records. People who attended the trial on Sandy's behalf agreed that the feds had simply not proved their case. The jury, however, found Sandy guilty. Sandy's indictment and conviction has caused polarization in the adoption reform movement; people either support her or denounce her "tactics" in doing adoption searches. Many people who do not support Sandy cite the fact that she was making "so much money" in her search work. When the federal judge sentenced Sandy October 1st, he took into account her business records from The Musser Foundation. Originally the court wanted to use Sandy's husband's income in computing any fine. Sandy, however, convinced the court that the charges for which she was convicted were based only on work that she did from The Musser Foundation. Any fines, therefore, should be based solely on the finances of that business.

Sandy received no fine in her sentencing because the court reviewed the financial records of The Musser Foundation and determined that a fine was simply not warranted. The fees collected in searches went to pay for researchers, for adoption reform publications, for business overhead (like an 800 number that received thousands of calls after The Musser Foundation reunited three sets of twins on the Maury Povich Show), for family preservation efforts and for numerous other adoption reform activities. Sandy Musser was not in the search business to make money. Sandy did searches because she believed that families have a right to be reunited. It's as simple as that. Anyone who claims that money motivated Sandy or that she profited from this enterprise is seriously misguided and grossly misinformed.

Others in the adoption reform movement who condemn Sandy's work question her methods of obtaining information. Some have claimed that, in some ways the resources she uses for searching are inappropriate and might negatively influence the public perception of efforts to reunite families. Many of those who take this position have, at one time or another, done searches themselves and know the disingenuousness of their statements.

The adoption reform movement should rally totally and unconditionally behind Sandy and protest this abuse by a federal agency that is working on behalf of a special interest group - the pro-closed adoption organizations. Instead of devoting years of effort to preventing the reunification of families, why not redirect the time and energy to preventing the interstate and international trafficking in babies? The federal government clearly has its priorities wrong. Let's let our federal legislators and Attorney General Janet Reno know that suppressing search efforts on behalf of a special interest group must be stopped immediately.

Nancy Verrier, M.A. is an adoptive mother, psychotherapist, and author. Until recently few people have given much thought to the wound which results from the separation of babies from their mothers. It has been assumed that babies are too tiny and insensitive to know what's happening to them and that so long as they get some kind of nurturing, they will be OK. Nancy has taken issue with this assumption in her book entitled **The Primal Wound: Understanding the Adopted Child.**

AN INTERVIEW WITH NANCY VERRIER
AUTHOR OF PRIMAL WOUND
Reprint from *Adoption Circles* - Spring '94

Q. Your belief is that the natural evolution of bonding by postnatal separation from the biological mother is indelibly imprinted upon the unconscious minds of babies, thus causing the Primal Wound?

A. My definition of the Primal Wound is the trauma of separation from the mother, which interrupts the bonding that should have just been a continuation from pre to postnatal life. It's not going to change that primal wound to have the mother separate from the child later. I think that the baby would be better off being with the mother for as long as possible because a lot of things happen right at birth, that helps the baby feel secure with her. The longer the mother is with the baby, the better it is for the baby. The trauma will happen anyway if she separates, but the baby can be further along in the evolution of its development which will be an advantage.

Q. A very important fact you mentioned in this book, is that society has certain misconceptions regarding adoption and how to separate a child from their birthmother. But indeed, it forgets that the adoptee was there. Why is this overlooked?

A. I think it's still overlooked today in a lot of ways. Babies are not given credit that all of their senses are working. Nothing is ever lost in the psyche or in the body cells. It's often thought that somehow, if a baby can't say anything, he/she can't know what is happening. Many babies can go into shock or just go numb. That's the sense of being lost or of all hope being gone of the mother ever coming back.

Q. In a way it's like the sexual abuse survivor, they set up one part of their brain to not remember.

A. That's right. The same can apply to adoptees, that is, they can suffer a trauma and then suffer from post-traumatic stress disorders. We need to look at our society and stop and think about what's being done to our children in order to know why they are responding in certain ways. To take a baby away from its mother is not normal. Many birthmothers and adoptees experience denial or numbness.

Q. You can say that babies bond in utero for the 40 weeks of gestation. In your experience, who would deny this?

A. Well, one Mothers' Day I read an article by a psychologist who said the birthbond is nonexistent and it's only something that people talk about to make mothers who put their kids in daycare feel guilty. Halfway through the article, she then admits that she's never been a mother. I thought, why was she even talking about this? Because she couldn't see it on some kind of graph? I know that a birthbond exists. There are a lot of people who are in denial about the birthbond. The denial is more convenient rather than taking responsibility for the fact that children are devastated upon separation.

Q. Why do reunited birthmothers find it so hard to deal with the part of their child's life that they missed? For example, looking at pictures of their child through the growing up years.

A. That's because all this time she has created the denial that this child was actually a baby, or even grew up. Society really appreciates it if you go along with that denial. You aren't as big of a problem if you go along with society. But, if you talk about it enough, you're considered pathological.

Q. Why is abandonment a major issue?

A. When a baby is separated from its mother for any reason, it feels abandoned. The reason that adoptees say they need to find their birthmother, to find their sense of self is that they not only feel that the mother was lost, but also part of themselves was lost. Abandonment is just simply "going away". When adults feel they are going to be abandoned, it is different because they can't be left helpless to die. But a baby can actually die from being abandoned.

Q. Will you differentiate between attachment and bonding?

A. I think the key is security and safety. Most children attach to their caregivers because it is necessary to do so, to be taken care of. They need that person so much that they become very attached to that person. It's a dependent relationship. The baby who is not separated from the mother feels very secure about him/herself and doesn't anticipate anything terrible or dreadful happening to them. That's bonding. It's falling in love with your baby and the baby responding to that. A baby who has been separated once from its mother, whether it's because of an incubator or adoption, can never feel that security.

Q. So someone like Jessica DeBoer will have a difficult time adjusting.

A. She already did. One of the things that people don't understand about that case is that this is the second time she has been devastated by separation. The first time, she was so tiny that people didn't notice. It was perhaps even more devastating because she was still so much a part of her birthmother.

Q. The idea of searching to reconnect with a birthmother is filled with conflict and anxiety. It should not be regarded as pathological, but as healthy. Could it take awhile for society to get used to that theory?

A. I think that some talk shows who televise reunions have a good effect in general, on society. When people see the emotion, they can feel that there's something there. It can be mysterious and mystical because the audience sees it as two strangers meeting. It may be hard for some

231

people to have any idea of what it feels like to not know your relatives. But I think everyone has to stop polarizing around the two mothers and realize that the adoptee is in the position of trying to please both mothers, as well as trying to do what's right for themselves. The most positive reunions are ones which the adoptive mother and the birthmother feel that they want to do what is best for the child.

Q. How many adoptees have you met who say they have no interest in searching for their birth relatives?

A. The ones I meet say that because they're unsure. I say it's fine and that's the way it is. It's hard to believe them because it doesn't make sense, even logically. Who wouldn't be interested in the people who gave birth to them and all the things that go along with it? They may be afraid. Fear drives a lot of people and can even paralyze them.

Q. Many birthmothers were told that they would forget. You also hear of many adoptees being told that they shouldn't search. Why the negativeness?

A. People need to be educated in this area. Ignorance is what got us into this pickle in the first place. I certainly didn't know as an adoptive parent that my child was in pain when we adopted her. I did not know that because I wasn't told. I don't believe the social workers at that time knew either. They probably didn't acknowledge the fact that babies knew their mothers at birth. Now, there's hardly any question to the fact. Also, there has always been a denial towards the importance of birthfathers. I haven't heard of too many children who say they're glad they don't have a father in their life. They need to know who those two parents are.

Q. The loss of a birthmother can erode the values of basic trust in an adoptee. How can adoptive parents overcome this?

A. It's very difficult. The best thing that adoptive parents can do is to validate the child's feelings. The child needs to feel that someone understands his pain. If a child can not handle certain feelings, they may do what we call projective identification, where they sort of inject the parents with those feelings. This can make the parent feel angry, confused and aggressive in a matter of minutes. Instead of flying off the handle, the parent can say "I'm beginning to feel angry, I'm wondering if you're angry too". When the parent can name the feeling and own it, this can help the child own it for themselves, too. If for example, a child says "I really miss my real Mom", rather than the adoptive parent saying, "I'm your real Mom!" or "She didn't want you and I came to rescue you", it's better to say, "Yes, you must miss her a lot", and let it go at that. The child's feelings are validated and he feels understood.

Q. You believe that adoption should serve children who need parents, not childless couples who seek children. What kind of feedback do you receive from this statement?

A. Not many people disagree with me. In fact, no one has even argued with me about that point. My book has surprised some readers because it pushed some sensitive buttons.

MUSINGS OF A BIRTHPARENT
by Sandy Musser
April 24, 1991
Open Adoption as Standard Practice Conference
Traverse City, MI

From the moment I received Jim's invitation to speak to you, I've pondered over various issues that I felt were important to share. I know that within a day or two of this conference, no one will remember most of what has been said, but since I never know when I might be making my last speech for adoption reform, it is always my hope and prayer that each person present will recall at least one point that will provide them with a new and fresh perspective.

Today I want to draw analogies from two historical events, which began during the late 50's and early 60's - the civil rights movement and the Viet Nam War. Though both these events are forever written in our minds, as well as our history books, the adoption reform movement has been slower to take hold or to gain the momentum needed for real reform. But the adoption reform movement also began in the 50's. As many of you know, it was Jean Paton -a 42 year old adoptee - former social worker, who finally broke the silence and wrote a book by the same title. Just like John the Baptist, she was a lone voice crying in the wilderness for many, many years. Now in her 80's, she continues the struggle she began back in 1953. It was not until the early 70's that the mantle she carried so high was finally picked up by new runners who, out of their own pain, began to forge a new kind of adoption.

I am going to take the liberty today to speak on behalf of white middle class birthmothers. Why? Because I was one and because I believe most of the millions of babies placed for adoption during the last four decades were from white, middle-class families. It is we who can probably best relate to sitting in the back of the bus. You see, we were sent to the back roads of America and placed in homes for the degraded - where our names were changed, the rules were strict, and we were taught what our place was - a lowly and lonely place - one of punishment and pain for the unpardonable act we had committed. The crime? Being an unwed

233

mother! The penalty? Losing our child to adoption forever. Like the blacks in the 50', we were relegated to the back of the bus. We did as we were told; we obeyed the rules and believed we had no choice; that's just the way it was. We did what we had to do - we "surrendered". We paid the ultimate price. We gave up our babies.

With the cleansing process complete, we were told to go on with our lives; within a few short years 25% of us had married the birthfather and had other children - full siblings to the child we surrendered; another 25% of us never had any other children, either by choice or because we were unable to conceive - we gave our only child to an infertile couple and we remained forever childless - we may have been the ones to make the greatest sacrifice; many of us were encouraged to go on to college to get our Masters' and PhD's - and as Elizabeth, a birthmother from Philadelphia, so aptly stated, "It didn't take me long to realize that I had traded my child for a piece of paper, and that I had been duped into believing that my degree was more important"; most of us went on to marry, have other children, became active in our communities and tried very hard to prove ourselves worthy as upstanding citizens. In order to accomplish this great feat, we had to deny "the experience". We pretended "as though it never happened". It appeared to our family and friends that we had forgotten. Most of you know by now that we never forgot and, like the Viet Vets years and years later, many of us are suffering or have suffered from post-traumatic syndrome. A few of the Vets did return from the war unscathed, but the majority returned with missing limbs, twisted bodies, confused minds and no glory. Like them, we returned from our war with missing pieces - empty wombs, pierced hearts, and hollow souls -and without our children.

You look at those of us who are angry and you have difficulty understanding why. You remind us that it was our decision, but you forget that there were no other choices. You told us we would be doing a wonderful, sacrificial deed, but neglected to tell us that we'd hurt for the rest of our lives. Maybe you just didn't know any better. Maybe you, too, were simply pawns in this scenario called adoption. We were told it was in our and our child's best interest - and then some of us found that our children did not fare nearly as well as we had been promised. Even those who did fare well still have a deep desire and longing to know us - their birthparents, but now these adult children of adoption are told that it's NOT in their best interest to know us. And you made sure that they never would! You, the child welfare system, sealed the records and even today most of you will do nothing toward helping to unseal them. And so we adoptees, birthparents and some concerned adoptive parents have joined forces as we seek to reclaim our lost rights. While we cannot possibly change the events of the past, we can at least try to right the wrongs that were done. We can remold the future so that no adoptee will ever have to wonder from whence they came - no birthparent will have to wonder if their child is alive or well - and no adoptive parent will need to fear the special person who gave them the opportunity to raise a child.

That is what this conference is about. An open, honest approach to adoption. Is this open adoption we keep talking about a new concept? No, not really. In the early part of this century, we knew it by a different name - it was called guardianship. Guardians were those special people who took over as caretakers for families who were struggling financially and/or emotionally from the war-torn depression years. Not too much different from today. The haves and the have-nots. The major difference was that guardianship never denoted ownership. There was no such thing as an amended birth certificate, a final decree, or the need for a "facilitator". It was just simply people helping people. Idealistic you say? Maybe, but if it was indeed possible then, why not now?

Since we've come this far, why don't we agree to go one step further; why don't we agree to redirect the millions of $ now being spent on the foster care system and expend it for the preservation of the natural family. Imagine how many families could remain together if those funds were used to teach parenting skills, provide programs to help increase a family's standard of living, etc. **The trauma of separation from one's family of origin is, I believe, one of the most agonizing traumas we suffer as human beings. It affects us for our entire lives.** The statistics have proved over an over that our jails, our mental health facilities, and our treatment centers are filled with those who become separated from their family of origin at an early age.

The most startling statistic of all is that 7 out of 10 mass/serial murderers over the past 20 years were adopted. By removing children from their original families, we have added to these alarming statistics. Many adoptees and foster children are filled with rage. Louise Armstrong, author of *Solomon Says,* states "Today's foster children are tomorrow's adults. They are our future - enraged, alienated, desperate young wards of a system that offers to 'help' mothers by taking away their children..."

It makes me wonder what will become of little Wesley who got caught up in the system and lost his entire extended family a year and a half ago. Let me tell you briefly what happened. I received a call from a man in his early 30's asking if we had taken his nephew? We had no idea what he was talking about and so we asked him to explain. He said he hadn't seen his nephew for a few weeks and suspected that his sister had given up her 5 year old son for adoption through us. We immediately assured him that it was not us, since we are in the business of reuniting

235

families - not separating them. We suggested a few other agencies in the area for him to call.

Within a short period of time, he was able to establish that one of our local agencies did, in fact, take a surrender from his sister on October 17, 1989. On October 30th (less than two weeks from the time the surrender was taken), Wesley's Uncle Dave, his Aunt Gale, his Uncle Jimmy, his grandparents from Illinois, and three close friends of the family wrote to the agency requesting custody of little Wesley. The agency refused claiming they had already placed him, had a valid consent from the birthmother, and there was nothing that could be done.

We question the MORALITY of an agency accepting a child for adoption to be placed in a stranger-home when there were family members willing and able to raise this little boy. The family did not have the money to fight, and we tried every attorney in the county, but could not find one to take the case - or to even talk about it! The director of the agency has strong political connections in the community, which may have been the reason.

My contention is this. We don't take a child just from a mother; we take a child from an entire family system - the root system - and unless we make a sincere effort to find someone in that family to help out, we are guilty of kidnapping. Yes, there was a surrender, but this very distraught birthmother was not the only person to be considered. This child had an entire extended family who cared about him.! Why weren't they contacted? Is it because the agency wouldn't have gotten their fee if they put their efforts toward keeping this child within the family unit? Let's call a spade a spade - the price on Wesley's head was approximately $5,000! Similar cases occur throughout our country on a daily basis.

My heart aches for little Wesley. I think about out him often and wonder how the social worker who took the surrender can sleep at night. How long does a small boy wait for a familiar looking face to come and get him? How much anger builds up within a child who has suddenly lost contact with every single person he has ever known? Think of it! Every single human being you have ever known is suddenly gone out of your life! What an atrocity! Is this really in the best interest of the child?? And when he's 18 and wants to know who his family is - what will we tell him then? Sorry, Wesley, but your records are sealed and they are sealed forever! You have no right to know! It's then that he realizes that he has no control, not now or ever, over this most important aspect of his life-his genetic connection - his entire history has been stolen and sealed.

Is it this built-up anger that one day explodes and causes the deaths of innocent people. What are the chances that this little guy might become a Son of Sam - a Hillside or Boston Strangler, a Joseph Kallinger, Arthur

Goode, Ken Bianchi, Albert DeSalvo, David Berkowitz - all adopted and filled with rage. Is there any connection? Is it nature or nurture that causes these heinous acts. Listen my friends - I don't believe it's genes or environment that set the stage for criminal acts, but I do believe that **the repressed anger that results from the trauma of separation is the most toxic emotion known to man.** And I believe the sooner we recognize this fact and decide that we're not going to be a party to it anymore, the better off our society will be.

Traditional, closed, sealed adoption has got to stop. Too many lives have been devastated in its wake. No longer should we be taking babies from mothers or children from parents simply because they are too young or too poor. Somehow we need to find new programs that will prevent this terrible loss from ever occurring in the first place. As Hal Aigner, author of *Adoption in America* says- "Healing is wonderful, but the better path is not to contract the disease."

Now that Open Adoption is becoming recognized and accepted, we need to proceed with caution - we need to be careful that it doesn't become just another avenue for us to support our chosen profession. How much better to put our energies into family preservation. Prior to records being sealed, the main focus and original purpose of child welfare was to preserve families. But once the sealed record was in place, the number of private placement agencies and fees both increased tremendously. What exactly was adoption originally intended for - what was its purpose? The purpose and intent of adoption was to provide a means to care for children who were truly orphans - orphans were children who had no families. It is time that we as professional leaders made a commitment to keeping families intact - open adoption is a beginning, but it's just that - a beginning.

In closing a little parable to strike home the point. As Jesus was making his way through the hills of Galilee, there was a group of men who decided they would try to trick him. One had captured a small bird which fit right in the palm of his hand. The plan was to ask Jesus if the bird was dead or alive. If He said the bird was alive, then the man would crush it and kill it, but if He said it was dead, the man would open his hand and let the little bird fly away. They asked "Master, is the bird I hold in my hand dead or alive?" Without a moments hesitation, Jesus replied "My friend, that decision is in your hands!"

Friends, the face of adoption is constantly changing. Most of the changes appear to be good. Since the social work profession has always controlled and structured the child welfare institution - and because there are so many of you here today - I submit to you that open adoption, guardianship and family preservation is in your hands. It is my sincere hope that you will let them live.

237

Lynn Giddens and I first met when she invited me to speak at an Adoption Information Exchange Conference in North Carolina. Lynn had established branches of AIE throughout the state of NC until she took a sabbatical in 1986. When she returned to reform work in 1991, the face of AIE had changed drastically so she founded a new organization known as NC Adoption Connections. During my dark hours, she became a stalwart of support.

THE LEGACY OF A LEADER

I came into what we now refer to as the Adoption Reform Movement in 1979. At that time, I think I was simply known as a 'disgruntled adoptee" who couldn't leave well enough alone.

As any adoptee who has been on a difficult and time-consuming search, one quickly begins to see life differently. I was no exception. I became angry with the system - the same system that tried to pretend "closed records" were in "my best interest." I became angry with those around me - feeling that it was a situation we all bore responsibility for - after all, years had not removed the injustice.

My discontent - not with my adoption - but with the system, who provided the rules for the adoption, motivated me into the founding of the Adoptee's Rights Group. It was organized in Chapel Hill in 1981 and the name was later changed to the Adoption Information Exchange including all members of the triad. During the next five years, I would remain actively involved as AIE's Director/Coordinator. My friend, Marion, joined me in 1983 as the Western Coordinator.

Due to a series of unfortunate circumstances, I left AIE in 1986 - vowing never to return to "adoption" work again. I did not return until 1991.

I met Sandy in 1983 when she was passing through North Carolina on her way to Florida. Sandy's vision was similar to mine. She wanted to see records opened. She had a message to tell - one that I believed then as I do now - is valuable for everyone to hear - whether or not they had suffered the pain of loss or separation.

During the years to follow, Sandy became a 'regular' at the forums and conferences I hosted. In 1991 upon returning after my "absence", I called Sandy. I was happy to see her work had continued, and that she was now a "nationally known entity". She was getting "the word out" any which way she could. My only disappointment was that it was taking the reform movement such a long time to make any legislative changes.

I first learned of Sandy's indictment via a telephone call from a friend advising me that Sandy was in trouble. I had always maintained my

238

friendship with her - we were in my opinion, more than just comrades in a fight for justice - we were also friends. When I left AIE in 1986, I had left with feelings which would later be dealt with - and "adoption" was not part of my agenda. Sandy had not forgotten me - we continued to keep in touch and after I had my son in 1988 (after seven miscarriages), I was touched when she sent him a gift! She has remained in my heart.

I called Sandy at home on the Sunday I first learned of the indictment and she confirmed my worst fears - she was in trouble but we didn't know the extent. I knew that although I was but one person, I wanted to be there. I had always known her motivations in the adoption reform movement were pure - she cared about people - she worked to help them and she rejoiced in their happiness when they were reunited. It was clear-cut and it was genuine and my high respect for her was due to her pure motivations. I had seen others whose motives I questioned - she was not one of them!

The following year was painful. Many tears were shed for a friend. I often heard people say "she is serving time for me". They were right. Sandy Musser went to jail for all of us who believe records should be open. As difficult as it was for me to accept she was in prison - what was even more perplexing was why our national organization did not rally at this critical time. The "unity" feelings that existed when our movement first began had apparently waned. But the support she received from individuals around the country, many who she did not even know, was the inspiration she needed to see it through.

Today Sandy is out of prison. I stand proud when I stand beside her. She represents survival to me - on many different levels. Is my thanks to her enough - probably not. There are no words that I know of that can ease pain of such an experience.

But I do have a vision - I have a vision that the movement will pull together and stand as one because of the sacrifice that Sandy Musser made. I have a vision that the greed, selfishness, conceit, arrogance and backstabbing methods that I have seen consume many will soon cease, and we will remember our ultimate aim - to make adoption a more humane loving institution and to provide access to open records! That is what Sandy Musser's legacy will be.

WHAT NOW?

"The adoptee position rests on two principles that must remain inflexible. The first is that each person has a right to his own human history and identity. The second is that adult adoptees have the same competence and right as non-adoptees to manage their own affairs without supervision of the State through its agencies. The underlying principle of the adoption movement is the determination to be free of those limitations that have not been imposed on non-adopted citizens. The issue is whether adoptees are to be allowed to emancipate from the chattel-child status into autonomous adults or are they to continue to be infantilized by the ongoing control of State and agency, birthparents and adoptive parents? Would legislators either seek or accept social work supervision of their own personal affairs? On what evidence do they decide that they are capable of managing without supervision, but adult adoptees are not? Slavery is the condition of having to submit to the power of others to control over their lives. Undoubtedly legislators fail to see a significant violation of human rights in this proposal because they do not realize the adversary relationship between power and liberty, and they do not realize that investing social work professionals with so much discretionary power is inappropriate to the goal."

Margaret Lawrence
1979 AAC Conference
Washington, DC

Having been through this experience has naturally given me a totally different perspective of things. I have ambivalent feelings about my government as never before, because their actions both in and out of prison have caused my trust and faith to waiver. I've seen family members pitted against family members, friends against friends, and organizations against organizations as the investigative government agencies go about their business of seeking more and more inane and asinine indictments, sometimes with trumped up charges and often with enticements.

Millions of people in our country were outraged over the way the WACO situation was handled. To see our military tanks crashing through a building where innocent women and children resided is not only a disgrace to our country, but it shows that our nation is in a sad state of affairs. Our "police agencies" (DEA, AFT, FBI, CIA) seem to have lost all sense of reason. To see Rodney King beaten beyond recognition by the men in blue is, of course, a scandal in and of itself, but had it not been captured on video, no one would ever have known; how many more have there been?

The world certainly appears to be topsy-turvey. I do not fear the women I served time in prison with, but I do fear what my government, **through their agents' abusive use of power,** can do to me and/or my loved ones. Trust in our justice system no longer exists. What is it going to take to change it?

A Reform Platform for Consideration

Aside from that - many have asked "**Sandy, where do we go from here as a movement and what needs to happen next?** I believe we need to agree upon a policy statement we can all get behind and then go forward with it.

When I read the following treatise, it reminded me of the process our own movement has gone through as we've struggled to find a platform palatable to the masses or even to a few legislators. This is no easy task, especially in light of the fact that drastic changes are so desperately needed and needed immediately!

Many individuals in our movement have settled for "gradual emancipation". i.e. passive registries, intermediaries, etc. But there are many of us who can no longer settle for halfway measures. The following article by William Garrison draws a perfect analogy. I believe this is where we need to be in our fight to free all triad members from the bondage of the "sealed record".

Just as Garrison called an end to the immoral institution of slavery, I am calling for the abolition of adoption as we have known it in this country for the past 50 years. (And I realize "them are fightin' words!")

In 1829 William Lloyd Garrison began his attack on slavery calling for gradual emancipation. In 1931, he published the first issue of *The Liberator and called for 'an immediate end to an immoral institution..'* Take note of the analogies to our cause:

242

"Assenting to the self-evident truth maintained in the American Declaration of Independence 'that all men are created equal and endowed by their Creator with certain inalienable rights - among which are life, liberty and the pursuit of happiness,' I shall strenuously contend for the immediate enfranchisement of our slave population. In Park Street Church, on the 4th of July 1829, in an address on slavery, I unreflectively assented to the popular, but pernicious, doctrine of gradual abolition. I seize this opportunity to make a full and unequivocal recantation, and thus publicly to ask pardon of my God, of my country, and of my brethren the poor slaves, for having uttered a sentiment so full of timidity, injustice and absurdity.

I am aware that many object to the severity of my language; but is there not cause for severity? I will be as harsh as truth, and as uncompromising as justice. On this subject, I do not wish to think or speak, or write, with moderation. Tell a man whose house is on fire, to give a moderate alarm; tell him to moderately rescue his wife from the hands of the ravisher; tell the mother to gradually extricate her babe from the fire into which it has fallen; - but urge me not to use moderation in a cause like the present. I am in earnest. I will not equivocate - I will not excuse - I will not retreat a single inch - AND I WILL BE HEARD.

The apathy of the people is enough to make every statue leap from its pedestal, and to hasten the resurrection of the dead. It is pretended, that I am retarding the cause of emancipation by the coarseness of my invective and the precipitancy of my measures. The charge is not true. On this question my influence, - humble as it is, - is felt at this moment to a considerable extent, and shall be felt in coming years - not perniciously, but beneficially - not as a curse, but as a blessing; and posterity will bear testimony that I was right. I desire to thank God, that he enables me to disregard 'the fear of man which bringeth a snare,' and to speak his truth in its simplicity and power...."

William Lloyd Garrison

Making a Beginning

The following press release was sent to the media soon after my trial. It sums up what we need to be emphasizing. The first part deals specifically with opening sealed records. The second part is a platform for abolishing closed adoption. We need to be working on both fronts simultaneously if we are going to move forward for reform and family preservation.

Recently Sandy Musser, Director of The Musser Foundation was found guilty of "conspiracy to obtain confidential information" in her work of reuniting families. In the meantime, the Foundation is asking anyone interested in adoption reform to join the "**Awareness**

243

Project" by sharing the following information which is clear cut and to the point:

America's Family Problem

1) Adoption records i.e. original birth certificates, court records, hospital records, agency records, etc. are "sealed forever" in all but two states - Kansas and Alaska.
2) 135,000,000 million extended families are affected by this archaic law.
3) Medical histories, heritage, culture and genealogy have been wiped out by virtue of the adoption process causing **ancestricide.**
4) This denial of basic human birthrights affects our divorce population as well; step-parent adoption records are also "sealed". Millions of young people are seeking their natural fathers or, in some cases, mothers.
5) Confidentiality always equals cover-up, providing the avenue for the falsification and alteration of birth certificates and adoption records.
6) Adoption is one of America's billion $ businesses, flourishing because of secrecy and confidentiality; this, in turn, has created the LEGAL baby-selling market.
7) The adoption lobbyist in Washington is the NCFA, a national organization supported by private agencies who are dedicated to secrecy and confidentiality, allowing the profitable baby-selling market to continue to flourish. (See 5 & 6 above).

America's Family Solution

The 14th Amendment

1. All persons born or naturalized in the U.S., and subject to the jurisdiction thereof, are citizens of the United States and of the State wherein they reside.

No state shall make or enforce any law which shall abridge the privileges or immunities of citizens of the United States; nor shall any State deprive any person of life, liberty, or property, without due process of law; nor deny to any person within its jurisdiction the equal protection of the laws.

On July 28, 1868 the 14th amendment was ratified giving the federal government the right to intervene when states or local governments deprive citizens of their rights.

This crucial amendment has become the basis for all the civil rights legislation in the last 100 years. Since **adoptees as a class** are being discriminated against by being denied basic birthrights, this is already a civil rights issue and is, therefore, applicable under the 14th amendment.

We propose the following:

1) An immediate **Federal Mandate** that would supersede state laws based upon the Civil Rights Act and the 14th amendment which gives equal access under the law. This mandate would allow adoptees, birthparents, adoptive parents, siblings and other extended family members to have access to one another.
2) Closed, sealed, secret, confidential adoptions should be abolished. If we are really the Pro-Family Society we claim to be, then we can no longer support family separation using the present form of adoption. Guardianship and Family Preservation measures should immediately be put into place.
3) We must sign the UN Treaty on Children's Rights. Our own United States has still not signed this treaty which emphasizes that every child shall have knowledge of, and access to, their birth family. America needs to get out of the lucrative baby business - it's the right of every child to know their origins and family connections.

A POLICY STATEMENT FOR OUR CONSIDERATION

1) Closed, sealed, secret adoption must be abolished because it is **un-American, unconstitutional, immoral and unworkable** for all those it directly affects;
2) Those we term "birth family" are already a family whose preservation should be our top priority;
3) The "Privacy Act" was intended to protect individuals from government intervention into their lives. Privacy cannot and should not be imposed when it concerns family and kin because it is in direct conflict with the Constitution and Bill of Rights;

245

4) Rights of those touched by adoption are Human Rights which may be categorized by Articles 3, 4, 6, 7, 12, 15, 16, 25, and 29 of The Universal Declaration of Human Rights (Covenant of 1948 of Amnesty International).

5) Human Rights cannot be legislated or voted upon because they are moral issues; however, it is every citizen's obligation to support legislation which upholds Human Rights;

6) Human Rights have no "legal age" limitations. The appropriate age for asserting one's Human Rights is the age at which one accepts responsibilities incumbent upon the exercise of one's rights;

7) Adoption injustices are a national disgrace which must be opposed in every possible way; i.e. altering and falsification of legal documents and sealed, secret, closed adoptions.

8) Adoption is actually the business of selling human beings (or "baby-selling") and therefore repugnant to any American citizen by whatever name it is called;

9) For purposes of simplifying what the Open Records Movement represents - "The Right To Know" shall refer to the rights of all; any attempt to infringe upon this right of any one individual does, as a matter of course, diminish the rights of another; that "The Right To Know" about one's self or one's family is a family matter and the extent of family knowledge and contact is a matter of individual and family conscience - not of societal, statutory, political or any other type of restraint;

10) That "open adoption" is a contradiction as long as records are falsified and the original record sealed, and as long as any of the parties profit from it; but we recognize open adoption as an effort to correct the injustices of adoption and support the effort as long as it seeks to reform itself toward legal agreements similar to joint custody situations in divorce and guardianships.

*Excerpts from AMFOR

If you are in agreement with this reform platform and policy statement, would you drop me a note and let me know. Send it to the National Adoption Awareness Convention, PO Box 2823, Chapel Hill, NC 27515. If you enclose a self-addressed stamped envelope, I will respond.

THE HOMECOMING

Release day had finally arrived. It was March 3, 1994 and the small calendar on the side of my locker now had a line drawn through each of the previous 117 days. Occasionally there were two or three women being released the same day, but on March 3rd, I was the happy lone ranger! I was told to be at R & D by 8:00 a.m. A few of my closest friends had escorted me to the door where we exchanged hugs and kind wishes. It was uncertain as to whether our paths would ever cross again.

My husband was waiting out front of the Administration Building. He was given permission to ride along in the van as we went to the "Big House" (FCI Main Office) to obtain whatever monies were still in my account. He had brought my wedding bands along and attempted to put them on me, but they wouldn't fit! I had been fed too well and had gained several pounds!

As we drove out of the driveway, I glanced back and felt a tinge of sadness. A part of me would always remain there in Marianna. There were so many women with whom I had bonded and who cross my mind on a daily basis. I long to reach out across the miles and communicate with them, but Big Bro says NO NO - not allowed!

Norm drove back to the motel where he had been staying to retrieve his belongings and check out. As soon as he opened the door, I flopped across the bed and tears welled up. I tried to choke them back, but they kept coming. What were these tears? Were they tears of joy, of relief, or a combination of both? Though I felt a great sense of relief, I also had feelings of sadness, anger, hurt, disappointment and a deep wound. Would I ever fully recover? I wasn't sure then and I'm not sure now.

Since my favorite breakfast meal consisting of eggs and corned-beef hash was seldom served in prison, we stopped at a little country restaurant right outside Marianna. It was a terrific feeling just to be able to place an order.

As we drove south on Rt.75 towards home, I talked about the little things we all take for granted - being able to sleep in my own bed, going to lunch with a friend, hugging my wonderful furry animals. As we pulled into our driveway in front of our house, yellow ribbons abounded. They were all over the yard - around every tree and on every bush. As soon as Norm had left the house to pick me up, my neighbors, Barb and Julie, started decorating it. It was a beautiful sight to my eyes and gave me a warm feeling of love. Baskets of flowers were sitting by the door from many well-wishers.

Party Time

A Homecoming party had been planned for Sunday afternoon. One of my friends in prison had made me a **Club Fed '94** shirt which was my attire for this special event. The back of the shirt says "**Not Invited Until Indicted!**" And it is peppered on the front and back with the names of the women I grew to care about while I was 'doing time'. My oldest son and his wife had come down from New Jersey. My brother and his wife came from Virginia. Several birthmothers were there - a few from MA and NY, and many local friends and family. As my grandfather used to say, "The whole fam damily" was present. It was a wonderful day. My daughters had prepared a little ceremony that, of course, made me teary. They presented me with a beautiful 11 x 14 black and white picture of 10 little orphans and it said Ten Good Reasons. It was engraved with ALARM.

They also shared special songs that were meaningful to them while I was away. They said they used to sing their hearts out as they drove to Marianna to visit their "convict" mother. One of their favorites was *Everything I Own*, written by David Gates. Though I had heard the song, I had never paid attention to the words. They said they thought of me whenever they heard it.

The words were very touching - "You sheltered me from harm, kept me warm. You gave my life to me, set me free. The finest years I ever knew were all the years I had with you - and I would give everything I own, give up my life, my heart, my home - just to have you back again. You taught me how to love, what it's of. You never said too much, but still you showed the way and I knew by watching you - that I would give everything I own - just to have you back again."

I had goose-bumps as the song played and I watched them sway to the music. The cake was also decorated with the words - Everything I Own - just to have you back again. Another song that meant a lot to them was *"The Hand That Rocks the Cradle."*

While I was in prison, I told several people that the one thing I was going to do when I got home was to just sit and soak in a nice warm bubble bath. I've always preferred baths to showers so I really missed not being able to take one. Somehow the word got around and I got lots and lots of bubble bath and accessories, which I've thoroughly enjoyed.

Pat, too, had a presentation. She had nominated me for a Giraffe Award several months before and the letter of commendation arrived in January, while I was still in prison. She and mother decided to keep it a surprise until I got out.

The Giraffe Project recognizes people who "stick their necks out". The beautifully framed commendation says:

Whereas: Sticking one's neck out for the Common Good is an inspiration to all;

Whereas: Such Risk-taking is vital to a compassionate, peaceful and just world;

Whereas: The Giraffe Project is commissioned to seek out such Risk-takers and to honor them for their deeds:

"The Giraffe Project herewith declares Sandy Musser to be a Giraffe whose courageous actions illumine all our lives making manifest the Truth that people who believe in themselves and care for others can meet any challenge life presents."

Not only was I being honored - I felt honored!

House Arrest & Renting Shackles

The first thing Monday morning, I was required to call the Probation Office and let them know I was home. Though I had expected to have the same officer as before, I had been assigned a new one. Mr. Hansen came to see me within a day or two and said I'd have two weeks 'reprieve' before getting my ankle bracelet. I guess I could have made the great escape during that time! House Arrest began March 15th.

House arrest is basically what it says; you are required to remain within the confines of your home. While I thought it would bother me to be confined, my home actually became a cocoon during those two months after prison and I found it to be comforting. I was only allowed to leave the house with prior permission and a legitimate reason. Job hunting, of course, was always a legitimate reason. Since the ankle bracelet is quite large, I wore slacks on the occasions I went out. The cost of 'renting these shackles' is $150 a month.

To explain as simply as possible how the process works - a box is attached to the phone line; if you wander past a certain distance from your home, a buzzer sounds an alarm and they know you've made an escape! House Arrest ended the middle of May. A week later, I went to see my two boys and grandchildren in NJ who I had not seen for a year.

I am now serving my three years probation which ends March, 1997. By the 5th of each month, I am required to send a form to the probation office listing my assets, expenses and whether I've been arrested during the month. Mr. Hansen has turned out to be a good friend and is beginning to restore my faith in "man" kind.

Hope Springs Eternal

Many have asked and many are wondering how I feel at this stage of the game. To state my feelings as succinctly as I can: I am happy to be free; I do not choose to go back to prison and will not risk doing so; I believe just as strongly as ever that sealed records are unconstitutional and that our entire child welfare system needs to be revamped; I am concerned about our future as a nation because we seem to have lost our bearings, but I haven't lost HOPE.

I have just returned from a conference in NC. It was my first "exposure" since the indictment. There I was able to rekindle and recapture the feelings of love and warmth reminiscent of earlier conferences. Two young adoptive mothers opened their hearts and, through tears of joy, told of their totally open adoptions and deep feelings they have for their childrens' birthparents. As I listened to them talk, I thought to myself "When this type of relationship among (all) parents becomes the norm, we will have created the type of society we want for all our children - one in which the love for OUR children does not divide, but rather a love that multiplies.

Some people in the movement believed I had gained excessive personal profit from my work of reuniting families, and they were speaking monetarily. Monetarily I did not fare well at all because money had never been my primary goal or purpose - except as it could further the cause. But I did fare a hundred-fold spiritually. Though I only played a small part in reconnecting many lives, the memories and joy will last me the rest of my life. Though my adversaries meant me harm, I am richer and wiser in spirit than ever before.

In closing, I want to share a quote by John Ruskin entitled *On the Need for A Rest* which was sent to me while I was still in prison by Sue, a birthmother friend:

ON THE NEED FOR A REST

There is no music in a "rest", but there is the making of music in it. In our whole life melody, the music is broken off here and there by "rests", and we foolishly think we have come to the end of the tune. God sends a time of forced leisure - sickness, disappointed plans, frustrated efforts - and makes a sudden pause in the choral hymn of our lives and we lament that our voices must be silent and our part missing in the music which ever goes up to the ear of the Creator. How does the musician read the "rest" ? See him beat time with unvarying count and catch up the next note true and steady as if no breaking place had come in between. Not without design does God write the music of our lives. But be it ours to learn the time and not be dismayed at the "rests". They are not to be slurred, not to be omitted, not to destroy the melody, nor change the keynote. If we look up, God will beat the time for us. With our eye on Him we shall strike the next note full and clear."

When I read this beautiful piece, I was profoundly moved. At the present time, I am enjoying a period of "forced leisure" and waiting to hear the next beat, which I know will strike loud and clear.

In this book, I have tried to open my heart and share with you, the reader, much of my personal life experience. It is being sent forth with a prayer that you will be able to glean something useful from its pages. If so, I would enjoy hearing from you.

Postscript: Sandy's appeal was turned down by the U.S. Court of Appeals, Sixth District, on March 16, 1994. Her appeal to the Supreme Court to hear the case was denied October 1, 1994.

251

Flanked by friends at my homecoming party, 3/5/94 - two days after my release. Front row L to R: Marcia Cohen, Lee Campbell (CUB Founder), Gail Hanssen, and Ann Henry. Back Row: My sister, Terry, Pat La Marco (Asst. Dir. of the Musser Foundation), and Alison Ward.

My supportive family - this was taken at a family reunion in August of '94. My brother, Stan; my 81 year old Mother; my sisters, Terry and Betty Ann.

HOW WE CAN HELP YOU
EDUCATE for AWARENESS

The primary purpose of The Awareness Press is to educate people to a new way of understanding and thinking about family issues - and to a more loving and caring way of relating.

If this book has given you some insights that you would like to share with a family member, a friend, a legislator, a social worker, a member of the clergy, or donate a copy to your local library, but cannot afford to purchase an extra copy of the book, we will send a free copy to the person of your choice. You need only send $5 to cover the cost of the packaging, shipping and handling, along with your name and address, and the name and address of the person you want the book donated to. We will be happy to include a gift card on your behalf and upon your request. (Only one per person please.)

Another suggestion is to loan your personal copy to a person you most want to educate, and attach a note or post-it in the particular section you would like them to read. There are many ways to educate for awareness.

To be kept informed of current events in the adoption reform arena, you may want to subscribe to a quarterly newsletter, written by the author, entitled *The Freedom Rider.* This quarterly newsletter will keep you abreast of adoption and family reform conferences, legislative bills, and reunion stories. Send your name and address and $25 subscription fee to Sandy Musser, 117 SE 44th Street, Cape Coral, FL 33910

Additional Copies of *To Prison With Love*
May be ordered by mail or phone:

1-800-356-9315 - for credit card orders only

Send me _____ copies of *To Prison With Love*
ISBN: 0-934896-37-2   Paperback $US14.95

Name _____

Address _____

City _____ State _____

ZIP Code _____ Phone (____) _____

Sales Tax: FL Residents add 6%
Shipping: Book Rate is $2.00 for first book and $.75 each additional
Mail to: Awareness Press, PO Box 41, Cape Coral, FL 33910

The Awareness Press distributes the following titles. For a free brochure, send a self-addressed stamped envelope to:
PO Box 41,
Cape Coral, FL 33910.

Adoption in America-Coming of Age / Aigner
Adoption Searchbook / Rillera
Adoption Triangle / Baran, Pannor, Sorosky
Adoption Without Fear / Gritter
An Adopted Woman / Maxtone-Graham
BirthBond / Gediman & Brown
Birth Mother / Kane
   (First Surrogate Mother Story)
Birthright / Strauss
By Order of Adoption / Downie
Chasing Rainbows / Lynn
Children of Open Adoption /Silber & Dorner
Dark Side of Adoption / Riben
Faces of Adoption / Giddens
Great Adoptee Search Book / Strauss
I Wish You Didn't Know My Name / Saunders
   (The Lisa Steinberg Story)
I Would Have Searched Forever / Musser
Lost & Found / Lifton
Missing Links / Begley
Mother, Can You Hear Me? / Allen
Primal Wound / Verrier
Sacred Bond / Chesler (Baby M Story)
Second Choice / Anderson
Synchronicity & Reunion / Stiffler
The Other Mother / Schaefer
The Solomon Decision / Pijanowski
To Prison With Love / Musser
Wake Up Little Suzie / Solinger
Wanted: First Child / Harsin
When Love Is Not Enough / Giddens

Index

AAC - 5, 18, 20, 21, 28, 36, 47-48, 50-51,
    91, 106, 198, 209, 213, 218, 227-228
activist - 14, 74, 158
adoptees - 24, 32, 41, 56, 58, 77, 150, 158,
    192, 200, 204-206, 223, 230, 235
adoption - 6, 25, 31, 39, 55, 78, 158-159,
    174, 199, 204
Adoption Forum.-. 17, 146, 217
adoptive parents - 41, 44, 52, 56, 65, 77, 88,
    189, 192, 203, 223, 232
agency(ies) -52, 56, 59, 118, 157, 182, 184,
    219, 236, 237, 244
Aigner, Hal - 2, 14, 74, 237
ALARM - 20-23, 30, 39, 52
America - 7, 32, 164, 179, 183, 185-186,
    244-245
Anthony, Susan B. - 223
arraignment - 54, 56-57
attorney - 10, 61, 69, 76, 77, 121, 144

Baran, Annette - 38, 211
bipolar - 142
birth Certificate - 22, 89, 235, 244
birthfather(s) - 34, 52, 75, 143
birthmother(s) 24, 30, 34, 43-45, 55-56, 70,
    80, 110, 176, 191, 207, 232-233, 235
birthparents(s) - 41, 77, 84, 223, 235
Broadcast News Network (BNN) - 9, 64, 71
Bureau of Prisons (BOP) - 151, 161, 163,
    170, 178-179, 185

camp - 64, 125, 162, 166-167, 171, 179-180
Campbell, Lee - 48, 51
CERA. - 48, 53, 71, 74, 77, 146
church. - 124-125
civil disobedience - 221
civil rights - 56, 192, 198, 223, 233, 245
Club Fed - 164,248
Cohen, Mary Anne -224
committed(ment) - 73, 157, 234, 237
commissary - 165-166, 171, 178
confidential(ity) - 22, 181, 203, 205, 225,
    244
conspiracy - 13, 30, 66, 69, 73, 157, 180-182,
    185, 196, 225
court - 36, 60, 146, 150, 152, 206, 228, 244
crime - 145, 151, 164, 186, 193, 228, 244
criminal - 39, 73, 108, 114, 149, 175, 200,
    206
CUB - 4, 18, 48, 53, 71, 127, 135, 136, 213,
    216

Dateline, - 8, 43, 64
defense - 11, 50, 53-54, 63, 116, 228
defraud - 157, 204
Department of Health - 34-35, 83, 88, 107,
    109, 143, 219

discovery - 59, 87, 159
disease(s) - 22, 135
drugs - 121, 137, 178, 180-181

Ensminger, Ray - 2

falsify, - 157, 205, 244
family(ies) - 14, 25-26, 45, 54, 77-78, 110, 118,
    120, 123, 144, 193, 196, 235
fees - 22, 26-27, 203, 228, 236-237
felony - 121
fictitious - 80, 87, 89
Flavin, Thomas - 34-35, 87, 92, 95, 101, 177

Ganz, Sheila - 16
genealogy, genetic - 22, 24-25, 123, 236, 244
Getz, Thomas - 61, 78-79, 90, 92, 102, 149, 227
Ghandi, Mahatma - 209
Giddens, Lynn - 168, 228
government - 11, 51-52, 69-70, 73, 76, 79, 82,
    89, 91, 108, 115, 161, 179,
Grimmie, Sandi - 48
Griffith, Rev. Keith - 204
Gritter, Jim - 209
guilty - 30, 61, 66, 122, 185

hospital - 52, 88, 128-129, 131-132, 134, 224,
    244
Haldol - 138
Harms - 70, 108,

identity -198, 210
indictment - 5, 79, 136, 140, 228, 239
iinterview - 64, 71, 145
investigator(tion) - 3, 8, 26-28, 34, 38, 69, 100,
    106-107, 144, 151, 177
isolation - 217

jail - 81, 91, 159, 204, 217
jury, jurors - 5, 54, 78-79, 150, 159, 185
judge - 30, 72, 77-78, 101, 114, 143, 146-147,
    152-154
justice - 121, 149, 182-183, 239, 242

Keith, George - 11, 60, 72-78, 86, 148, 152
King, Martin Luther - 209, 224

laws - 177, 192, 204, 216, 219, 222, 244
leaders - 214, 237-238
legal - 10, 177, 192, 197, 199, 214, 219, 223-224,
    244
legislators(tion), - 21, 23, 174, 204-205, 239,
    241, 246
lobby(ing) - 20-21, 205, 244

mail fraud - 108, 228

manic-depression(ive) - 90-91, 135, 142
marijuana - 181
media - 23, 65
medical information - 113, 172, 174, 178, 195,
    205
mental illness - 123, 141
misdemeanor - 121
movement - 12, 19, 46, 52, 174, 198, 229, 239,
    242
Musser Foundation - 5, 7, 17, 30, 48, 59, 63, 69,
    75, 79, 87, 92-94, 96, 99, 103, 109, 147,
    193, 226, 243
Musser, Stanton - 73

organization - 25, 33, 55, 125, 144, 158, 183,
    227, 238
open adoption - 106, 209, 211-212, 233, 246
open records - 21, 23, 126, 189, 222-223, 237,
    246

Pannor, Reuben - 215
Parks, Rosa - 198
Partridge, Penny - 146, 156, 168, 216
Paton, Jean - 52, 233
Peterson, Rebecca - 71, 145
police (state) - 174, 181-184, 242
Povich, Maury - 8, 38, 161, 229
preservation - 55, 127, 237, 244-245
pretrial - 63-65, 72
prison - 64, 67, 72, 87, 153-154, 164, 166, 168,
    174, 178-179, 186, 196, 219
probation - 13, 144, 152, 174

reform - 8, 11, 21, 23, 46, 55, 74, 158, 174, 177,
    189, 209, 239
relatives - 25, 217
reunions, reunited(ing) - 9, 30-31, 34, 38, 55,
    60, 73, 110, 153, 200, 217, 227
Rillera, Mary Jo - 18, 136
Rollenhagen, Mark - 6, 110
Ryan, Jon -156, 225

sealed records - 10, 24, 55, 89, 177, 216, 223
search(ing), searcher - 7-8, 12, 23, 29, 35, 45,
    68-69, 84-85, 196, 217, 226
secrecy, secret(s) - 69, 77, 170, 205, 210, 216,
    223, 244
segregation - 156-157, 173
sentence(ing) - 186, 220, 227
separation - 52, 235, 237
siblings - 32, 52, 234
Sixty Minutes - 8, 71, 91, 122, 145, 170, 174,
    177, 189, 190, 192, 194, 197, 219
Snyder, Tom - 64
Social Security Administration - 29, 59, 70, 74,
    79, 88, 104, 108, 110, 112.184, 225-227
solitary - 163, 167, 173-174, 197

Soll, Joe - 48
Stahl, Lesley - 145, 177, 189
Swanson, JoAnn -205

talk shows - 33, 37-39, 62, 165
Taylor, Dave & Judy - 48, 71, 77, 91, 114, 119,
    146
testify, testimony - 69, 80, 108, 110, 114, 219,
    228
Thorazine - 135
transcript - 80
travesty -121
trial - 72, 224

underground - 24, 35, 40, 218
UNICOR - 179-180

Verrier, Nancy -200, 229
vigilantes - 71
Vilardi, Emma May - 18
vital statistics - 52, 59, 92

Washington - 18, 28-29, 33, 36, 71
witnesses - 153